PROGRAMS
and
SERVICES
for
Gifted Secondary Students

A Service Publication of the National Association for Gifted Children

PROGRAMS
and
SERVICES
for
Gifted Secondary Students

A Guide to Recommended Practices

Edited by
Felicia A. Dixon, Ph.D.

PRUFROCK PRESS INC.
WACO, TEXAS

Library of Congress Cataloging-in-Publication Data

Programs and services for gifted secondary students : a guide to recommended practices / edited by Felicia A. Dixon.
    p. cm.
"A service publication of the National Association for Gifted Children."
Includes bibliographical references.
ISBN-13: 978-1-59363-348-6 (pbk.)
ISBN-10: 1-59363-348-3 (pbk.)
1. Gifted children—Education (Secondary)—United States. 2. Gifted teenagers—Education—United States. I. Dixon, Felicia A., 1945– II. National Association for Gifted Children (U.S.)
  LC3993.9.P754 2009
  371.95'73—dc22

2008029452

Copyright © 2009, the National Association for Gifted Children
Edited by Jennifer Robins
Cover and Layout Design by Marjorie Parker

ISBN-13: 978-1-59363-348-6
ISBN-10: 1-59363-348-3

Printed in the United States of America.

At the time of this book's publication, all facts and figures cited are the most current available. All telephone numbers, addresses, and Web site URLs are accurate and active. All publications, organizations, Web sites, and other resources exist as described in the book, and all have been verified. The authors and Prufrock Press Inc. make no warranty or guarantee concerning the information and materials given out by organizations or content found at Web sites, and we are not responsible for any changes that occur after this book's publication. If you find an error, please contact Prufrock Press Inc.

Prufrock Press Inc.
P.O. Box 8813
Waco, TX 76714-8813
Phone: (800) 998-2208
Fax: (800) 240-0333
http://www.prufrock.com

Contents

Foreword

IN **1993,** I addressed the annual convention of the National Association for Gifted Children with a keynote address titled, "Our Gifted Children: Are They Asking Too Much?" The title of my remarks came from an entry in a student's "thinking log"—a personal and reflective diary of ideas, concepts, and questions that captured each student's "thinking about their own thinking." The author was a 15-year-old, first-year student at the Illinois Mathematics and Science Academy in Aurora.

Her journal entry is as follows:

> I wish I could still draw. When I was in grammar school, I used to draw pretty decently. I loved to draw in pencil and chalk. Art of all kinds intrigues me, but I also love music and painting and carpentry and metal working and dancing and sewing and embroidery and cooking. I want to dance in my old ballet class, play my clarinet, draw thousands of pictures—really good ones—create beautiful poems and pieces of woodwork, cook and sew for my children, decorate my home, have a good marriage, be an active volunteer, go to church, be an astrophysicist, go to Mars, and understand all my questions about life. Now, that's not too much to ask, is it?

My remarks were structured around my response to her question and why my answer was, "No—it was *not* too much to ask."

In countless speeches after that, I repeated her journal entry and its poignant question, "Is that too much to ask?" The response pattern was sobering and gradually quite predictable, and in itself is a compelling reason why this book had to be written. In audiences of adults, there was always laughter—as if to say, "What a naïve question. Of course it's too much to ask and when you grow up and enter the real world, you will understand why." In audiences of young people—high school and college age—there was silence. The question was neither naïve nor funny.

Although more than 15 years have passed since that convention (and manned space flight to Mars is now a possibility), the question remains a fundamental one, and scores of gifted students are still asking it and hoping we are on their side.

Programs and Services for Gifted Secondary Students is scholarly, engaging, and thoughtfully written by some of our nation's most knowledgeable and respected practitioners, researchers, and policy leaders in gifted education. It provides a comprehensive survey of best policies and practices, yet wisely situates the imperative for meaningful multidimensional program and content differentiation in the context of advances in the learning sciences and the neuroplasticity revolution. We now know that thinking and learning can change the structure and function of the brain and alter its map. This has enormous implications for the learning environments that we create for our children—by design.

By presenting evidence and research-based practices, the mythologies traditionally surrounding the education of gifted children are eroded. The cognitive case is made that differentiated education for gifted students is *essential* to their development. Knowing this, our national policy toward gifted students cannot be "make it on your own." Talent must be ignited, nurtured, and sustained *by design*, through wise, knowledge-based policies and innovative best practices. This book tells us why and shows us how.

To develop expertise and strategic thinking and to invite intellectual energy and creative power to flourish requires decidedly different learning environments. These personalized, curiosity-driven, and inquiry-based environments immerse gifted students in advanced, accelerated, challenging, and complex curriculum; problem solving; abstract conceptual thinking; multidisciplinary collaboration; experimentation; and the pursuit of meaningful questions that matter to them— and they do so by design.

In addition to artfully describing the attributes framing the design and map of optimal learning experiences for Gifted Secondary students, the book also:

- provides evidence-based descriptions and assessments of the current state of gifted secondary education, focusing on issues such as stress, peers, perfectionism and fear of failure, cultural diversity, gender differences, and twice-exceptional students;
- summarizes some current reform efforts, such as high school restructuring, competency-based promotion, and early- and middle-college programming and their impacts on gifted students;

- explores some national policy initiatives and programs, such as NAEP (what it can and cannot report about gifted students) and the Javits Grant Program;
- describes promising programmatic options and best practices, such as specialized magnet schools, early college entrance and talent search programs, school-to-work and study abroad opportunities, and distance education; and
- frames the context and content of an expanded multistakeholder national conversation on the education of gifted students at the secondary level.

Grounded in both pragmatism and possibility, the authors remind us that the future of gifted secondary education does not lie in increasing and scaling what we currently are doing. In the absence of systemic options, supplemental programs provide critical programming for gifted adolescents, but they are inadequate preparation for coherently and comprehensively developing their talents over time.

The future of gifted secondary education lies in a new vision. The vision offered in this book rests upon four major commitments:

1. formal identification of student abilities and talents based on a variety of information and evidence including grades, assessment of significant products, observation of behaviors, and students' disciplinary interests;
2. commitment to advance students based on their prior knowledge;
3. an openness and flexibility with respect to student placement—not a rigid adherence to require prerequisites if students are performing exceptionally well; and
4. programs that have adaptive and flexible structures, well-qualified personnel, and multiple opportunities for professional experiences, such as mentorships and internships.

This is a future vision framed by what we now know about human learning, grounded in the unique intellectual, social, and emotional needs of Gifted Secondary students and congruent with the policies and practices that can develop the remarkable potentials of our students. We shape the world from the inside-out. The nature and quality of our thinking shapes who we become, and who we become shapes the world. Mind-shaping is world-shaping. The future prosperity and sustainability of the global community rests on the development of talent and the igniting and nurturing of our children's ethical and creative minds. This is our work, it must be our commitment . . . and, it is not too much to ask.

—Stephanie Pace Marshall, Ph.D.
Founding President and President Emerita,
Illinois Mathematics and Science Academy
November 2008

Acknowledgements

AS WITH ANY MAJOR PROJECT, this one began with an idea, which was to provide guidance for administrators and teachers regarding services for Gifted Secondary students. Although I first proposed this task force in 2004, I was not the first person who had expressed interest for such a group with a focus on gifted adolescents. I would like to both acknowledge and thank those who came before and provided encouragement for this project. I would especially like to acknowledge Rick Olenchak, Joyce VanTassel-Baska, and Del Siegle—three presidents of NAGC whose support and encouragement launched our work and sustained us over the past several years. I sincerely thank them and NAGC's Executive Director, Nancy Green, for their support.

The task force itself is composed of scholars who are both excellent researchers in the field of gifted education and are invested in ideas to improve the lives of gifted adolescents in schools. This work required commitment of time and energy in the lives of very busy professionals. I am both humbled and extremely proud of this work and I thank all of the members of the task force for their thoughtful and provoking chapters. Shelagh Gallagher added much expertise and thoughtful scholarship in her coverage of several important topics in this work. In addition, Susannah Wood contributed her expertise concerning counseling needs for careers and for social and emotional issues of gifted adolescents. Marcia Gentry and Scott Peters contributed important background for policy concerning gifted adolescents. Paula Olszewski-Kubilius' work on talent search, summer programs, special schools, and several other pieces provided essential information on what is currently available for students. In addition, Lisa Lindberg-Weber's work on Study Abroad provides programmatic consideration that may increase this viable option for gifted adolescents. Kathy Gavin's knowledge of the federally funded Javits projects, as well as current monographs about gifted adolescents, adds depth to what is available for administrators and practitioners alike. These were the writers of the sections of our project and they all made it happen. I would be absolutely remiss not to acknowledge the input and guidance provided by Bill Stepien, who has been a wise and committed member of the task force. His advice and suggestions improved the final product. I also want to acknowledge the early input provided by David Ehle as the task force developed the project outline.

Especially helpful to me was our staff liaison with NAGC, Jane Clarenbach. We could not have completed this project without Jane, who advised, monitored, encouraged, cheered us on, and especially was the voice of reason at many points during the project. Jane's services to us were catalytic in the success of this project. Her work in editing, serving as liaison to our publisher, and in keeping us on task was essential to our success. Thank you, Jane.

Finally, we began as a task force developing a monograph. We are completing that work as a task force who has developed a book. We give thanks to Joel McIntosh and Jennifer Robins at Prufrock Press for their interest in and support of this project, and to the NAGC Publications Committee, which provided critical reviews that helped improve key sections. In addition, we are grateful to Stephanie Pace Marshall for her insightful foreword that helps put this work into a greater context. As always, Sidney Moon offered valuable insight to the project; I appreciate her wisdom and advice. We had much to say about gifted adolescents and there is much more to say. To all of you who have supported us in our work, we thank you and hope that we have met your needs. Our long-term goal is improved services and greater understanding of gifted secondary students. We think our book is a positive step in that direction.

Felicia A. Dixon, Ph.D., Chair
NAGC Task Force on Gifted Secondary Students

National Association for Gifted Children

Task Force on Gifted Secondary Education

Felicia Dixon, Ph.D., Chair
Ball State University
Muncie, IN

Jane Clarenbach, J.D.
NAGC Staff Liaison
Washington, DC

David Ehle
Columbus, OH

Shelagh Gallagher, Ph.D.
Charlotte, NC

M. Katherine Gavin, Ph.D.
University of Connecticut
Storrs, CT

Marcia Gentry, Ph.D.
Purdue University
West Lafayette, IN

Paula Olszewski-Kubilius, Ph.D.
Northwestern University
Evanston, IL

Bill Stepien
Charlotte, NC

Susannah Wood, Ph.D.
University of Iowa
Iowa City, IA

Introduction

BY

FELICIA
DIXON, CHAIR

NAGC
TASK FORCE
ON GIFTED
SECONDARY
EDUCATION

THIS BOOK IS THE CULMINATION OF 2 YEARS of work by the NAGC Task Force on Gifted Secondary Education. It is divided into three sections: Part I defines the gifted adolescent and the cognitive dimensions that set him or her apart while establishing the need for unique programming. Additionally, social and emotional dimensions and career possibilities are presented in Part I. The focus is entirely on the individual gifted adolescent. Part II shifts the focus to current offerings for gifted students at the secondary level. Divided into two sections, Section 1 presents issues that impact secondary students while Section 2 describes the program options available for gifted adolescents in the majority of school settings. Part III is the visionary piece that delineates what the Task Force advocates for the future for the education of gifted secondary students.

We address the information here to gifted coordinators as well as teachers, administrators, parents, gifted students, and educators interested in gifted and talented education. There are answers, questions, descriptions, and suggestions for all. It is our hope to begin a dialogue with a range of professionals concerning the education of gifted students at the secondary level. We focus on the high-school-aged adolescent primarily although some sections address the need to engage students much earlier in their education. But it is high school, not middle school, that is the focus of this work.

It is essential that readers know that this volume differs from *The Handbook of Gifted Secondary Education* (Dixon & Moon, 2006) in that it is divided into different sections, has a different focus, and is meant to be used as a much speedier reference for options for practitioners, administrators, and coordinators of gifted programs. It is a companion piece rather than a competing piece. For example, we do not intend to replicate the extensive examination of curricular offerings presented in Part III of *The Handbook*. For specific suggestions on content areas, critical and creative thinking, and affective curriculum for the gifted adolescent, readers should consult the appropriate chapters of *The Handbook of Gifted Secondary Education* (Dixon & Moon, 2006). Rather, this book augments *The Handbook* by covering issues pertinent to gifted education in a changing world as well as by providing a vision of programs for the future. For a field that has had little available for either the teacher or the program planner in terms of secondary recommendations, these two companion pieces should serve as wise guidance. More than Advanced Placement and International Baccalaureate are available for secondary program options for gifted adolescents, and teachers, program planners, and administrators must consider the issues carefully. We offer the necessary guidance. Our hope as a Task Force is that our field will have two very different and very useable references for secondary issues. This volume has evolved into a piece that has great potential to help the field expand services and begin conversations with other national education content organizations with the goal of improving educational possibilities for Gifted Secondary students.

Reference

Dixon, F. A., & Moon, S. M. (2006). *The handbook of Gifted Secondary education*. Waco, TX: Prufrock Press.

PART I

Characteristics of the **Gifted** Adolescent

PART **I** FOCUSES ON THE GIFTED ADOLESCENT as an individual with unique needs that must be understood for maximum growth and development to occur. We begin with a rationale that attends to the cognitive characteristics of gifted adolescents in determining program considerations. In the first chapter, Shelagh Gallagher argues for a focus on the gifted adolescent's unique epistemology as educators and administrators craft programs that maximize cognitive strengths. In examining these ways of knowing, Gallagher reviews the literature and extends it, creating a plausible rationale that clearly understands these students in suggesting necessities for programming for them.

Chapter 2 continues the emphasis on the individual gifted adolescent, examining the social and emotional considerations that must be acknowledged as educators and researchers seek to maximize student potential. Susannah Wood reviews the literature on many of the issues that these adolescents face, using a counseling lens to focus on their needs and a wise "best practices" lens to suggest practical ways to attend to them. Again, we focus on the person, examining the uniqueness of the gifted adolescent and building a case for special attention to his or her issues to promote maximum growth.

Finally, Chapter 3 examines the issues explicitly tied to career choices for gifted adolescents. Susannah Wood and Kathy Gavin discuss multipotentiality, gender role issues, and career opportunities, reviewing the literature on each area and suggesting ways to meet these needs. All three chapters in Part I center on the individual's characteristics in considering how and why current programming may not be adequate for appropriate service.

Chapter 1

Designed to Fit

Educational Implications of Gifted Adolescents' Cognitive Development

BY

SHELAGH A.

GALLAGHER

ALL OF A SUDDEN John eats like a horse, Dwight brings new friends home, Tanya discovers existentialism, while Sarah discovers—and then loses—her temper. Welcome to adolescence. Although the external transformations capture our attention, the genesis of adolescent change is internal: an influx of hormones stimulates physical growth, moods shift as the body adjusts, and even the brain is expanding, opening the door to whole new vistas of understanding. The changes of adolescence are so numerous and far-reaching it is a wonder we try to teach these students at all, yet many secondary educators feel a sense of urgency about their instruction. The need to prepare students for college contributes to the urgency, as does the need to prepare them for work in the Information Age. The sense of urgency also is fed by the knowledge that in some way, the clock is running out on compulsory education for these adolescents, and before that happens, they must acquire enough dedication to seek the education they need independent of laws or parents. Ideally, they will have some vision of their future to guide their way.

All this urgency sometimes convinces teachers that there is too much at stake to take time to differentiate for their gifted students. Yet, adolescence is also the time when it is most likely that gifted students will abandon their gift because of a desire to be popular, of boredom with simple schooling, or of disenchantment with the lack of significance of their curriculum. How do we sustain gifted students' desire to learn while still preparing them for college and life? At the very least, how can we keep them from skipping class? The answers to these questions lie in the qualitative differences gifted students bring into the classroom. New research on the brain may well provide us with new ways to map and describe these differences (see Figure 1). Even now, evidence of qualitative differences from both psychology and education provide a strong rationale for modifying content, emphasizing thinking strategies, and using student perspective to create a meaningful differentiation: goals that are respectful and consistent with secondary instruction.

A Rationale for Multidimensional Content Differentiation

Copious Challenging Content

Gifted students' sponge-like absorption of new information is a defining trait. Cognitive scientists have isolated at least three skills related to IQ that combine to create an advantage in acquiring information. According to Steiner and Carr (2003), infants who: (1) react to new information quickly; (2) accommodate new information, or "habituate" quickly; and (3) leave "habituated" information to seek out new stimuli quickly, grow into children with high IQs. These same factors—rapid information processing, habituation, and preference for novelty—also are crucial to adult expert performance.

Between high-IQ children and the expert adults are gifted adolescents who also (1) learn better when taught two to three times faster than average (rapid response to stimuli); (2) remember better with fewer repetitions (Larson & Richards, 1991), which suggests habituation; and (3) respond better to open-ended, inquiry-oriented instruction (novelty seeking; Sak, 2004), preferring to learn something new even more than typically popular hands-on activities. Although it is impossible to make causal or developmental ties based on these separate bodies of research, the similarities are clear.

As gifted adolescents engage in the cycle of seeking, responding to, and accommodating new information, they acquire an extensive knowledge base, which contributes to academic success. Helping gifted students acquire a substantial knowledge base is the first essential component of an effective secondary program.

Should differentiation then focus on intensive memorization of facts? No. Gifted students consistently report that the dominant emphasis on factual learning leads to their disenchantment with school (Csikszentmihalyi, Rathunde, & Whalen, 1993; Gallagher, Harradine, & Coleman, 1997; Kanevsky & Keighley, 2003; Plucker & McIntire, 1996). The extensive knowledge base gifted students

Adults often wonder what happened to the mind of a new adolescent, as it often seems to have disappeared. Ironically, adolescents don't suffer from a lack of grey matter; rather, they have a surfeit. A decade of research using Magnetic Resonance Imaging (MRI) technology has revealed that brain development is much more dynamic than once thought, particularly during adolescence. Key findings include:

1. Just before the teenage years, the brain acquires a mass of new grey matter. Grabner, Neubauer, and Stern (2006) reported this new brain growth peaks at around 11 for girls and 12 for boys.

2. The new grey matter is deposited in the prefrontal cortex, which controls executive functions: impulse control, decision-making, reasoning, and planning.

3. Myelinization of an early adolescent's prefrontal cortex is significantly less developed than an adult's. Myelin, the insulation, helps make strong, efficient connections between neurons; the neural connections manifest as thought or action. Myelin develops as a result of exercising an area of the brain much as muscle develops as a result of exercising an arm or leg. New and unexercised, an adolescent's new prefrontal cortex—the area that controls executive function—is relatively flabby and in need of a workout (Sowell et al., 2003).

4. Unable to efficiently use their flabby prefrontal cortex, young teens rely on other regions of the brain, including the amygdala, which sends out impulsive gut reactions to respond to certain stimuli like facial expressions. Adults use their prefrontal cortex to respond to the same stimuli. Only in later adolescence does the teen brain begin to respond like an adult's (Yurgelun-Todd & Kilgore, 2006).

5. Individuals with high measured IQ also tend to have more grey matter in the prefrontal cortex than individuals whose IQ is average or below (Haier, Jung, Yeo, Head, & Alkire, 2004), suggesting the opportunity to develop more or stronger executive control function.

6. The preadolescent influx of grey matter is followed by attrition throughout adolescence. Grabner and colleagues (2006) called this a "pruning" process that weeds out weak neural connections and retains stronger connections.

For decades, the assumption has been that secondary educators have been adding to a work in progress, helping to mold a brain that has been around since a child's birth. Current research replaces this picture with another: 12-year-olds hurrying down crowded hallways, each carrying a mass of untrained brain. This image might serve as a call to action for any teacher, but it is particularly important for gifted educators, because the prefrontal cortex regions are "critical for essentially all higher order cognitive functions" (Grabner et al., 2006, p. 436). Grabner et al. noted the observed efficiency of prefrontal cortex activity in intelligent individuals suggests that they are malleable and responsive to training.

The key to changing an unpredictable, impulsive 12-year-old into a more self-possessed 22-year-old lies at least in part on the effective development of executive control processes. Given the relationship between prefrontal matter and intelligence, gifted students may well have more potential for executive control skill to develop—or waste. Because the adolescent brain also will engage in winnowing out unused or ineffective neural connections, it seems incumbent upon gifted educators to pay special attention to this area during the secondary years.

Figure 1. Neurological changes at adolescence.

develop is significant because "more leads to different" (Berliner, 1986, as cited in Shiever & Maker, 1997). With more content at their disposal, gifted students can make more connections and see more original relationships, for ". . . a strong knowledge base . . . facilitates and is facilitated by the development of advanced, domain-specific strategies and metacognitive knowledge" (Carr & Alexander, 1996, p. 214). Over time, these strategies accumulate and create an impetus toward complex and abstract levels of understanding.

Abstract, Complex Content

Another form of differentiation, particularly appropriate for gifted students, is exposure to abstract, conceptual ideas. Abstract reasoning creates its own form of new content to understand, encompassing intangible notions such as hypothesis posing, theorizing, and analogous reasoning. By implication, students must have access to abstract reasoning before they can succeed with curriculum that requires designing experiments, interpreting symbolic meaning, or comparing policy initiatives.

Students are generally thought to have access to abstract thought with the onset of adolescence and the acquisition of formal operational reasoning (Inhelder & Piaget, 1958). Systematic differences between groups in the acquisition of formal operational reasoning would provide compelling reasons to differentiate in order to capitalize on the early opportunity to begin honing these essential skills. Berninger and Yates (1993) present a thorough review of the literature on gifted students and formal operations, demonstrating that:

1. Children move through the Piagetian stages in the same order, but not on the same timeline. Gifted students acquire formal operational reasoning around ages 12–13; most other students are still in the transition to formal operations at age 15.
2. Gifted boys tend to enter formal operations earlier than gifted girls. The effect size of this difference is small, and the male advantage diminishes by late adolescence.
3. Gifted adolescents progress through substages of formal operations more quickly than their age-mates.

Gifted students have the capacity for abstract, conceptual reasoning as many as 3 years ahead of their peers—*the equivalent of their entire middle school careers.* Naturally, variability exists in both the gifted and average populations, but still the implications are clear: Gifted students are ready to grapple with qualitatively different content years ahead of their classmates. Once formal operations are achieved, instruction should be designed toward mastering this new form of content, as it is critical for success in secondary academics (Bitner, 1991; Gipson, Abraham, & Renner, 1989; Hurst & Milkent, 1996; Matthews & McLaughlin, 1994; McDonald, 1989; Niaz & Robinson, 1992; Wavering, 1989). Incorporating conceptual content with a plentiful factual base also provides a means of ensuring that learning will not fall into drill and rote memorization. Concepts help organize facts, resulting in more meaningful connections and expert-like thinking (Shore & Irving, 2005).

Disciplinary or Interdisciplinary Content?

Understanding the need for a deep, concept-centered knowledge base is only partly useful; it also is necessary to know how to focus the knowledge. Compelling arguments can be made in two directions. On one hand, opportunity for early specialization is essential for students with exemplary talent (Jarvin & Subotnik, 2006). Early specialization also makes sense for many students whose chosen career may require many years of schooling. On the other hand, the modern age is marked by unique combinations of traditional disciplines into new fields (Klein, 1993), and innovation is often the result of cross-disciplinary application, similar to the use of linguistics to decode the DNA sequence (Young, 2001). Ultimately, the most effective programs for gifted adolescents provide the choice to either go wide or deep while ensuring some exposure to deep disciplinary thinking and original interdisciplinary connections, regardless of the direction students take.

In sum, gifted students are capable of learning substantially more content than their peers. They also have early capacity for abstract thought, which both adds a layer of content and helps organize factual information. Building a gifted student's knowledge base makes sense, especially because this knowledge base is a predictor of academic success. Ensuring that gifted students, fond as they are of novelty, remain engaged in learning requires the presentation of content that:

- presents information using instructional models that facilitate identification and creation of meaningful connections,
- allows for inductive and deductive connections between facts and abstract ideas,
- incorporates time specifically for cultivation of abstract reasoning, and
- encourages either deep exploration of one discipline (with exposure to interdisciplinary thought) or wide exploration of several disciplines (with exposure to deep exploration in one field)—or both!

Frequent Opportunities for Higher Order Thinking

The knowledge base gifted students acquire may be impressive, but it is ultimately fairly useless unless they put that knowledge to work with the help of thinking strategies. Surprisingly, the research base on gifted adolescents' unique thinking attributes is thin in both gifted education and cognitive science; research on how cognitive differences *develop* is virtually nonexistent (Steiner & Carr, 2003). The research that is available tends to focus on three interrelated areas: (1) strategic thinking, (2) metacognition, and (3) expert thinking.

Strategic Thinking: Speeding up to Slow Down. Gifted students generally use the same set of strategies that other students use, so in terms of sheer number of strategies employed, they do not seem different from other students (Hong, 1999). However, gifted students learn more quickly, and when faced with a challenging task, they use more complex forms of strategies and often select sophisticated strategies (Steiner & Carr, 2006). Having more content at their disposal, they have the capacity to use thinking strategies to more original ends. As obvious as it may seem, however, it bears emphasizing that there is a difference between knowing a strategy and using a strategy. Evidence suggests that gifted students only use their critical thinking strategies when they perceive a need; that is, when the challenge of a task merits their use (Hong, 1999).

Gifted students' advantage with thinking strategies is especially apparent when they are engaged in problem solving. Gifted students tend to show a greater explicit knowledge of problem-solving stages, know more problem-solving strategies, and are more adept in selecting strategies to use when faced by an open-ended problem. They also are more inclined to switch from one strategy to another when necessary (Kanevsky, 1992). The strength gifted students demonstrate is evident even in the absence of direct instruction in problem solving; gifted students seem to "invent" strategies when needed (Montague, 1991). While they are problem solving, fast-learning gifted students slow down, taking more time to plan and strategize (Davidson & Sternberg, 1984; Shore & Lazar, 1996). In addition, they show early tendencies toward expert-like behavior when problem solving; content knowledge may strengthen this tendency (Cherney, Winter, & Cherney, 2005).

In summary, gifted students demonstrate superior performance in a wide range of thinking skills, which they use well and selectively. However, gifted students use these skills only when faced with meaningful challenges. Ensuring that gifted students develop their skills in critical thinking requires:

- constant exposure to challenging content;
- tasks more challenging than average, requiring the use of critical thinking;
- reflective time to engage in problem finding, planning, and conceptual reasoning; and
- an overall pace of curriculum and instruction in which time saved as a result of rapid content learning is spent on more difficult complex thinking.

Metacognition. In the early 1980s, Sternberg (1982) proposed that metacognition, the ability to oversee and manage thinking, is an important factor in gifted performance. After two decades of research, a more specific, but unexpected, picture has emerged of gifted students' use of metacognition. Although it is clear that metacognition is a component of exemplary performance, gifted students do not show a clear-cut performance advantage. In fact, there are only two areas of metacognition where gifted students consistently show superior performance: (1) gifted students' knowledge about specific learning strategies, and (2) their inclination to use a skill in a new, usual setting, also known as "far transfer" (Carr & Alexander, 1996; Robinson & Clinkenbeard, 1998; Span & Overtoom-Corsmit, 1986). Other studies of metacognition show only a slight advantage for gifted students;

some show inferior performance among gifted youth (Dresel & Haugwitz, 2005; Ludlow & Woodrum, 1982).

At first glance, these findings seem counterintuitive: Why wouldn't gifted students show the same advantage in metacognition that they have in learning content and using thinking skills? Carr and Alexander (1996) presented three plausible explanations. First, the tasks used in metacognitive research, especially research on near transfer, may be so easy that gifted students do well without monitoring their performance. This would explain why gifted students are similar to their peers in their use of metacognitive skills on near transfer tasks, but consistently perform better on far transfer tasks. Far transfer tasks offer a greater challenge, requiring gifted students to engage in self-monitoring. Dresel and Haugwitz (2005) conducted a classroom-based study that reinforces this notion, finding that gifted students did not use self-regulating behavior if they thought an assignment was easy. Based on their study, they concluded, ". . . the finding that students with high abilities use strategies less frequently in regular school lessons can be seen as an indication that their learning environment is inadequately low . . ." (p. 15). In order to provide gifted students with the same amount of practice in self-regulation as average students, they must work as frequently with tasks they find challenging. The alternative is to leave these skills undeveloped, underdeveloped, or poorly developed.

Second, the relationship between metacognition and IQ may have a "threshold effect": IQ may predict skilled use of metacognition up to a point. Once the threshold is crossed, IQ ". . . does not guarantee that children will acquire or use cognitive skills, such as metacognition, believed to promote high achievement. These cognitive skills appear to develop, instead, out of emerging expertise" (Carr & Alexander, 1996, p. 214).

Third, the generic, content-free nature of research tasks may be both unrealistic and unlikely to reveal gifted performance differences. Research on expert performance suggests that cognitive monitoring really is only necessary after the student develops a deep and significant body of discipline-based content (Chi, Glaser, & Farr, 1988; Rabinowitz & Glaser, 1985).

In sum, gifted students have access to self-regulatory behaviors but use them inconsistently. Effective self-regulation is related both to academic success and to adult expert performance. Ensuring that gifted students have adequate practice with a wide range of metacognitive skills requires

- constant exposure to challenging content,
- learning tasks sufficiently difficult to require self-regulation, and
- immersion in disciplinary-based content.

Expertise and Giftedness. Insight into expert performance provides a guidepost for planning programs for gifted adolescents because we aspire for them to become experts or innovators in their chosen field. Research findings continue to strengthen the tie between gifted students' thought processes and that of domain-specific experts (Gorodetsky & Klavir, 2003; Kaufman, Gentile, & Baer, 2005; Shore, 2000). Common characteristics already discussed include rapid acquisition of content, skill and flexibility in critical thinking, and self-regulation. Gifted students seem to intuitively have some expert-like skills (Kaufman et al., 2005), while others are only acquired through training (Cherney et al., 2005).

Reviewing the literature on expertise, Carr and Alexander (1996) pointed out that it takes more than skill and ability to be an expert: "Although experts need sufficient general ability (IQ) to perform at a high level, other factors such as task commitment, a strong knowledge base and social support are more important for developing expertise and promoting achievement through expertise. . . ." (p. 214). The list of requirements for expertise also includes perspective, forward problem solving, persistence, risk taking, and tacit knowledge (e.g., professional language and behaviors; Jarvin & Subotnik, 2006; Shore, 2000; Sternberg, 2003). Expertise in this larger sense can be developed using curriculum and instruction that emphasize problem solving, open-ended questions, construction of ideas, multiple perspectives, and exposure to disciplinary experts (Gallagher, 2006; Shore & Irving, 2005; Sternberg, 2003; Subotnik, 2003).

In sum, gifted students' cognitive characteristics parallel those of adult experts. Ensuring that gifted students continue to develop expert-like skills requires

- exposure to explicit and tacit disciplinary knowledge;
- time to engage in flexible thinking with disciplinary and interdisciplinary content;
- curriculum and instruction that incorporate inquiry, conceptual learning, and authentic contexts; and
- opportunities for problem solving and mentorships.

The Role of Student Perspective: Epistemology

Still missing is perhaps the most important factor about the education of gifted adolescents. Efforts to design effective programs and promote new kinds of practice will be for naught if the students themselves do not recognize the significance or value in the tasks assigned.

The form of perspective in question is *epistemology*, one's belief about the nature of knowledge. Perry (1970) presented a developmental scheme that made direct and pragmatic application to the classroom, for it described both how students' views of knowledge change over time and also the powerful effect differing views have in the classroom. Perry's scheme presents nine distinct "positions" that can be collapsed into four broad stages, as summarized by Gallagher (2006):

Dualism: Marked by a black-and-white perspective, students at this stage believe all legitimate questions have certain answers. So-called questions without answers are just nonsense questions, pointless.
Multiplicity: Students acknowledge that there are a few unanswered questions, but believe that in the absence of an answer, all opinions on the matter are equally valid.

Contextual Relativism: Unanswered questions are investigated using the tools provided by each discipline; each discipline approaches questions in a different way. Certain answers are unlikely, but a "best answer" can be achieved using the proper tools.

Commitment/Dialectic: Theories are used to set directions for important questions, most of which have no right or wrong answers. Gaining understanding requires building upon the possibilities presented by data as interpreted by a consciously selected point of view, but with willingness to change perspective if the need arises. (p. 436)

Table 1 presents the four stages aligned with the beliefs about learning that accompany each stage.

For a more concrete example, consider Carl and Cedric, two students waiting for class to begin. Carl believes that knowledge means facts, and being knowledgeable means remembering lots of facts. Cedric, on the other hand, thinks that knowledge is the ability to combine facts to create ideas. For Cedric, being knowledgeable isn't about the number of facts he knows, it's about how the facts can form and reform to create different ideas. Their teacher, Ms. Morgan, starts her lecture on the Trail of Tears, focusing on the sequence of events, detailing what, who, and when. Carl picks up his pen and starts studiously taking notes; Cedric slumps down in his desk, grumbling, "factoids." The two boys hear the same lecture from the same teacher, but their different beliefs about knowledge affect how willing they are to accept the information as meaningful or valid.

A number of theories now attempt to describe aspects of epistemological development (Baxter Magolda, 1987; King & Kitchener, 1994; Schommer, 1994). Each theory describes sequential, developmental movement from a low or "naïve" stance in which knowledge is equated with factual information and memorization, to a high or "mature" stance in which facts are used to build theories from ". . . a consciously selected point of view, but with willingness to change perspective if the need arises" (Gallagher, 2006, p. 436). In the example above, Carl holds a naïve stance and thus is happy to gather up a list of facts from the lecture; Cedric's stance is more mature, and he wishes the facts had been embedded in more meaningful ideas.

The Comprehensive Impact of Epistemology. At one level, the impact of Carl's and Cedric's differing beliefs is immediately apparent: Students are not likely to learn what they do not believe to be meaningful—or at least, they won't learn it for long. After two decades of research into the effect of epistemology on learning, it is clear that the impact extends beyond whether students like what they learn to a number of other important academic outcomes.

Epistemological stance affects academic achievement. Using a structural equation analysis, Cano (2005) found that high school students' epistemological stance had both direct and indirect effects on academic achievement. Similar results have been

Table 1

Perry's Stages/Positions of Epistemological Reasoning and Related Instructional Strategies

Stages of Epistemological Development	Dualism	Multiplicity	Relativism	Commitment/Dialectic
Beliefs Associated With the Position	Knowledge is certain (right or wrong) and unambiguous. Authorities (teachers) know "The Truth."	Some questions have no certain answers; in these cases, knowledge and "truth" are subjective, so everyone's opinion is equally valid.	Knowledge is interpreted in context; distinguishing better from worse answers requires selecting theories that best fit the question.	Knowledge, theories, and methods are imperfect and uncertain. Choices require analysis and values.
Instruction That Matches Epistemological Stage	Activities that help students develop skill in memorization and recall: mnemonics, etc.	Practice in comparing hypotheses and theories; acknowledging all possibilities.	Practice in creating, comparing, and selecting preferable theoretical models; practice in expert behaviors.	Mentorship.
Instruction That Encourages Movement to a Higher Stage	Exposure to problems with more than one right answer and/or more than one approach to a solution.	Exposure to the tools used in different disciplines to conduct research, construct theories, and make decisions.	Exposure to models of paradigm shifts (chaos theory), personal choice (Gandhi's personal commitment to nonviolence), interdisciplinary problem solving.	

Earlier Positions →

Range of Typical High School Senior

Range of Gifted High School Senior

Later Positions

found with middle school students (Schommer-Aikins, Duell, & Hutter, 2005). Students at lower levels may have trouble correcting misconceptions, and draw only fact-based information from inquiry-oriented environments (Ryan, 1984).

Epistemological stance affects advanced academic performance. Students with more advanced beliefs have an easier time building logical arguments (Weinstock, Neuman, & Tabak, 2004); they tend to choose thinking strategies that support deep, rather than surface, learning (Cano, 2005; Zhang & Watkins, 2001). Kitchener (1983) also suggested that students' selection of metacognitive strategies can be affected by their epistemological beliefs. Support for this idea comes from a study by Ruban and Reis (2006), who found that high-achieving students tended to select "enhancement" oriented learning strategies while lower achieving students selected "survival" oriented strategies.

Instruction can encourage movement to higher epistemological levels. Teachers can affect changes in students' epistemological thinking through intentionally structured learning experiences (Kloss, 1994; Kronholm, 1993). Strategies recommended to develop epistemological thinking include using ill-structured problems and instructional strategies that allow students to examine their assumptions; analyze data that present different, conflicting perspectives; and then make decisions (King & Kitchener, 2004). Devoting some time to direct instruction about the nature of the discipline helps develop higher levels of reasoning (Bell, 2004).

Mismatch between instruction and epistemological stance (perspective) contributes to frustration and disillusionment. Cedric didn't respond well when Ms. Martin started a fact-based lecture. Over time he will simply decide that school is trivial, or worse, meaningless. Had Ms. Martin started instead with a discussion of the violation of Native Americans' sense of personhood, Cedric would have been thrilled and Carl would have been lost. This kind of disparity creates barriers to learning (Nelson, 1996; Perry, 1970). Neber and Schommer-Aikins (2002) found that a mismatch between instruction and stance caused work avoidance among some high school physics students. Lovell and Nunnery (2004) found that students even found small-group work more satisfying when they were grouped according to stance (perspective).

Gifted students tend to be ahead in epistemological development. Studies of adolescents document that epistemological beliefs mature in a predictable developmental sequence (Cano, 2005; Zhang & Watkins, 2001). In parallel to formal operational reasoning, gifted adolescents move through epistemological stages in the same sequence (Thomas, 2008), but tend to be a stage or two ahead of others the same age (Arlin & Levitt, 1998; Goldberger, 1981; Schommer & Dunnell, 1997; Thomas, 2008; Wilkinson & Maxwell, 1991; Wilkinson & Schwartz, 1987). Table 1 provides a general sense of the distribution of senior year students based on existing research.

Adult experts tend to hold advanced epistemological views. The epistemological framework also provides a connection to another aspect of expertise. Across the disciplines, the behaviors and attitudes associated with mature epistemology are considered essential for advanced, authentic work (Buehl & Alexander, 2005; Felder, 1997; Henderson, 1995; Kloss, 1994; Muis, 2004).

Connections With Gifted Education. Evidence that gifted students tend to be somewhat ahead of their age-mates in epistemological development follows naturally from the data on formal operations reported above. However, other interesting connections bring this theory into cohesion with existing knowledge of gifted students. For example, there is some indication that people who prefer Intuition on the Myers-Briggs Type Inventory tend to have higher epistemological stances (Zhang, 1999). Gifted students overwhelmingly report this preference (Sak, 2004), and the connection gives further evidence that gifted students will respond best to open-ended inquiry-oriented learning environments. Similarly, it explains gifted adolescents' positive response to mentor relationships. Like all adolescents, gifted teenagers want to see similarities between themselves and others; in mentors, they find kindred spirits who think about ideas from similar frames of mind.

Most exciting, perhaps, is the connection between epistemology and expertise. Not only do gifted students show early potential to achieve the experts' high levels of reasoning, but also, epistemological models provide a guide to help explain how to move all students closer to authentic higher order reasoning. Gallagher (1998) suggested that models such as these would make effective frameworks for designing high school curriculum, providing an organic model for differentiation. Based on his study of adolescent epistemological beliefs, Cano (2005) concurred:

> . . . it is necessary to take into account not only students' previous knowledge and learning strategies . . ., but also their learning approaches and epistemological beliefs. . . . Secondly, we should work directly to try to enhance the depth of learning approaches and the complexity of epistemological beliefs, as a way of improving academic achievement. (p. 217)

Finally, this framework reinforces the notion that the outcomes for ignoring students' beliefs are grave. Students have trouble accepting the relevance of instruction that is out of sync with their stage (Perry, 1970), a finding that is consonant with the well-established knowledge that gifted adolescents reject mundane, repetitive curriculum. Further, gifted students operating at higher levels than other students find instruction oriented towards the majority uninspiring, and communicate their feelings through underachievement. More seriously perhaps, Nelson (1989) cautioned that excessive time spent in low-level curriculum actively builds a wall of habits that blocks the path to higher level reasoning. Even rapid acceleration can have this damaging effect if students are only accelerated into new low-level content. To provide a climate ready for higher order thinking, educators must present content that is accelerated vertically as well as horizontally.

Complete Coherence:
Evidence-Based Recommendations for
Differentiation in Secondary School

Each of the perspectives considered in this rationale is championed by different researchers operating from different paradigms and using different research techniques. Even so, their respective findings are remarkably similar.

1. Gifted adolescents need exposure to a larger quantity of content that they find challenging. Beginning at least in middle school, abstract content should be a standard part of their curriculum. The importance of developing a plentiful, high-quality well of information is essential as it is a precursor to using higher order thinking, metacognitive thinking, and abstract thinking. Gifted students will not adequately develop their thinking skills without this knowledge base.

2. A quality knowledge base is necessary, but not sufficient, for developing thinking skills. Gifted students must be presented with learning experiences that require them to engage their critical thinking skills and metacognitive skills. If they do not find their assignments challenging, their brains will not engage their higher order functions. Together, content and strategy used along with metacognition predict academic performance, making the simultaneous development of these three paramount.

3. Gifted students show early promise for developing expertise. Capitalizing on that early promise requires instruction where students can practice the qualities of expertise including open-ended instruction, inquiry-based instruction, problem-oriented instruction, field experiences, and mentorships, all centered on high-quality disciplinary or interdisciplinary content. Gifted students are most likely to see this instruction as relevant and draw maximum value from it.

4. Expertise requires more than content and skill; habits of mind and advanced epistemological reasoning also are essential. If we aspire for gifted students—or for any student—to become creative, productive leaders in their chosen field, curriculum and instruction should be selected to develop these simultaneously, and include exposure to the philosophies and ethics of the disciplines.

The absence of a quality differentiated secondary program for gifted students is not a neutral position; it is a choice that will result in deficit skill development and student apathy. At worst, it will result in the disillusionment of some of the best minds in the country.

References

Arlin, P. K., & Levitt, L. (1998). A developmental perspective on giftedness. *Creativity Research Journal, 11,* 347–356.

Baxter Magolda, M. B. (1987). Comparing open-ended interviews and standardized measures of intellectual development. *Journal of College Student Personnel, 28,* 443–448.

Bell, P. (2004). Promoting students' argument construction and collaborative debate in the science classroom. In M. C. Linn, E. A. Davis, & P. Bell (Eds.), *Internet environments for science education* (pp. 115–143). Mahwah, NJ: Lawrence Erlbaum.

Berninger, V., & Yates, C. (1993). Formal operational thought in the gifted: A post-Piagetian perspective. *Roeper Review, 15,* 220–224.

Bitner, B. L. (1991). Formal operational reasoning modes: Predictors of critical thinking abilities and grades assigned by teachers in science and mathematics for students in grades nine through twelve. *Journal of Research in Science Teaching, 28,* 265–274.

Buehl, M., & Alexander, P. (2005). Motivation and performance differences in students' domain-specific epistemological belief profiles. *American Educational Research Journal, 42,* 697–726.

Cano, F. (2005). Epistemological beliefs and approaches to learning: Their change through secondary school and their influence on academic performance. *British Journal of Educational Psychology, 75,* 203–221.

Carr, M., & Alexander, J. (1996). Where gifted children do and do not excel on metacognitive tasks. *Roeper Review, 18,* 212–216.

Cherney, I. D., Winter, J., & Cherney, M. G. (2005). Nuclear physics problem solving: A case study of expert-novice differences. *Transactions of the Nebraska Academy of Sciences, 30,* 1–7.

Chi, M. T. H., Glaser, R., & Farr, M. J. (Eds.). (1988). *The nature of expertise.* Hillsdale, NJ: Lawrence Erlbaum.

Csikszentmihalyi, M., Rathunde, K., & Whalen, S. (1994). *Talented teenagers: The roots of success and failure.* Boston: Cambridge University Press.

Davidson, J. E., & Sternberg, R. J. (1984) The role of insight in intellectual giftedness. *Gifted Child Quarterly, 28,* 58–64.

Dresel, M., & Haugwitz, M. (2005). The relationship between cognitive abilities and self-regulated learning: Evidence for interactions with academic self-concept and gender. *High Ability Studies, 16,* 201–218.

Felder, R. (1997). Meet your students: Dave, Martha and Roberto. *Chemical Engineering Education, 31,* 106–107.

Gallagher, J., Harradine, C. C., & Coleman, M. R. (1997). Challenge or boredom? Gifted students' views on their schooling. *Roeper Review, 19,* 132–136.

Gallagher, S. A. (1998). The road to critical thinking: The Perry scheme and meaningful differentiation. *NASSP Bulletin, 82*(595), 12–20.

Gallagher, S. A. (2006). Guiding the gifted to science expertise. In F. A. Dixon & S. M. Moon (Eds.), *The handbook of Secondary gifted education* (pp. 426–460). Waco, TX: Prufrock Press.

Gipson, M., Abraham, M., & Renner, J. (1989). Relationships between formal-operational thought and conceptual difficulties in genetics problem solving. *Journal of Research in Science Teaching, 26,* 811–821.

Goldberger, N. R. (1981). Developmental assumptions underlying models of general education. *Liberation Education, 67,* 233–243.

Gorodetsky, M., & Klavir, R. (2003). What can we learn from how gifted/average pupils describe their processes of problem solving? *Learning & Instruction, 13,* 305–326.

Grabner, R., Neubauer, A., & Stern, E. (2006). Superior performance and neural efficiency: The impact of intelligence and expertise. *Brain Research Bulletin, 69,* 422–439.

Haier R. J., Jung, R. E., Yeo, R. A., Head, K., & Alkire, M. T. (2004). Structural brain variation and general intelligence. *Neuroimage, 23*(1), 425–433.

Henderson, S. (1995). "Why do I have to be here? The Advanced Placement student in first-year composition: Problems and issues in cognitive development. *Journal of Secondary Gifted Education, 7,* 324–332.

Hong, E. (1999). Studying the mind of the gifted. *Roeper Review, 21,* 244–252.

Hurst, R., & Milkent, M. (1996). Facilitating successful prediction problem solving in biology through application of skill theory. *Journal of Research in Science Teaching, 33,* 541–552.

Inhelder, B., & Piaget, J. (1958). *The growth of logical thinking from childhood to adolescence.* New York: Basic Books.

Jarvin, L. & Subotnik, R. (2006). Understanding elite talent in academic domains: A developmental trajectory from basic abilities to scholarly productivity/artistry. In F. A. Dixon & S. M. Moon (Eds.), *The handbook of Secondary gifted education* (pp. 203–220). Waco, TX: Prufrock Press.

Kanevsky, L. (1992). Gifted children and the learning process: Insights on both from the research. In F. Mönks & W. Peters (Eds.), *Talent for the future* (pp. 155–161). Assen, The Netherlands: Van Gorcum.

Kanevsky, L., & Keighley, T. (2003). To produce or not to produce? Understanding boredom and the honor in underachievement. *Roeper Review, 26,* 20–28.

Kaufman, J. C., Gentile, C. A., & Baer, J. (2005). Do gifted student writers and creative writing experts rate creativity the same way? *Gifted Child Quarterly, 49,* 260–265.

King, P. M., & Kitchener, K. S. (1994). *Developing reflective judgment: Understanding and promoting intellectual growth and critical thinking in adolescents and adults.* San Francisco: Jossey-Bass.

King, P. M., & Kitchener, K. S. (2004). Reflective judgment: Theory and research on the development of epistemic assumptions through adulthood. *Educational Psychologist, 39*(1), 5–18.

Kitchener, K. S. (1983). Cognition, metacognition and epistemic cognition: A three-level model of cognitive process. *Human Development, 26,* 222–232.

Klein, J. T. (1993). Blurring, cracking and crossing: Permeation and the fracturing of discipline. In E. Messer-Davidow, D. R. Shumway, & D. J. Sylvan (Eds.), *Knowledge: Historical and critical studies in disciplinarity* (pp. 185–211). Charlottesville: University of Virginia Press.

Kloss, R. J. (1994). A nudge is best: Helping students through the Perry scheme of intellectual development. *College Teaching, 42,* 151–158.

Kronholm, M. M. (1993). The impact of developmental instruction on reflective judgment. *Review of Higher Education, 19,* 199–255.

Larson, R. W., & Richards, M. H. (1991, August). Boredom in the middle school years: Blaming schools versus blaming students. *American Journal of Education, 99,* 418–443.

Lovell, C. W., & Nunnery, J. (2004). Testing the adult development Tower of Babel hypothesis: Homogeneous by Perry position collaborative learning groups and graduate student satisfaction. *Journal of Adult Development, 11,* 139–150.

Ludlow, B. L., & Woodrum, D. T. (1982). Problem-solving strategies of gifted and average learners on a multiple discrimination task. *Gifted Child Quarterly, 26,* 99–104.

Matthews, D., & McLaughlin, T. (1994). Effects of learner-centered laboratory activities on achievement and students' preferences in two high school biology courses. *Perceptual and Motor Skills, 78,* 285–286.

McDonald, J. (1989). Cognitive development and the structuring of geometric content. *Journal for Research in Mathematics Education, 20,* 76–94.

Montague, M. (1991). Gifted and learning disabled gifted students' use of knowledge and use of mathematical and problem solving strategies. *Journal for the Education of the Gifted, 14,* 393–411.

Muis, K. (2004). Personal epistemology and mathematics: A critical review and synthesis of research. *Review of Educational Research, 74,* 317–377.

Neber, H., & Schommer-Aikins, M. (2002). Self-regulated science learning with highly gifted students: The role of cognitive, motivational, epistemological, and environmental variables. *High Ability Studies, 13*(1), 59–74.

Nelson, C. E. (1989). Skewered on the unicorn's horn: The illusion of the tragic tradeoff between content and critical thinking in the teaching of science. In L. W. Crow (Ed.), *Enhancing critical thinking in the sciences* (pp. 17–27). Washington, DC: National Science Teachers Association.

Nelson, C. E. (1996). Student diversity requires different approaches to college teaching, even in math and science. *American Behavioral Scientist, 40,* 165–175.

Niaz, M., & Robinson, W. (1992). From "algorithmic mode" to "conceptual gestalt" in understanding the behavior of gases: An epistemological perspective. *Research in Science & Technological Education, 10,* 53–64.

Perry, W. G., Jr. (1970). *Forms of intellectual and ethical development in the college years: A scheme.* New York: Holt, Rinehart, & Winston.

Plucker, J. A., & McIntire, J. (1996). Academic survivability in high-potential, middle school students. *Gifted Child Quarterly 40,* 7–14.

Rabinowitz, M., & Glaser, R. (1985). Cognitive structure and process in highly competent performance. In F. D. Horowitz & M. O'Brien (Eds.), *The gifted and talented: A developmental perspective* (pp. 75–98). Washington, DC: American Psychological Association.

Robinson, A., & Clinkenbeard, P. R. (1998). Giftedness: An exceptionality examined. *Annual Review of Psychology, 49,* 117–139.

Ruban, L., & Reis, S. (2006). Patterns of self-regulation: Patterns of self-regulatory strategy use among low-achieving and high-achieving university students. *Roeper Review, 28,* 148–156.

Ryan, M. (1984). Monitoring text comprehension: Individual differences in epistemological standards. *Journal of Educational Psychology, 76,* 248–258.

Sak, U. (2004). A synthesis of research on psychological types of gifted adolescents. *Journal of Secondary Gifted Education, 15,* 70–79.

Schommer, M. (1994). An emerging conceptualization of epistemological beliefs and their role on learning. In R. Garner & P. A. Alexander (Eds.), *Beliefs about texts and instruction with text* (pp. 25–40). Hillsdale, NJ: Lawrence Erlbaum.

Schommer, M., & Dunnell, P. A. (1997). Epistemological beliefs of gifted high school students. *Roeper Review, 19,* 153–156.

Schommer-Aikins, M., Duell, O. K., & Hutter, R. (2005). Epistemological beliefs, mathematical problem-solving beliefs, and academic performance of middle school students. *The Elementary School Journal, 105,* 289–304.

Shiever, S., & Maker, C. J. (1997). Enrichment and acceleration: An overview and new directions. In N. Colangelo & G. A. Davis (Eds.), *Handbook of gifted education* (pp. 99–110). Boston: Allyn & Bacon.

Shore, B. M. (2000). Metacognition and flexibility: Qualitative differences in how gifted children think. In R. C. Friedman & B. M. Shore (Eds.), *Talents unfolding: Cognition and development* (pp. 167–187). Washington, DC: American Psychological Association.

Shore, B. M., & Irving, J. (2005). Inquiry as a pedagogical link between expertise and giftedness: The high ability and inquiry research group at McGill University. *Gifted and Talented International, 20*(1), 37–40.

Shore, B. M., & Lazar, L. (1996). IQ-related differences in time allocation during problem solving. *Psychological Reports, 78,* 848–849.

Sowell, E. R., Peterson, B. S., Thompson, P. M., Welcome, S. E., Henkenius, A. L., & Toga, A. W. (2003). Mapping cortical change across the human life span. *Nature Neuroscience 6,* 309–315.

Span, P., & Overtoom-Corsmit, R. (1986). Information processing by intellectually gifted pupils solving mathematical problems. *Educational Studies in Mathematics, 17,* 273–295.

Steiner, H. H., & Carr, M. (2003). Cognitive development in gifted children: Toward a more precise understanding of emerging differences in intelligence. *Educational Psychology Review, 15,* 215–243.

Steiner, H. H., & Carr, M. (2006). *The development of problem solving strategies in gifted and average-ability children: Bringing research from cognitive development to educational practice.* Hauppauge, NY: Nova Science.

Sternberg. R. J. (Ed.). (1982). *Handbook of human intelligence.* New York: Cambridge University Press.

Sternberg, R. J. (2003). A broad view of intelligence: The theory of successful intelligence. *Consulting Psychology Journal: Practice and Research, 55,* 139–154.

Subotnik, R. F. (2003). Adolescent pathways to eminence in science: Lessons from the music conservatory. In P. Csermely & L. Lederman (Eds.), *Science education: Talent recruitment and public understanding* (pp. 295–302). Burke, VA: IOS Press.

Thomas, J. A. (2008). Reviving Perry: An analysis of epistemological change by gender and ethnicity among gifted high school students. *Gifted Child Quarterly, 52,* 87–98.

Wavering, M. (1989). Logical reasoning necessary to make line graphs. *Journal of Research in Science Teaching, 26,* 373–379.

Weinstock, M., Neuman, Y., & Tabak, I. (2004). Missing the point or missing the norms: Epistemological norms as predictors of students' ability to identify fallacious arguments. *Contemporary Educational Psychology, 29*(1), 77–94.

Wilkinson, W. K., & Maxwell, S. (1991). The influence of college students' epistemological style on selected problem solving processes. *Research in Higher Education, 32,* 333–350.

Wilkinson, W. K., & Schwartz, H. H. (1987). The epistemological orientation of gifted adolescents: An empirical test of Perry's model. *Psychological Reports, 61,* 976–978.

Young, E. (2001, May/June). Analyzing the building blocks of life. *The Courier,* 46–48.

Yurgelun-Todd, D. A., & Kilgore, W. D. (2006). Fear-related activity in the prefrontal cortex increases with age during adolescence: A preliminary fMRI study. *Neuroscience Letter, 406,* 194–199.

Zhang, L. F. (1999). Further cross-cultural validation of the theory of mental self-government. *Journal of Psychology, 133,* 165–181.

Zhang, L. F., & Watkins, D. (2001). Cognitive development and student approaches to learning: An investigation of Perry's theory with Chinese and U.S. university students. *Higher Education, 41,* 239–261.

Chapter 2

The Socioemotional Needs of Gifted Students in Secondary Schools

BY

SUSANNAH
WOOD

N **1997,** Moon, Kelly, and Feldhusen investigated what parents, counselors, teachers, and related professionals believed were important differentiated services for gifted youth and families and how those services could be developed. One of the greatest perceived needs for differentiated services was that of counseling for gifted adolescents. As Gallagher (Chapter 1, this volume) emphasized, adolescence is the unique and pivotal time of life in which gifted students experience many challenges while attending secondary schools; it comes with exciting life changes as well as significant challenges.

The fields of gifted education and counseling have investigated several of the most common experiences and challenges faced by gifted adolescents. Robinson (2002a) suggested that social and emotional challenges facing the gifted student would stem from one of three areas: asynchronous development, affective regulation based on the typical traits of gifted students as described above, or membership in a special group within the gifted population, such as twice-exceptional students. Several of these stressors or challenges have been suggested in the literature as "predictable" because they are challenges that gifted students will most likely encounter during the development of their talent (Blackburn & Erickson, 1986). The type, nature, and characteristics of these challenges have expanded as the research base has increased. Although each gifted adolescent encounters a range of social and emotional concerns as he or she matriculates through the secondary school experience and engages in the process of resolving identity, not all students encounter precisely the same ones.

This chapter addresses several common areas of concerns and challenges that some gifted students might encounter during adolescence. Finally, the literature concerning common best practices designed to meet the gifted students' social and emotional needs is synthesized. Future systematic outcome research is warranted, focused on examining which of these best practices are effective and why.

Adolescence: A Delicate Juncture

Adolescence has been targeted as a critical period in the development of gifted students. This stage of life is typified by rapid physical changes due to hormonal fluctuations and growth spurts, including changes in neural functioning and changes in social and emotional functioning such as individuation from parents, independence, and the beginning definition of personal identity, values, and philosophy (Clark, 2002). Adolescence comes with great upheavals as well as opportunities for students to determine a sense of how their individual gifts will contribute to the future (Schultz & Delisle, 2003).

One of the primary tasks of adolescence is to resolve the dilemma between identity and role confusion (Erikson, 1963); in essence, gifted adolescents must answer the question of "Who am I?" This question is multifaceted and rests in relationships, work, and in the concept of self with regard to culture and gender. Additionally, with adolescence comes the onset of struggles with identity, the balancing of expectations of self and of others, decision-making that can impact future plans such as career and college choice, achievement, the individuation from parents and acceptance into social groups, as well as exploration and ownership of talent (Clark, 2002; Schultz & Delisle, 2003). For the gifted adolescent, several challenges exist within this primary question including ownership of talent, dissonance between self-expectation and performance, risk-taking, competing expectations, impatience, and premature identity (Buescher & Higham, 1990).

Adolescence is also a delicate juncture in the talent development process. As raw gifts are practiced, honed, and nurtured into talent domains, gifted students are affected by a variety of influences, such as their own personalities, their community, their families of origin, their social mores, and their educational environments (Gagné, 2003). For gifted students, adolescence is a time of questioning and making sense of their gifts, exploring how those gifts will be translated into product and performance, as well as envisioning what those products will look like in the future in their quest for a meaningful and authentic life.

Engagement and Achievement

Adolescence is a time in which gifted students can choose to engage or disengage on a variety of fronts including school, family, and community. Within the context of the school, this engagement often is contingent on the level of rigor and challenge in middle and high school coursework, which sometimes is lacking for gifted students (Clark, 2002; Gallagher, Chapter 1). Lack of challenge, denial of giftedness, and the immense need to blend in may drive a gifted student to disengage. One reason for underachievement is the fact that gifted students' intellectual and affective needs are not being met in school (Rimm, 2003). Students who go unchallenged and uncared for typically become bored, discouraged, angry, and depressed, and they may suffer from physical and psychological pain (Carlson, 2004; Clark, 2002; Davis & Rimm, 1997). The cause can be the mismatch between student ability and classroom curriculum, which can result in disengagement and dropping out of school (Reis & McCoach, 2000).

Other characteristics of gifted underachievers include low self-esteem and self-concept; alienation and withdrawal; fear of failure and fear of success; locus of control; hostility or negative attitudes towards school; high degrees of self-criticism and perfectionism; and lack of coping or self-regulation skills (Reis & McCoach, 2000). Other stressors that may lead to underachievement include the inability to handle nonsuccess coupled with a change from lack of challenge to rigorous work (Reis & McCoach, 2002). Additionally, peer messages about acceptable behavior, families characterized by discord, inconsistent parenting styles, manipulation and sibling rivalry, "masking" of low self-esteem with bravado, rebellion, open criticism of teachers, and the sense of low personal control (Rimm, 2003) are contributing factors. As gifted students approach adolescence, they naturally are concerned about being popular and want to be well-liked and admired by peers (Rimm, 2003). This need for acceptance may cause gifted students to quietly underachieve to maintain peer support.

Stress

One of the greatest myths gifted adolescents encounter is that they are so competent due to their giftedness, that they do not encounter stress, boredom, or frustration (Cross, 2002). If they do, their giftedness must compensate for these experiences. Adolescents who expect that they can do everything often struggle when they do encounter difficulties and challenges. This myth also is exacerbated by the fact that many gifted students are smart enough to hide how they feel, even if they despair of having it all together or are experiencing exhaustion from performing at such high levels. Gifted students may experience stress, dissonance, and frustration when they attempt new things for the first time and do not immediately encounter success (Buescher & Higham, 1990; Dweck, 2000). This anxiety can be compounded by implicit messages by others who state that because they are gifted, they should be able to be successful on the first attempt. In addition, they also may encounter the "imposter syndrome" or the idea that they must work over and beyond their limitations so that they are not "caught" or thought of as a fake (Kaplan, 1990). Students may experience a great deal of stress trying to "prove" they are gifted or can meet expectations. No one can do everything all at once, completely perfectly, happily, and without challenges or obstacles. Study and practice are required in order to develop in any one area of talent, interest, or passion (Cross, 2002). Encouragement, nurturance, education, and training all require the input and aid of other people such as parents, teachers, counselors, mentors, and friends.

Stress for gifted students is not limited to the academic environment. Socializing in the secondary school experience can be fraught with perils. Gifted adolescents, like all adolescents, encounter the concept of the "imaginary audience" of peers who judge, critique, and assess them on a variety of fronts (Santrock, 1996). However, this audience may not be as imaginary as it seems. The high school experience is filled with harsh assessments of beauty, ability, and intelligence. Because of their advanced abilities, gifted students understand this readily and early. Kaplan (1990) listed several stressors that gifted adolescents encounter, including testing, demanding extracurricular activities, multiple and competing expectations, loneliness, difficulty in finding appropriate peer groups, and decision-making in the face of incomplete information or ambiguity. Because of their extraordinary abilities, gifted adolescents also can be "stressed" by the complex decisions of college and career, and how they will choose to engage their talents.

Individuation From Parents

The family of the gifted student is the "essential context" of his or her talent development (Freeman, 2000, p. 573). It is the context in which the talent was first identified and encouraged or not encouraged (Bloom, 1982; Colangelo, 2003; Freeman, 2000). Families have been the primary source of resources that encourage talent, which include early education, books and mentor teachers, the encouragement of educational practice, and the navigation of school climate (Bloom, 1982; Freeman, 2000). The family culture, norms, and belief systems, or the way it values gifts and talents, greatly affects a gifted student's achievement (Freeman, 2000). Studies suggest that parents react in various ways to the identification of giftedness of their child, ranging from ambivalence about the label of "gifted," to pride, denial, feelings of burden, or worry over the child's rejection (Keirouz, 1990). Parents of culturally diverse gifted students may not wish to question the educational status quo by requesting gifted services, in order to maintain good relationships with the school. An additional reason for not seeking gifted services is that parents may feel that by identifying their child as gifted, they will lose control of him or her, or that the adolescent will forsake his or her cultural heritage (Evans, 1993).

Parenting gifted adolescents presents its own challenges. As part of the natural progress of individuation, the gifted adolescent establishes a sense of self in relationship to the family unit and peer network. Adolescents, as part of determining their identity must ask, "Who am I in relation to you?" Adolescents naturally push boundaries and desire more freedom and participation in the rules and decision-making of the family unit (Ruf, 2004). In addition, gifted adolescents must confront their own ideas about giftedness. Bombarded by multiple and often conflicting messages, gifted adolescents must wrestle with who owns their talent and how that talent will be applied. Students may want to "try on" a variety of personalities, peer networks, activities, and possible career paths. However, doubt, frustration, discouragement, and anxiety are all a part of this searching. Parents may encounter the student's lack of patience and frustration over the ambiguity of multiple options, decisions, or a lack of definitive answers (Buescher & Higham, 1990). Gifted adolescents can challenge the family or parent's ability to parent, causing questions about parenting efficacy and the ability to provide enrichment and stimulation (Keriouz, 1990; Ross, 1979). Parents of the gifted may need support and guidance as their gifted children progress from childhood into adolescence and adulthood.

Peers

A critical question gifted adolescents must answer is which they would choose if faced with the options of being smart or being popular (Delisle, 2002). Traditionally, gifted students have been challenged to find peers of the same intellectual level. Younger gifted students seem to be socially accepted, but this acceptance usually changes with the onset of adolescence (Rimm, 2002). However, this generality may not hold true for highly gifted children with IQ's above 160 who reported that despite their efforts, including purposely hiding their gifts or underachieving for social acceptance, had few or no friends within the regular education classroom (Gross, 2002; Robinson, 2002a). The number and type of friendships may vary depending on the level of introversion or extraversion and the desire for friendships demonstrated by the student. Not having many friends or acquaintances is not necessarily a sign of social deviance; it simply may be a sign of the difficulty gifted students have finding others who have similar abilities.

Although casual conversation regarding sports, movies, and popular music and bands are just as enjoyable to gifted students as they are to their nongifted peers, these students still need to discuss, read, and ponder issues of fairness, justice, physics, literature, societal mores, or existentialism (Schultz & Delisle, 2003). The problem is the small pool of peers with whom these higher order conversations can occur. Some gifted students cannot or do not choose to make same-age friends, but rather choose students who are older and share either abilities or interests. Gifted students may worry about how they will be perceived if they opt for a few significant friends rather than a room full of casual acquaintances.

In addition, gifted adolescents may experience conflicts between achievement and affiliation and peer rejection (Clark, 2002). Research suggests that they seem to believe giftedness was positive with regard to personal growth and academics, but negative in terms of peer relationships (Kerr, Colangelo, & Gaeth, 1988).

Although gifted students do not mind being known as academically oriented, they do not want to have that orientation highlighted to the point at which it sets them apart from their peers (Kerr et al., 1988). Dauber and Benbow (1990) noted that students with verbal talents reported having the lowest feelings of importance and social standing, possibly due to students' complex verbal skills that are readily apparent in social situations. Students with mathematic or quantitative ability, however, report that their peers would rate them higher on importance; they also have a higher opinion of their own importance than the verbally talented children (Dauber & Benbow, 1990).

By the time gifted students reach adolescence, they realize that peer relationships come with a price (Rimm, 2002). Gifted students who believe that they will be treated differently based on their giftedness if their peers learn of it also may believe that they have the ability to manage how much their peers know about them, in an effort to increase their social desirability (Coleman, 1985; Cross, 2004). Gifted students base their chosen social coping strategies and degree of information disclosure about being gifted on the level of potential stigmatization or threat for being gifted in that social situation (Cross, Coleman, & Terhaar-Yonkers, 1991). For some students, giftedness is not something to self-disclose, especially in a perceived hostile social environment. Various means of coping have included denying giftedness, using humor, maintaining a high activity level, denying a negative impact of giftedness on peer acceptance, conforming to others' standards, helping others, and minimizing one's focus on popularity (Swiatek, 1995, 1998, 2001).

Even the most capable gifted adolescent may have difficulty finding friends and romantic partners. Because adults often see these students as more mature, they may not give the adolescent the time, dialogue, support, and guidance they need to successfully pursue friendships and romantic connections (Ruf, 2004). Students who are comfortable with Byron or Einstein may not know "party" etiquette, "small talk," or how to ask someone for a date. Adults in the lives of gifted students have the wisdom and experience to help them not only practice certain social skills, but also to help them process and reflect on issues of dating, male and female perspectives, consequences, and peer pressure (Fahlman, 2000).

Perfectionism and Fear of Failure

Perfectionism has been and continues to be a highly discussed and researched topic in both gifted education and in psychology. Over time there have been different beliefs regarding perfectionism: viewing the trait as either one dimensional or multidimensional, positive or negative, or as a continuum of behaviors and feelings (Schuler, 2002). From one perspective, perfectionism has been seen as a neurotic, debilitating, unhealthy, and destructive trait (Hamachek, 1978; Pacht, 1984); while from a second perspective, it has been seen as an adaptive behavior indicating high standards, and a striving toward excellence and personal potential (Hamachek, 1978; LoCicero & Ashby, 2000; Pacht, 1984; Parker & Adkins, 1995; Parker & Mills, 1996; Schuler, 2002). Disabling or neurotic perfectionism has been associated with guilt, procrastination feelings of "I should," self-deprecation, face-saving behavior, writer's block, and mental health concerns such as depression (Hamachek, 1978; Pacht, 1984). However, "normal" perfectionists feel good about their effort involved with a task (Hamachek, 1978), and there may be a sense of an internal striving, and a desire to maximize potential, to hold high personal standards, and to self-actualize (Parker & Adkins, 1995). Analyses on the lives of eminent people point to the fact that perfectionism is a consistent theme described both as the dedication and desire to work, stressing the importance of high levels of aspiration, holding high personal standards, and the dissatisfaction with accomplishments (Parker & Adkins, 1995).

One research study focused on gifted adolescents at a specialized secondary school and examined the relationship between the typology of adolescent perfectionism and mental health. Dixon, Lapsley, and Hanchon (2004) found four perfectionism types (i.e., Mixed-Adaptive, Pervasive, Nonperfectionist, and Mixed-Maladaptive) in which students varied on their level of confidence, standards, reactions to mistakes, and parental expectations as well as their psychiatric symptoms, feelings of mastery and coping, competence, and self-image. The Mixed-Adaptive types had confidence in their ability to complete tasks, held high standards, and had parents who had high expectations but did not criticize and did not react negatively to making mistakes. Pervasive and Mixed-Maladaptive perfectionistic types were associated with poor adjustment and mental health concerns, displayed low self-image and personal security, dysfunctional coping, and more psychiatric symptoms (Dixon et al., 2004). In addition, Speirs Neumeister (2004) suggested two types of perfectionists: socially prescribed and self-oriented. Socially prescribed perfectionists experienced an increase in other's expectations of them based on past successes, and perceived their perfectionism as a result of their parents' expectations, high demands, and authoritarian parenting style. Self-oriented perfectionists, in contrast, experienced a desire for perfection and increased expectations for themselves based on earlier successes, but did not experience an expectation of perfection by their parents; rather, self-oriented perfectionists adopted characteristics by watching their parents' model perfectionistic behaviors (Speirs Neumeister, 2004).

In her review of the literature, Schuler (2002) wrote that as a group gifted students are more perfectionistic than their average age-mates and that their perfectionism can be a positive force behind achievement. LoCicero and Ashby (2000), citing Parker and Mills (1996), contend that gifted students are more perfectionistic in adaptive ways but their behaviors can be misconstrued by adults or school professionals. Misconception about the topic may stem from the language used to describe a student. A child described as a high achiever or as exhibiting high standards is seen as engaging in positive behaviors while another child described as Type A, obsessive, or anal retentive is seen as engaging in negative or even debilitating behaviors.

Clark (2002) wrote that at the heart of perfectionism is fear, typically the fear of failure. For many gifted students, there is an inherent need to do everything "right" so that they are validated as "good" people. Perfectionism and fear of failure are not just the province of academics or schools; gifted adolescents also may experience social anxiety and feelings of discomfort, frustration, self-doubt, or ineptitude. Being less than perfect is equated to not being good enough, and most students who experience this feeling do everything in their power not to encounter situations in which failure is an option (LoCicero & Ashby, 2000). Fear of failure and perfectionism can stem from self-expectations. Gifted adolescents are challenged by the self-expectation that they should be able to meet each new situation or new challenge expertly (Dweck, 2000; Robinson, 2002b). In situations that are overly challenging or could result in a lack of success (Blackburn & Erickson, 1986; Silverman, 1993b), gifted students simply may choose to avoid or not to take risks in areas outside their comfort zone. To avoid the risk of committing to paper words or thoughts that aren't articulated precisely, gifted students also can adopt procrastinating behaviors (Rimm, 2003). Adolescents who have an established track record of success can be very surprised by situations that don't result in success and subsequently can experience self-doubt, feelings of helplessness and vulnerability, questioning, and a drop in self-concept (Dweck, 2000). As a result, gifted students may be confronted by the fact that they lack skills or emotional responses needed to handle these "unsuccessful" events (Dockery, 2005; Reis & McCoach, 2002).

Experiences of Culturally Diverse Students

Clark (2002) defined culture group as "any group of people who share a common value structure, belief system, language and/or world view" (p. 497) and which typically encompasses students who differ from the White middle-class norm, such as children from African American, Asian American, Native American, Pacific Islander, and Latino descent (Evans, 1993). Culturally diverse gifted students must contend with unique challenges in secondary schools. Ford and Harris (1999) outlined several important issues that impact the academic, social, and emotional lives of culturally diverse gifted students including self-concept (academic and social), students' experiences of injustice and discrimination, and racial identity development.

Ford and Harris (1999) wrote that culture is the

aggregation of beliefs, attitudes, habits, values and practices that form a view of reality. These patterns function as a filter through which a group of individuals view and respond to the environment. Learning styles are experienced by individuals in terms of acting, feeling and being. (p. 1)

Hence, the way students learn and how they feel about education and achievement is directly tied to the concept of culture. The learning and achievement of gifted students from culturally diverse backgrounds is impacted by several factors.

First is the type of educational experience these students encounter. The educational experience of gifted students from culturally diverse backgrounds is influenced by the type of curriculum, the educators who teach them, and the attitudes and beliefs those educators have. Ford and Harris (1999) noted that African American gifted students are represented disproportionately among underachievers and experience negative attitudes toward school because they experience a curriculum that does not augment their racial and cultural identity, the subjects taught lack meaning and significance, and in general, these students are not being educated to live in a society that is culturally and racially diverse.

Because American educational institutions have been built on White Western European ideas of what are "normal" or "appropriate" values, behaviors, and ideas, educators often have failed to acknowledge that what is considered appropriate student behavior in White Western European culture may not be appropriate behavior for students from culturally diverse backgrounds (Evans, 1993). Gifted students from diverse cultural backgrounds often have been seen as inferior to White gifted students. This concept of "cultural deficiency" or a "deficit thinking" model has perpetuated myths about students from culturally diverse backgrounds and has influenced gifted educational practices in a variety of ways, including identification measures and procedures, the lack of encouragement to develop gifts and talents, and the labeling of the gifted child as "defiant" or a having a "behavior problem" for behaviors different from the cultural norm (Evans, 1993; Ford, 2003).

If this attitude is modeled by educators, it may lead to students' skewed beliefs about their own learning and achievement. Deficit thinking has enabled American educators to assume that the reason why culturally diverse children do not perform well on standardized tests, a traditional method of identification, is because there is something wrong with them or that they are "cognitively inferior" or "culturally deprived" (Ford, 2003; Evans, 1993; Ford, Harris, Tyson, & Trotman, 2002). The examination of potentially culturally biased assessments and instruments and their implementation in order to include more culturally different students in gifted programs has been criticized by some as "lowering rather than broadening standards" (Evans, 1993, p. 281). Deficit thinking also contributes to educators' inability or decreased desire to identify these students for screening and identification or to see them as gifted (Ford et al., 2002). Culturally diverse students remain severely underrepresented in gifted programs, by anywhere between 50% to 70% (Ford, 2003).

Some students experience both teacher and student skepticism regarding their legitimacy of placement in gifted programs and lowered expectations of success and achievement (Townsend & Patton, 1995). The academic self-concept of diverse gifted students can be eroded with this critique to the point where they may be confused as to whether they are actually gifted (Colangelo, 1985, as cited in Evans, 1993) or become unable to correctly assess their giftedness and talent (McIntosh & Greenlaw, 1986, as cited in Evans, 1993).

This erosion, in turn, leads to underachievement through gifted students' doubt about their ability to satisfy expectations of parents and teachers or to execute academic assignments in the traditional manner (Whitmore 1980, 1986, as cited in Ford & Harris, 1999). Ford and Harris described their own studies that demonstrate that underachieving African American students hold incongruous or paradoxical attitudes and behaviors regarding achievement: Although they have positive beliefs about achievement, the behaviors do not match or support those beliefs. The student's internalization of deficit thinking can lead to the questioning of abilities, self-sabotage, hiding talent, refusal to participate in gifted education programs, and the avoidance of achievement proscribed by peer pressure (Ford et al., 2002). Other students may encounter the "stereotype threat" described by Steele (1997) in which African American test performance suffers due to over-whelming anxiety and anxiety related to confirming stereotypes about African American IQ (Ford et al., 2002).

The learning, achievement, and personal success of culturally diverse gifted students is derailed by "prevalent and persistent" social injustices and discrimination (Ford & Harris, 1999). With their advanced cognitive abilities and perception, these students learn about injustices at an early age through experience, and they acutely feel the pain related to them (Lindstrom & VanSant, 1986). Many cultur-ally diverse gifted students are in classrooms or schools that are predominantly White and experience the pressure to "code switch" or change their behavior in order to meet the particular demands or social mores of a specific setting (Perry, 1993, as cited in Patton & Townsend, 1997). A "clash of cultures" in the classroom may lead to a lack of appreciation of or respect for the cultural assets of diverse gifted students. For example, the cultural assets of African American gifted students such as spirituality, harmony, movement, verve, oral tradition, expressive individu-alism, affect, communalism, and social time perspective (Boykin, 1994) may be brought in to direct conflict with White Euro-centric behavioral expectations of conformity, passivity, quietness, and competition (Harmon, 2002).

Adolescence is also a pivotal time in identity development. For culturally diverse gifted students, this means the development of a sense of racial identity. Racial identity "concerns one's self-concept as a racial being, as well as one's beliefs, attitudes, and values relative to other racial groups" (Ford & Harris, 1999, p. 132). There have been several racial identity development models proposed, and it is beyond the scope of this chapter to address them all; however, the priority is for culturally diverse gifted students to develop positive racial identities in the face of multiple challenges including those issues discussed above, such as implicit mes-sages, educational practices, overt discrimination, cultural misunderstanding, and challenges to social affiliation.

Minority students are traditionally socially oriented and need belonging and affiliation as well as bonding with others who have similar experience, concerns, and interests (Ford & Harris, 1999). But, as discussed above, gifted students also experience isolation, loneliness, and alienation based on the stigma of giftedness and the perceptions of others. In order to gain access and belong to a peer group, minority students may feel pressure to not engage or participate in gifted programs or to deliberately underachieve in order to avoid accusations of "acting White," "selling out" their cultural heritage to the dominant culture, or behaving in ways traditionally identified with White European cultural norms (Evans, 1993; Ford, 2002). This "opting out" stems from a seeming forced choice dilemma: academic achievement or social acceptance (Ford, 2002; Lindstrom & VanSant, 1986). Hence, underachievement may grant the gifted student social acceptance. Academic achievement wins culturally diverse students the pleasure of the educational system and future benefits while costing them loneliness, isolation, social ostracism, and accusation from their peer groups (Ford, 2003). Gifted students from diverse backgrounds also must attempt to fit in among different and competing cultures and values including mainstream culture, the students' culture of origin, and the gifted culture (Patton & Townsend, 1997).

Gender and Giftedness

A gifted adolescent's quest for identity and talent development is further complicated by conflicting societal messages regarding gender (Fahlman, 2000). Differences regarding life aspirations begin to manifest between young men and women during adolescence (Delisle, 1992) and both gifted girls and gifted boys encounter new challenges. Parental influences, issues relating to teachers, and grades in school become external barriers for gifted girls, while loss of belief in their abilities, social problems and isolation, concerns about future education, multipotentiality, perfectionism, and issues of achievement become internal obstacles that must be confronted (Reis, 2002). Gifted males also face their own set of unique challenges such as defining their identity, transitioning to manhood with a lack of initiation rites, and receiving conflicting messages regarding masculinity, engagement, and intimacy (Kerr & Cohn, 2001; Kerr & Nicpon, 2003).

Gifted Girls. Although there are no standard skills or attributes for navigating the female talent development process, there are some consistent characteristics and resiliencies that gifted women who have achieved eminence seem to have. These characteristics include passion, single-mindedness, and the willingness to make difficult decisions (Reis, 2003); the intensity to pursue one's passions (Kirschenbaum & Reis, 1997); the identification of a chosen field, leadership, maturity; and the necessity of falling in love with an idea (Kerr & Kurpius, 2004). Lerner (1993, as cited in Reis, 2003) suggested that inner assurance, serenity, and the ability to disregard patriarchal constraints allowed women with talent to withstand discouragement, isolation, and loneliness. Other attributes, such as flexibility and reflection in both emotional and cognitive domains; having the willingness to dream, take risks, change courses, and make mistakes; and the commitment to hard work and the nurturance of ambition are cited by Noble, Subotnik, and Arnold (1996). Moreover, patience, persistence, and disciplined practice are the defining characteristics that make a difference between raw ability and potential, and reality and product (Noble et al., 1996). In her studies on gifted women, Reis (2005a, 2005b) found that traits such as determination, insight, independence, initiative, humor, commitment, and creativity characterized the lives of talented women. Additional factors such as strong family and relationship ties, friendships with both men and women, love of work, and a passion to persevere in doing what they loved all contributed to these women's success and resilience (Reis, 2005a, 2005b).

Reis (2005a) suggested that in order for talented young girls to become successful women, they need the ability to challenge convention, to question authority, to speak out, to assert themselves, and to control their lives. However, the development of these assets can be a confusing process for gifted girls because they conflict with the traditional parental and often educational messages of what a gifted girl should be and how she should act (Reis, 1987, 2005a). Teachers of both sexes were found to perceive gifted boys as more competent in critical and logical thinking skills than gifted girls, who were more competent in creative writing (Cooley, Chauvin, & Karnes, 1984; Reis, 2002). In fact, teachers often liked smart girls less than other students, and some male teachers viewed girls as being more high strung, emotional, and gullible (Reis, 2002). Gifted girls who demonstrate curiosity, eagerness, and questioning may encounter labels of aggressiveness, lack of femininity, or obnoxiousness, unlike gifted boys who demonstrate the same characteristics (Reis, 1987).

For gifted girls, adolescence heralds subtle changes in expectations, achievement, attitudes, and aspirations (Kerr & Nicpon, 2003). Kerr and Nicpon wrote that moderately gifted girls remain well adjusted in adolescence like their male counterparts, but that some gifted girls experience a decline in self-confidence as well as experience social anxiety. The belief that girls must work harder to earn academic achievement may begin to be internalized by smart girls at an early age, contributing to gifted girls' beliefs that they are not innately as smart as their male counterparts and must work harder to succeed (Reis, 2002). The self-confidence of gifted girls appears to decrease from elementary school through high school. By adolescence, gifted girls become chameleons and choose adaptive behaviors to fit in with various groups (Silverman, 1993b). To be accepted by girls her own age, the gifted girl may opt to "dumb down" and hide her abilities in order not to be a "show off" or alienate this group (Reis, 2002). To avoid being unpopular with young men, gifted girls often choose to avoid competition with them (Reis, 2002).

Parents may become confused by the differences in their gifted girls' behavior between home, in which complex work is displayed proudly, and school, where girls may demonstrate their abilities with timidity (Silverman, 1993b). Research in self-concept and academic achievement with gifted females emphasizes the fact that parental opinions are highly important to these gifted learners (Reis, 2002). Mothers especially have a profound impact on how gifted females think about issues such as the development of their talent, financial security, and the world of work, relationships, and marriage (Kirschenbaum & Reis, 1997; Reis, 2005a, 2005b; Zimmerman, 1995).

Gifted Boys. "The gifted boy usually enters adolescence already knowing what his 'role' is going to be in high school . . . most gifted boys, however, inwardly aspire to something more than this superficial role" (Kerr & Cohn, 2001, p. 126).

In their studies on gifted males, Kerr and Cohn (2001) found that they felt pressure to have a "normal" life in order to relieve feelings of social isolation stemming from their giftedness. The choice between "excellence" and "normality" for gifted men required them to blend in and "be one of the guys" or accept the gifted label at the cost of appearing to be an "intellectual" (Kerr & Cohn, 2001). In order to survive their peer culture, gifted young men may put enormous pressure on themselves to compete and succeed athletically in order to avoid being labeled "geeks" (Kerr & Cohn, 2001). This pressure can lead to the creation of an impossible ideal to attain self-image of masculinity, while at the same time causing a hatred, fear, or distrust of their gifts and academic accomplishments. Gifted men from both small towns and diverse cultural backgrounds had the additional burden of being the paragon of the "scholar athlete" and shouldering the hopes of their communities (Kerr & Cohn, 2001).

On one hand, gifted men face ostracism by not committing to the culture of sports, while on the other they experience a limited number of leadership activities due to an increase of participation by females (Kerr & Cohn, 2001). Adolescent gifted boys may also choose to "opt out" or disengage from academic or leadership pursuits like their female counterparts but for different reasons. From an early age, gifted boys are taught that any activity labeled "female" is automatically "unmanly" (Kerr & Cohn, 2001). Ergo, if the fact that increasing numbers of females are achieving and engaging leadership positions in schools means that leadership is now a "female" or a "girl thing," then gifted boys will choose to leave the leadership arena (Kerr & Cohn, 2001). The perception that activities or even fields of work and career paths are more feminine than masculine also perpetuates the myth that they are then of lower status, are less prestigious, or emphasize the emotional (Kerr & Cohn, 2001). Hence, gifted men may disengage in order to protect their masculinity if they perceive it is being threatened in those academic or leadership domains by young women.

Interactions with females during adolescence can be challenging in their own right. Many gifted young men are indoctrinated at early ages to the idea that finding a perfect and beautiful young woman is the ultimate achievement and the key to success and happiness (Kerr & Nicpon, 2003). However, finding appropriate mates from the opposite sex can be difficult if gifted men feel threatened by competition, or if the pool of candidates with the same level of ability is small (Kerr & Nicpon, 2003). These young men may be confused as to how to engage with gifted females, especially if the females display characteristics such as power, questioning, and assertiveness that are considered traditionally "unfeminine" but may be valued in the work place or in many classes (Kerr & Nicpon, 2003; Reis, 2005a). Many gifted men are unhappy about being alone but may not know how to find a young woman whom they consider their equal (Kerr & Nicpon, 2003).

Another factor that may challenge gifted young men is their reluctance to seek help even though these students also experience boredom, social isolation, depression, and self-destructive behaviors (Kerr & Cohn, 2001). Some special populations of gifted young men that may be at risk for these challenges are those who are highly creative and exhibit unhealthy perfectionism and experience social isolation, gay and bisexual men, those who use substances, and those young men who have been abused either sexually or physically (Kerr & Cohn, 2001). Of these young men, many can hide their struggles from parents, educators, and peers by engaging and performing academically even if they are experiencing isolation, ostracism, alienation, or depression (Kerr & Cohn, 2001). Many of these young men feel that they have no one to listen to or support them, and that "real men" can carry these burdens silently and on their own (Kerr & Cohn, 2001). Kerr and Cohn noted that "these boys need meaningful relationships with others in which they feel understood, accepted, and valued" (p. 146)

Meaningful relationships may be hard to find for these young men. Some experience a lack of connection with their fathers and/or their communities, while others experience a sense of helplessness in the face of seemingly overwhelming challenges and hypocrisy in the world that they cannot change (Kerr & Nicpon, 2003). Mentors and guides are desperately needed by these young men, as are rites of passage that indoctrinate these young men into the responsibilities and privileges of adulthood (Kerr & Cohn, 2001).

Gifted men also have strengths and resiliencies that can help them work though and overcome many of the challenges discussed above. Although intensity and sensitivity, predominant gifted traits, are not always valued in American men, gifted men realize that being able to be emotionally expressive could make them more likely to be successful later in life (Hébert, 2002). "Belief in self" seems to be the most important factor influencing these gifted young men's future success (Hébert, 2000a). Hébert (2000b) discovered that gifted men recognized that characteristics such as empathy—although typically considered feminine traits—were appreciated and valued because they "allowed them to be better men and professionals" (Hébert, 2002, p. 140). This androgynous psychology, or the ability "to be at the same time aggressive and nurturant, sensitive and rigid, dominant and submissive, regardless of gender" (Csikszentmihalyi, 1996, p. 71), enables gifted men to have a broader understanding of human behavior with the belief that these characteristics in no way diminish masculine identity (Hébert, 2002).

Twice-Exceptional Students

Twice-exceptional students, or those students who are gifted but also have a disability, can encounter their own unique set of challenges as they progress through secondary education. Statistics suggest that between 120,000 and 180,000 individuals are both talented with a learning disability, and the incidence rate of gifted individuals with a learning disability is just as high as the general population (10–15%; Davis & Rimm, 1985, as cited in Olenchak & Reis, 2002; Silverman,

2003). Traditionally, the identification of both giftedness and disability occurs in elementary schools, when many high-ability students with learning disabilities are referred by teachers and parents as having reading and writing difficulties; however, some students are not identified as having a disability until later in middle or high school (Reis, Neu, & McGuire, 1997). Determining which student is gifted with a disability can be difficult.

Finding gifted students with disabilities generally includes the identification of discrepancies, such as differences between intelligence and ability test scores, differences in intelligence tests subtest scores (e.g., Verbal vs. Performance), or differences between IQ measures and academic performance (Olenchak & Reis, 2002; Silverman, 2003). However, reliance primarily on test measures for identification may cause educators to miss students who are eligible for services based on their twice-exceptionality; additional information is needed to ascertain a picture of the whole individual's functioning (Olenchak & Reis, 2002). Twice-exceptional students can be described as individuals who require special programming to accommodate functional limitations related to a disability that will allow him or her to fully develop the potential for exceptional achievement for one or more areas in which the student is talented (Whitmore, 1981, as cited in Szymanski & Corn, 1989). Yewchuk and Lupart (1988, as cited in Assouline, Nicpon, & Huber, 2006, p. 14) suggested an alternate definition: twice-exceptionality occurs "when [a student] is identified as gifted/talented in one or more areas while also possessing a learning, emotional, physical, sensory, and/or developmental disability."

Research regarding twice-exceptional students usually has focused on gifted individuals with learning difficulties (Reis & Colbert, 2004), ADHD (Zentall, Moon, Hall, & Grskovic, 2001), Asperger's syndrome (Neihart, 2000), dyslexia (Hishinuma, 1993), or emotional and behavioral concerns (Rizza & Morrison, 2003) because these areas are traditionally served in the schools. However, sensory integration dysfunction, auditory processing disorder, visual processing deficits, and spatial disorientation are also disabilities (Silverman, 2003), yet there has been little attention drawn to other areas of disability, such as gifted individuals who are deaf (Vialle & Paterson, 1998), blind (Corn, 1986), or who experience other physical challenges (Whitmore, 1981). If the student identified has one or both of the exceptionalities, services can be provided by an array of educators. But, for these students, the secondary school experience is not always smooth, even when services are provided.

For many twice-exceptional individuals, experiences with peers and educators can be painful and embarrassing. Twice-exceptional students have reported experiencing late identification of either the gift or the disability, placement in self-contained special education classes, retention, punishments for not finishing work when they were unable to, repeated admonishments to work harder, receiving detentions or being denied recess in order to finish school work, and being denied opportunities to learn or use needed compensation strategies (Reis et al., 1997). This paradoxical learner may be bombarded by the labels of lazy, unmotivated, undisciplined, defiant, or "retard" (Reis et al., 1997). Twice-exceptional students have frequently reported anxiety, frustration with the inability to articulate their knowledge in a useful manner and the physical manifestation of that frustration, lack of self-confidence, and the avoidance of competition or of certain tasks in which failure may occur (Reis & Colbert, 2004; Vespi & Yewchuk, 1992). Educators should be aware that the twice-exceptional student can be wrestling with "the continual conflict between [the student's] expectations and [his or her] achievement" (Vespi & Yewchuk, 1992, p. 68), which may lead to anger based on the conflicting beliefs in both their inability to reach their own goals and their beliefs that they are failures if they cannot (Silverman, 1989; Vespi & Yewchuk, 1992). These students may not know what to believe about themselves and try to reconcile the conflicting messages they have received from educators, peers, and parents with regard to both their gift and their disability. One individual described this experience as like having "two different people in the same body . . . one competent and bright and the other blocked that person from communicating" (Reis et al., 1997, p. 472).

For twice-exceptional individuals, the socialization that takes place with the peer group can be equally as painful and include ridicule and teasing for not being able to complete perceived "easy" school work (Reis & Colbert, 2004). Participants in Reis and Colbert's study reported hiding to avoid teasing and bullying or not answering questions in class for fear of not having the right answer or using the wrong words.

Once appropriate academic placements have occurred, additional services that focus on both gifts and disability needs should be provided for these students as a means of developing new, or nurturing existing, coping skills or resiliencies (Assouline et al., 2006; Gardynik & McDonald, 2005; Reis & Colbert, 2004; Stormont, Stebbins, & Holliday, 2001). Probably the greatest challenge educators will encounter is ensuring they express the desire to hear and understand their twice-exceptional students. Because of the negative experiences in educational systems, twice-exceptional students may feel anxiety or trepidation working with educators and counselors. These experiences should be explored so that students understand how they have impacted their view of education, work, and their thoughts and feelings about self-concept; use of compensation strategies; motivation; and frustration. Dialogue pertaining to students' conflicting feelings about the identification of both gift and disability and how they impact their constructed identity should be a primary consideration. Service providers should be prepared for mistrust, withdrawal, and anger from their students during these conversations.

Additional literature on twice-exceptional individuals suggest exploring a variety of inter- and intrapersonal issues such as stereotypes, multiple expectations, stress, identification and expression of emotions, burnout, self-blame, stress reduction, goal-setting, and the identification of ways and times for releasing emotions appropriately (McEachern & Bornot, 2001; Reis & Colbert, 2004). These issues can be addressed through a variety of therapeutic paradigms and can include simulations, role-plays (McEachern & Bornot, 2001; Reis & Colbert, 2004), and support groups (Assouline et al., 2006). Service providers and educators also should consider multiple venues for partnerships including school counselors, parents, and, when students are ready for transition to the world of work, rehabilitation counselors (McEachern & Bornot, 2001; Scarborough & Gilbride, 2006).

Current State of Counseling and Services to the Gifted

Traditionally, there have been three primary types of counseling available for individuals: family counseling, individual counseling through private practitioners, and counseling in the schools. In addition, concurrent with the rise of gifted education were centers throughout the United States that focused on gifted psychology and development; these centers also have traditionally provided counseling services. Each has its own strengths in serving the gifted child.

Teachers and Educators of the Gifted

Typically, it has been the teacher who has acted as the "wise friend" and nurturer of talent for the gifted student because he or she has the appropriate level of training in gifted psychology and education (VanTassel-Baska, 1991, 1993, 1998a). Teachers who have been trained in gifted psychology and education are in a unique position to meet the social and emotional needs of their gifted students as well as, and often through, meeting their intellectual and academic needs (VanTassel-Baska & Baska, 1993).

Undoubtedly, gifted students sense or acknowledge when a teacher is supportive of both their academic and social-emotional needs. Baldwin, Vialle, and Clarke (2000) found that important characteristics of teachers of the gifted included the following traits: having a mission, feeling empathy, having rapport, possessing the ability to see and perceive students on an individual basis, listening, having an investment in students, communicating excitement about learning, activating learning, encouraging innovation, providing gestalt, having objectivity, and providing focus. Educators of the gifted have the skills and resources to provide intervention skills and techniques such as modeling, bibliotherapy, discussion groups, special projects, career exploration, tutorials, and role-playing, which can be facilitated inside the classroom (VanTassel-Baska & Baska, 1993). Teachers are also in the position to act as advocates for their gifted students' needs within the school environment, which provides reassurance to parents who might be confused about how best to help their child. In addition, they are active listeners and informal advisors on a variety of topics because teachers know the gifted student (VanTassel-Baska & Baska, 1993).

Centers for Talent Development

Centers for talent development also have supported the needs of gifted students by providing career guidance, assessments, and counseling. These centers have acknowledged the importance of social-emotional development as an integral part of the gifted student's development and have worked with gifted students to nurture their overall potential for excellence (Colangelo, 2003; Sajjadi, 2000). Many of the founders and supporters of these centers for gifted learning and development conceptualized their beliefs about the importance of guidance and counseling and how these services played a critical role in the education of the gifted (Colangelo & Davis, 2003).

Some centers for talent development provide counseling at their sites. Educators who are interested in learning more should contact the center closest to them to receive information on the services offered. Although the following is not an exhaustive list of centers for talent development, they do provide support for identification, assessment, and service for gifted students:

- Ball State University's Center for Gifted Studies and Talent Development (http://www.bsu.edu/gifted);
- The Connie Belin and Jacqueline N. Blank International Center for Gifted Education and Talent Development (http://www.education.uiowa.edu/belinblank);
- Center for Talented Youth at Johns Hopkins University (http://www.cty.jhu.edu/gifted/dcc);
- Davidson Institute for Talent Development (http://www.ditd.org);
- Gifted Education Resource Institute at Purdue University (http://www.geri.soe.purdue.edu);
- Gifted Development Center (http://www.gifteddevelopment.com);
- Neag Center for Gifted Education and Talent Development at the University of Connecticut (http://www.gifted.uconn.edu);
- Northwestern's Center for Talent Development (http://www.ctd.northwestern.edu); and
- Talent Identification Program at Duke University (http://www.tip.duke.edu).

In addition, several national organizations may be of help to educators of the gifted who are seeking additional counseling supports and resources in schools, or need a referral for a counselor in their area. These include:

- National Association for Gifted Children (NAGC; http://www.nagc.org);
- Supporting Emotional Needs of Gifted (SENG; http://www.sengifted.org);
- American Counseling Association (ACA; http://www.counseling.org); and

- American School Counselor Association (ASCA; http://www. schoolcounselor.org).

Family Counseling

Given the challenges that parenting a gifted adolescent may present, one means of providing counseling services and support is through family counseling. Moon and Thomas (2003) suggested that family counseling and therapy have been effective means of working with adolescent concerns, and they recommend these services for families of gifted children who are experiencing challenges. The family system and the institution of the school at times clash over beliefs about the gifted student and how he or she should be served. This clash can cause considerable stress on the family system, which may cause families to seek support and encouragement from counselors in a family therapy setting. In a review of family counseling and therapy, Moon and Hall (1998) underscored the need for differentiated counseling for families because of the unique stressors parents of gifted children face due to the child's giftedness as well as the challenges encountered in seeking and attaining appropriate services in schools.

Individual Counseling

Individual counseling, as provided by private practitioners such as psychiatrists, psychologists, and licensed counselors, offers a wide variety of treatment modalities based on the counselor's theoretical orientations and beliefs about the client and counselor relationship. In his or her master's program, every practicing counselor is trained in a variety of theoretical orientations to counseling, including both basic and advanced techniques of the counseling process (Council for Accreditation of Counseling and Related Educational Programs, 2001). This training is required prior to becoming a professional counselor. Theoretical orientations from which counselors can choose are diverse in assumptions about human functioning, pathology and wellness, counseling techniques, treatment modalities, and the definitions of the client-counselor relationship. Examples of orientations include traditional psychoanalytic counseling as proposed by Freud and object-relations theory; Adlerian counseling that stresses personality and family roles; existential counseling based on the work of Victor Frankl and Rollo May, which emphasizes the quest for meaning and value; behavioral counseling based on the premises of B. F. Skinner; and Rational-Emotive Behavior counseling conceptualized by Albert Ellis, which focuses on identifying and refuting irrational or faulty cognitions and substituting these with rational and healthy thoughts (Corey, 1996).

School Counselors

Recently, the school counseling profession has drawn attention to and highlighted the school counselor's involvement with gifted students (Milsom

& Peterson, 2006; Peterson, 2006). Professional school counselors are leaders, advocates, and specialists in delivering comprehensive developmental guidance and counseling curricula that provides an array of services and collaborative partnerships, and whose effectiveness and impact on both student achievement and school culture can be measured (American School Counselor Association [ASCA], 2003a). The professional school counselor is a key person in the advocacy of special populations in schools and an important part of the talent development of gifted students (ASCA, 2003b; Gagné, 2003). The ASCA's National Model (2003a) provides the foundation for school counselors to advocate for all students, including their gifted students, in identifying systems or issues that may impede the gifted student's academic, career, or personal/social development. In addition, this model gives school counselors the vocabulary and professional stance that lends itself naturally to leadership positions that can promote changes to benefit gifted students in their schools.

Suggested Best Practices

"Numerous strategies have been suggested for enhancing the social and emotional development of gifted students" (Reis & Moon, 2002, p. 252). Strategies and techniques have been scattered through the literature on gifted and talented learners, but few have been comprehensively employed by school counselors or even private practitioners (Reis & Moon, 2002). What follows is a synthesis of current practices in serving the gifted student, including strategies and techniques that have been suggested in the gifted literature. This list has been developed from the following sources, which are also suggested for further reading and resources: Colangelo (2003); Ford (2002); Hébert (2002); Keiley (2002); Moon (2002); Nugent (2000); Peterson (2006); Reis (2002); Robinson (2002a); Rysiew, Shore, and Leeb (1999); Silverman (1993a, 1993b, 1993c, 1993d); and Van Tassel-Baska (1991, 1993, 1998a, 1998b). This list is not exhaustive, but may provide educators with a place to start when working with gifted adolescents who are encountering one or more concerns or challenges as described above.

The Relationship

Silverman suggested that what gifted students need is a good listener who can offer insight, a new perspective, recognition, and development of individual strengths; in addition, they need help from those who can see problems from the student's view, and provide room for self-exploration and growth. Consequently, those who counsel the gifted student should have an "understanding of the affective needs of the gifted as wedded to knowledge of counseling skills" (Silverman, 1993c, p. 85).

Academic Best Practices

Because many of the socioemotional issues experienced by gifted students are outgrowths of academic concerns, the following issues should be addressed by counselors and educators alike:

- *Correct identification* of student strengths, talents, and abilities. This includes examination of possible cultural biases, the use of culturally sensitive tests, multiple assessment data points, and proper testing protocols.
- *Appropriate placement* in classes and consideration of honors classes, Advanced Placement, International Baccalaureate, and early entrance to college programs.
- *Differentiated curriculum* designed to meet the intellectual needs of gifted students.
- Formulation of *academic blueprints* that help students navigate a course of study that best matches their strengths and abilities (VanTassel-Baska, 1993, 1998b). When outlining course offerings and potential 3- or 4-year plans, educators can discuss the "fit" between options and choices that best meet student needs and would benefit the student in the future when considering colleges and future career choices. To minimize anxiety, educators and students should discuss the concept of blueprints being flexible and not "set in stone."
- Guidance in *decision-making skills*. These skills are typically glossed over because of the assumption that if students are gifted, they already know how to make positive and healthy decisions. Counselors must consider teaching students this invaluable skill, using "pros and cons," lists, hypothesizing outcomes, considering personal values and ethics, and other methods.
- Guidance in *organization and time management skills*. Both of these are concrete skills that can be modeled, taught, and reinforced. Adults can take these skills for granted in their gifted students, but many students need to have these explicitly taught like any other academic skill. Time management and organization are crucial in coping with multiple classes and assignments, as well as scheduling extracurricular activities typical of secondary schooling. Techniques for studying, use of calendars and dayplanners, filing systems, and other skills hopefully will increase achievement and decrease student stress.
- Knowledge about *gifted students' experiences in the heterogeneous classroom*. Some students risk peer disapproval if they appear academically successful, so hiding gifts and talents is not an uncommon coping strategy for them. The pressure to hide gifts and abilities or to underachieve is problematic, especially for gifted girls and students from diverse cultural backgrounds.

- Provision of an *open and safe forum* in which students can discuss the level of rigor and challenge in the classroom and/or feelings of boredom or anxiety.
- Guidance in *common negative perfectionistic behaviors*. For some gifted students, the need to have precision and perfection can create paralysis when it comes to completing assignments or even putting one or two words on paper. Teachers and counselors need to teach and discuss the ideas of *multiple rough drafts and editing*.
- *Guidance in the use of inventories* for students' better understanding of their own abilities, learning preferences, and leadership styles.
- *Provision of multicultural gifted educators* who are trained in providing appropriate curriculum, knowledgeable about racial identity, skillful in addressing racism and discrimination, understand the needs of culturally diverse student groups, aware of their own perceptions and beliefs, and respect and appreciate students' cultural assets. Schools must create inclusive and safe environments for each student to learn about his or her cultural heritage in an integrative manner.

Career/College Best Practices

Social and emotional needs and concerns are naturally intertwined with future planning and decision-making regarding college and career choices (see Chapter 3, this volume). The following are suggested best practices:

- *Provide mentors* who can speak knowledgeably about specific fields in which the students are interested.
- *Provide the opportunity for shadowing, internships, volunteerism, and part-time employment* as ways for students to learn from experts in the field while gaining on-the-job skills and determining whether or not that specific job is a good fit for them.
- *Facilitate open and honest dialogue* about influencing factors such as self/other expectations, societal pressures, gender identity, and beliefs about what constitutes success.
- *Offer parent education* to introduce parents to potential career paths, college choices, and scholarships with which they may not be familiar.

Personal/Social Best Practices

Helping gifted students explore their identity as a gifted and talented person is paramount to serving their social and emotional needs. The following suggestions may assist educators in helping students address their thoughts and feelings pertaining to being a gifted student, as well as facilitate the learning of new skills to help students cope with their experiences.

- Provide a comprehensive and developmentally appropriate *affective curriculum* as both a preventive and interventive service.

- Address the issue of being gifted and how it affects the student's world view and experiences. Address the *meaning of giftedness* with students in small groups, classroom activities, or individual discussions. Discuss and provide activities surrounding topics such as intelligence, creativity, performance and production, motivation, and achievement. Be familiar with *multiple conceptualizations of giftedness* as well as the working definitions utilized by states and local school districts.

- Anticipate and support students' experiences of feelings of *loneliness or feeling different*. One of the top concerns experienced by gifted students is being perceived differently and being misunderstood because of their giftedness (Delisle & Galbraith, 2002; Galbraith, 1985). Provide small groups as a safe forum for gifted students to meet each other and talk about their experiences. Teaching communication skills, perspective taking, and working with role-plays and scenarios may increase student self-efficacy when it comes to making friends. Educators must be prepared for the fact that not only are the majority of gifted students introverts, but many students prefer few friends and more time alone, while others may choose friends among older nongifted students who are their cognitive and intellectual "age." Therefore, those who work with the gifted need to explore resources and forums that might have a larger "pool" of possible friendship candidates through summer and enrichment programs, safe and secure online groups, and community-based groups.

- *Actively address the needs of culturally diverse students.* Include discussions of cultural assets, community, affiliation, conflict and cooperation, leadership, self-determination, power, authority, control, and student choices involving social acceptance and achievement (Ford & Harris, 1999; Patton & Townsend, 1997). Be knowledgeable about different cultural groups and different paradigms of racial identity development, be aware of biases and stereotypes, and be aware of the continual need for further training and education. Don't be afraid to address racism and discrimination, and ensure a safe environment in which to discuss these issues. Work toward open communication, honesty, and respectful and appreciative collaborative relationships with the families and communities of these students. Form partnerships with local community groups that can help promote positive racial and cultural identity.

- Teach *positive communication skills*. Many gifted students are precocious in their vocabularies and can be extraordinarily talented when talking to adults. However, others encounter difficulty in "casual conversation" skills. These students would benefit from doing role-plays, writing "scripts," exploring multiple outcomes for each new social interaction, and then debriefing and discussing after having tried new communication skills. Some students may need access to media to learn more about popular culture, music, movies, and sports in order to facilitate "small talk."

- Teach appropriate *boundary setting and perspective taking* and how to work with hostile people. Some gifted students are very insightful and also can feel what other people feel. Appropriate boundaries and healthy give-and-take in relationships should be explored so that students do not "take on" the emotions of others, and learn to define how they think and feel apart from others. Perspective taking can challenge students to consider that others may not know what they know or see the world as they do. By "walking a mile in another's shoes," gifted students learn to value and appreciate another perspective than their own and may learn patience when other students aren't as "quick" as they are. Gifted students also can be met with hostility from others, both peers and adults. Hence, teaching students how to negotiate, compromise, and how to use humor and appropriate assertiveness skills needed for tough situations would be beneficial.

- Help students *identify negative thoughts* that may interfere with self-confidence or performance, and replace them with positive self-talk. Automatic negative thoughts (Amen, 1997) can plague gifted students in a variety of ways, especially with regard to perfectionism. Types of negative thinking can include the following: all or nothing thinking, overgeneralizations, distortions ("I failed one test so I am a failure"), focusing on the negative, "fortune telling" the worst case scenario, mind reading or hypothesizing what others think, deletions or forgetting past successes, and guilty and/or absolutist thinking (such as "must," "should," "ought"; Amen, 1997; Ellis, 2001). Other irrational thinking as hypothesized by Albert Ellis includes the absolute necessity for being loved, and the belief that a person should be totally competent and perfect all of the time. Teaching students to identify these thoughts, dispute them through experimentation or discussion, and then replace them with positive self-talk may increase self-concepts in multiple domains, positive performance, and overall self-esteem.

- Be creative in the *methods of exploring topics* and engaging in conversation. Some students may be wary, anxious, or in pain such that talking about personal experiences may be difficult. *Use books and movies* as a way for students to identify with characters, point out similarities and differences in characters' experiences and behaviors, and hypothesize characters' thoughts and feelings. The use of biblio- and cinematherapy (Halstead, 2002; Hébert & Kent, 2000; Hébert & Speirs Neumeister, 2002) may help gifted students open up about their own experiences and identify personal coping skills while learning new ones.

- *Use both play and art* as means and ways of calming upset students and activities with which students can engage while talking. Working with clay, drawing mandalas, constructing collages, engaging in mask-making, or simply sketching gives students some "space" when exploring painful, frustrating, or anxiety-provoking topics and can provide a venue for talking about multifaceted concepts such as identity.

- Help students keep track of positive changes through the *use of journaling or reflective writing*. Putting thoughts, feelings, and situations on paper may help gifted students to think about experiences more objectively, to identify recurrent thought patterns, and to document past successes that may be forgotten as a result of stress or perfectionism. Writing also facilitates the identification of common themes, concerns, and issues that students may not be able to observe or vocalize at the time of experience.
- Help students *identify emotional responses* to a variety of sources. Students need to be able to identify triggers and experiences with frustration and anxiety, including physical reactions, immediate thoughts, feelings and reactions, and reactions to people and things.
- Model and teach *stress reduction and relaxation techniques*. Counting to 10, deep breathing, visualization, and active muscle tensing and relaxing all are useful relaxation techniques that can be utilized both in and out of school. Students need to be able to identify times that they are likely to feel stress and pressure and what their preferred way of coping is, as well as people and places that they can rely upon to help reduce stress.
- Work with students to *view mistakes as learning experiences* and opportunities for future growth. No one likes to discuss experiences with failure, incompetence, bad choices, or mistake-making; however, these experiences, if left unresolved or unexplored, may create paralysis when similar situations arise. Students who experience intense feelings of perfectionism or fear of failure also may feel paralyzed and unable to act, and therefore choose to procrastinate if they have encountered perceived failure once. In addition, they may be hesitant to take risks or opportunities that may be outside their comfort zones. Students should have a safe forum to *discuss and explore outcomes of these experiences, as well as to generate and hypothesize alternative choices*, actions, and outcomes so that the situations are seen as chances to learn and grow—and opportunities to avoid making similar decisions.
- Be sensitive to gifted *adolescents' moral concerns, beliefs about justice, and keen sense of fairness*, some aspects of which society does not necessarily prize or desire. Many gifted students are acutely empathetic and "in tune" with the feelings of people and animals. These students often wish to alleviate pain and suffering and have remarkable ideas for helping others on both the micro and macro level. *Service-learning and volunteerism* may encourage these students to see these abilities as true gifts that can be used for society's benefit. These abilities also should factor heavily into career exploration and future lifestyles.
- Work with students as they wrestle with their *self-expectations and the perceived expectations of others*. Gifted students may entertain a vast array of expectations for themselves and perceive that others also have expectations or place demands on them.

- *Form partnerships* with families of gifted students, community members, local businesses and agencies, and universities. Working with gifted students provides incredible opportunities as well as many challenges. Partnering with other individuals and entities can provide more resources and decrease educator stress and concern about providing needed services. Inside the school and school system, gifted educators may be able to identify several likely partners, such as the school psychologist, school counselor, reading specialist, librarian, media resource personnel, and others who could help gifted educators advocate for and serve their students. Churches, businesses, counseling agencies, community services such as the YMCA and park districts, and local universities and community colleges may be able to provide additional information, resources, and avenues for programming for gifted students' needs.
- *Consider additional training.* Gifted educators encounter many students who are experiencing the challenges described above, and some may feel that they are unprepared for working with these students and issues. In this case, they should investigate training and workshops offered not only through the school district but also through mental health agencies, counseling services, and local universities that offer graduate training in counseling.

Summary

Adolescence can be both a challenging and exciting time for gifted students. Their quest for an identity and an answer to the question "Who am I?" contains obstacles that can create both crises and opportunities. Navigating the rocky waters of gender and cultural identity, achievement, engagement, perfectionism, and the relationships between peers and parents can create stress, but also provides a challenge to adolescents to grow and develop during their secondary school experience. Astute guidance counselors are a necessity for their maximal growth during this catalytic period.

Suggested Readings

Buescher, T., & Higham, S. (1990). *Helping adolescents adjust to giftedness* (Digest No. E489). Reston, VA: ERIC Clearinghouse on Handicapped and Gifted Children. (ERIC Document Reproduction Service No. ED321494)

Colangelo, N. (2003). Counseling gifted students. In N. Colangelo & G. A. Davis (Eds.), *Handbook of gifted education* (3rd ed., pp. 373–387). Needham Heights, MA: Allyn & Bacon.

Cross, T. (2004). *On the social and emotional lives of gifted children: Issues and factors in their psychological development* (2nd ed.). Waco, TX: Prufrock Press.

Delisle, J., & Galbraith, J. (2002). *When gifted kids don't have all the answers: How to meet their social and emotional needs.* Minneapolis, MN: Free Spirit.

Kaplan, L. S. (1990). *Helping gifted students with stress management* (Digest No. E488). Reston, VA: ERIC Clearinghouse on Handicapped and Gifted Children. (ERIC Document Reproduction Service No. ED321493).

Neihart, N., Reis, S., Robinson, N., & Moon, S. (Eds.). (2002). *The social and emotional development of gifted children: What do we know?* Waco, TX: Prufrock Press.

Ruf, D. (2004). *Independence and relationship issues in intellectually gifted adolescents.* Retrieved April 1, 2008, from http://www.educationaloptions.com/gifted_adolescents.htm

Silverman, L. (Ed.). (1993). *Counseling the gifted and talented.* Denver, CO: Love.

Suggested Web Sites

American Counseling Association—http://www.counseling.org
American School Counselor Association—http://www.schoolcounselor.org
Council for Accreditation of Counseling and Related Educational Programs—http://www.cacrep.org
Hoagies' Gifted Education Page—http://www.hoagiesgifted.org/counseling.htm

References

Amen, D. G. (1997). *ANT therapy: How to develop your own internal anteater to eradicate Automatic Negative Thoughts (ANTs).* Retrieved April 1, 2008, from http://ahha.org/articles.asp?Id=100

American School Counselor Association. (2003a). *The ASCA National Model: A framework for school counseling programs.* Fairfax, VA: Author.

American School Counselor Association (ASCA). (2003b). *Position statement: Gifted programs.* Retrieved April 1, 2008, from http://www.schoolcounselor.org/content.asp?contentid=209

Assouline, S. G., Nicpon, M. F., & Huber, D. H. (2006). The impact of vulnerabilities and strengths on the academic experiences of twice exceptional students: A message to school counselors. *Professional School Counselor, 10*(1), 14–24.

Baldwin, A., Vialle, W., & Clarke, C. (2000). Global professionalism and perceptions of teachers of the gifted. In K. A. Heller, F. J. Mönks, R. J. Sternberg, & R. F. Subotnik (Eds.), *International handbook of giftedness and talent* (2nd ed., pp. 565–572). Amsterdam: Elsevier.

Blackburn, A. C., & Erickson, D. B. (1986). Predictable crises of the gifted student. *Journal of Counseling and Development, 64,* 556–557.

Bloom, B. (1982). The role of gifts and markers in the development of talent. *Exceptional Children, 48,* 510–522.

Boykin, A. W. (1994). Afrocultural expression and its implications for schooling. In E. R. Hollins, J. E. King, & W. C. Hayman (Eds.), *Teaching diverse populations: Formulating a knowledge base* (pp. 225–273). Albany: State University of New York Press.

Buescher, T., & Higham, S. (1990). *Helping adolescents adjust to giftedness* (Digest No. E489). Reston, VA: ERIC Clearinghouse on Handicapped and Gifted Children. (ERIC Document Reproduction Service No. ED321494)

Carlson, N. (2004) School counselors' knowledge, perceptions, and involvement concerning gifted and talented students. (Doctoral dissertation, University of Maryland, College Park, 2004). *Dissertation Abstracts International, 65*(04), 04B. (UMI No. 3128875)

Clark, B. (2002). *Growing up gifted* (6th ed.). Upper Saddle River, NJ: Prentice-Hall.

Colangelo, N. (2003). Counseling gifted students. In N. Colangelo & G. A. Davis (Eds.), *Handbook of gifted education* (3rd ed., pp. 373–387). Needham Heights, MA: Allyn & Bacon.

Colangelo, N., & Davis, G. A. (2003). Introduction and overview. In N. Colangelo & G. A. Davis (Eds.), *Handbook of gifted education* (3rd ed., pp. 3–10). Needham Heights, MA: Allyn & Bacon.

Coleman, L. J. (1985). *Schooling the gifted.* New York: Addison Wesley.

Cooley, D., Chauvin, J., & Karnes, F. (1984). Gifted females: A comparison of attitudes by male and female teachers. *Roeper Review, 6,* 164–167.

Corey, G. (1996). *Theory and practice of counseling and psychotherapy* (5th ed.). Albany, NY: Brooks-Cole Publishing.

Council for Accreditation of Counseling and Related Educational Programs. (2001). *CACREP 2001 Standards.* Retrieved April 1, 2008, from http://www.cacrep.org/2001Standards.html

Corn, A. L. (1986). Gifted students who have a visual handicap: Can we meet their educational needs? *Education of the Visually Handicapped, 18*(2), 71–84.

Cross, T. (2002). Competing myths about the social and emotional development of gifted students. *Gifted Child Today, 25*(3), 44–48.

Cross, T. (2004). *On the social and emotional lives of gifted children: Issues and factors in their psychological development* (2nd ed.). Waco, TX: Prufrock Press.

Cross, T., Coleman, L., & Terhaar-Yonkers, M. (1991). The social cognition of gifted adolescents in schools: Managing the stigma of giftedness. *Journal for the Education of the Gifted, 15,* 44–55.

Csikszentmihalyi, M. (1996). *Creativity: Flow and the psychology of discovery and invention.* New York: HarperCollins.

Davis, G. A., & Rimm, S. B. (1997). *Education of the gifted and talented* (4th ed.). Needham Heights, MA: Allyn & Bacon.

Dauber, S., & Benbow, C. (1990). Aspects of personality and peer relations of extremely talented adolescents. *Gifted Child Quarterly, 24,* 10–14.

Delisle, J. (1992). *Guiding the social and emotional development of gifted youth.* New York: Longman.

Delisle, J., & Galbraith, J. (2002). *When gifted kids don't have all the answers: How to meet their social and emotional needs.* Minneapolis, MN: Free Spirit.

Delisle, J. R. (2002). *The gifted adolescent.* Retrieved April 1, 2008, from http://www.naesp. org/ContentLoad.do?contentId=865

Dixon, F. A., Lapsley, D. K., & Hanchon, T. A. (2004). An empirical typology of perfectionism in gifted adolescents. *Gifted Child Quarterly, 48,* 95–106.

Dockery, D. A. (2005). Ways in which counseling programs at specialized high schools respond to social and emotional needs of gifted adolescents (Doctoral dissertation, University of Virginia, 2005).

Dweck, C. S. (2000). *Self-theories: Their role in motivation, personality, and development.* Philadelphia: Taylor & Francis.

Ellis, A. (2001). *Overcoming destructive beliefs, feelings, and behaviors: New directions for rational emotive behavior therapy.* Amherst, NY: Prometheus Books.

Erikson, E. H. (1963). *Childhood and society* (2nd ed.). New York: Norton.

Evans, K. M. (1993). Multicultural counseling. In. L. Silverman (Ed.), *Counseling the gifted and talented* (pp. 263–276). Denver, CO: Love.

Fahlman, S. (2000). *Actualization of giftedness: Effects of perceptions in gifted adolescents.* Retrieved April 1, 2008, from http://www.metagifted.org/topics/gifted/ giftedAdolescents/researchActualizationOfGiftedness.html

Freeman, J. (2000). Families: The essential context for gifts and talents. In K. A. Heller, F. J. Mönks, R. J. Sternberg, & R. F. Subotnik (Eds.), *International handbook of giftedness and talent* (2nd ed., pp. 573–595). Amsterdam: Elsevier.

Ford, D. (2002). Racial identity among gifted African American students. In M. Neihart, S. M. Reis, N. M. Robinson, & S. M. Moon (Eds.), *The social and emotional development of gifted children: What do we know?* (pp. 19–30). Waco, TX: Prufrock Press.

Ford, D. (2003). Equity and excellence: Culturally diverse students in gifted education. In N. Colangelo & G. A. Davis (Eds.), *Handbook of gifted education* (3rd ed., pp. 506–520). Needham Heights, MA: Allyn & Bacon.

Ford, D., & Harris, J. J., III. (1999). *Multicultural gifted education.* New York: Teachers College Press.

Ford, D., Harris, J., Tyson, C., & Trotman, M. F. (2002). Beyond deficit thinking: Providing access for gifted African American students. *Roeper Review, 24*(2), 52–59.

Gagné, F. (2003). Transforming gifts into talents: The DMGT as a developmental theory. In N. Colangelo & G. A. Davis (Eds.), *Handbook of gifted education* (3rd ed., pp. 60–74). Needham Heights, MA: Allyn & Bacon.

Galbraith, J. (1985). The eight great gripes of gifted kids: Responding to special needs. *Roeper Review, 4,* 15–18.

Gardynik, U. M., & McDonald, L. (2005). Implications of risk and resilience in the life of the individual who is gifted/learning disabled. *Roeper Review, 27,* 206–214.

Gross, M. (2002). Social and emotional issues for exceptionally intellectually gifted students. In M. Neihart, S. M. Reis, N. M. Robinson, & S. M. Moon (Eds.), *The social and emotional development of gifted children: What do we know?* (pp. 19–30). Waco, TX: Prufrock Press.

Halstead, J. W. (2002). *Some of my best friends are books: Guiding gifted readers from preschool to high school.* Scottsdale, AZ: Great Potential Press.

Hamachek, D. E. (1978). Psychodynamics of normal and neurotic perfectionism. *Psychology, 15,* 177–197.

Harmon, D. (2002). They won't teach me: The voices of gifted African American inner-city students. *Roeper Review, 24,* 68–76.

Hébert, T. (2000a). Defining belief in self: Intelligent young men in an urban high school. *Gifted Child Quarterly, 44,* 91–114

Hébert, T. (2000b). Gifted males pursuing careers in elementary education. *Journal for the Education of the Gifted, 24,* 7–45.

Hébert, T. (2002). Gifted males. In M. Neihart, S. M. Reis, N. M. Robinson, & S. M. Moon (Eds.), *The social and emotional development of gifted children: What do we know?* (pp. 137–144). Waco, TX: Prufrock Press.

Hébert, T., & Kent, R. (2000). Nurturing social and emotional development in gifted teenagers through young adult literature. *Roeper Review, 22,* 167–178.

Hébert, T., & Speirs Neumeister, K. L. (2002). Fostering the social and emotional development of gifted children through guided viewing of film. *Roeper Review, 25,* 17–21.

Hishinuma, E. S. (1993). Counseling gifted/at risk and gifted/dyslexic youngsters. *Gifted Child Today, 16*(1), 30–33.

Kaplan, L. S. (1990). *Helping gifted students with stress management* (Digest No. E488). Reston, VA: ERIC Clearinghouse on Handicapped and Gifted Children. (ERIC Document Reproduction Service No. ED321493)

Keiley, M. K. (2002). Affect regulation and the gifted. In M. Neihart, S. M. Reis, N. M. Robinson, & S. M. Moon (Eds.), *The social and emotional development of gifted children: What do we know?* (pp. 41–50). Waco, TX: Prufrock Press.

Keirouz, K. S. (1990). Concerns of parents of gifted children: A research review. *Gifted Child Quarterly, 34,* 56–63.

Kerr, B., & Cohn, S. (2001). *Smart boys: Talent, manhood, and the search for meaning.* Scottsdale, AZ: Gifted Psychology Press.

Kerr, B., Colangelo, N., & Gaeth, J. (1988). Gifted adolescents' attitudes towards their giftedness. *Gifted Child Quarterly, 32,* 245–247.

Kerr, B., & Kurpius, S. E. R. (2004). Encouraging talented girls in math and science: Effects of a guidance intervention. *High Ability Studies, 15*(1), 85–102.

Kerr, B., & Nicpon, M. F. (2003). Gender and giftedness. In N. Colangelo & G. A. Davis (Eds.), *Handbook of gifted education* (3rd ed., pp. 373–387). Needham Heights, MA: Allyn & Bacon.

Kirschenbaum, R. J., & Reis, S. M. (1997). Conflicts in creativity: Talented female artists. *Creativity Research Journal, 10,* 251–263.

Lindstrom, R. R., & VanSant, S. (1986). Special issues in working with gifted minority adolescents. *Journal of Counseling and Development, 64,* 583–586.

LoCicero, K. A., & Ashby, J. S. (2000). Multidimensional perfectionism in middle school age gifted students: A comparison to peers from the general cohort. *Roeper Review, 22,* 182–185.

McEachern, A. G., & Bornot, J. (2001) Gifted students with learning disabilities: Implications and strategies for school counselors. *Professional School Counseling, 5,* 34–42.

Milsom, A., & Peterson, J. (2006). Introduction to special issue: Examining disability and giftedness in schools. *Professional School Counseling, 10,* 1–2.

Moon, S. M. (2002). Counseling needs and strategies. In M. Neihart, S. M. Reis, N. M. Robinson, & S. M. Moon (Eds.), *The social and emotional development of gifted children: What do we know?* (pp. 213–222). Waco, TX: Prufrock Press.

Moon, S. M., & Hall, A. S. (1998). Family therapy with intellectually and creatively gifted children. *Journal of Marital and Family Therapy, 24,* 59–80.

Moon, S. M., Kelly, K., & Feldhusen, J. (1997). Specialized counseling services for gifted youth and their families: A needs assessment. *Gifted Child Quarterly, 41*(1), 16–25.

Moon, S. M., & Thomas, V. (2003). Family therapy with gifted and talented adolescents. *Journal of Secondary Gifted Education, 14,* 107–113.

Neihart, M. (2000). Gifted children with Asperger's syndrome. *Gifted Child Quarterly, 44,* 222–230.

Noble, K. D., Subotnik, R. F., & Arnold, K. D. (1996). A new model for adult female talent development: A synthesis of perspectives from *Remarkable Women.* In K. D. Arnold, K. D. Noble, & R. F. Subotnik (Eds.), *Remarkable women: Perspectives on female talent development* (pp. 427–439). Cresskill, NJ: Hampton Press.

Nugent, S. A. (2000). Perfectionism: Its manifestations and classroom-based interventions. *Journal of Secondary Gifted Education, 11,* 215–222.

Olenchak, F. R., & Reis, S. M. (2002). Gifted students with learning disabilities. In M. Neihart, S. M. Reis, N. M. Robinson, & S. M. Moon (Eds.), *Social and emotional development of gifted children: What do we know?* (pp. 177–192). Waco, TX: Prufrock Press.

Pacht, A. R. (1984). Reflections on perfectionism. *American Psychologist, 39,* 386–390.

Parker, W., & Adkins, K. (1995). Perfectionism and the gifted. *Roeper Review, 2,* 173–175.

Parker, W. D., & Mills, C. (1996). The incidence of perfectionism in gifted students. *Gifted Child Quarterly, 40,* 194–199.

Patton, J., & Townsend, B. (1997). Creating inclusive environments for African American children and youth with gifts and talents. *Roeper Review, 20,* 13–18.

Peterson, J. S. (2006). Addressing counseling needs of gifted students. *Professional School Counseling, 10,* 43–51.

Reis, S. M. (1987). We can't change what we don't recognize: Understanding the special needs of gifted females. *Gifted Child Quarterly, 31,* 83–89.

Reis, S. M. (2002). Gifted females in elementary and secondary school. In M. Neihart, S. M. Reis, N. M. Robinson, & S. M. Moon (Eds.), *The social and emotional development of gifted children: What do we know?* (pp. 125–136). Waco, TX: Prufrock Press.

Reis, S. M. (2003). Gifted girls, twenty-five years later: Hopes realized and new challenges found. *Roeper Review, 25,* 154–159.

Reis, S. M. (2005a). External barrier experienced by gifted and talented girls and women. In S. K. Johnsen & J. Kendrick (Eds.), *Teaching and counseling gifted girls* (pp. 9–30). Waco, TX: Prufrock Press.

Reis, S. M. (2005b). Internal barriers, personal issues, and decisions faced by gifted and talented girls and women. In S. K. Johnsen & J. Kendrick (Eds.), *Teaching and counseling gifted girls* (pp. 31–63). Waco, TX: Prufrock Press.

Reis, S. M., & Colbert, R. (2004). Counseling needs of academically talented students with learning disabilities. *Professional School Counseling, 8,* 156–167.

Reis, S. M., & McCoach, D. B. (2000). The underachievement of gifted students: What do we know and where do we go? *Gifted Child Quarterly, 44,* 152–170.

Reis, S. M., & McCoach, D. B. (2002). Underachievement in gifted students. In M. Neihart, S. M. Reis, N. M. Robinson, & S. M. Moon (Eds.), *The social and emotional development of gifted children: What do we know?* (pp. 81–92). Waco, TX: Prufrock Press.

Reis, S. M., & Moon, S. M. (2002). Models and strategies for counseling, guidance, and social and emotional support of gifted and talented students. In M. Neihart, S. M. Reis, N. M. Robinson, & S. M. Moon (Eds.), *The social and emotional development of gifted children: What do we know?* (pp. 251–266). Waco, TX: Prufrock Press.

Reis, S. M., Neu, T. W., & McGuire, J. M. (1997). Case studies of high-ability students with learning disabilities who have achieved. *Exceptional Children, 64,* 463–479.

Rimm, S. (2002). Peer pressures and social acceptance of gifted students. In M. Neihart, S. M. Reis, N. M. Robinson, & S. M. Moon (Eds.), *The social and emotional development of gifted children: What do we know?* (pp. 13–18). Waco, TX: Prufrock Press.

Rimm, S. (2003). Underachievement: A national epidemic. In N. Colangelo & G. A. Davis (Eds.), *Handbook of gifted education* (3rd ed., pp. 424–443). Needham Heights, MA: Allyn & Bacon.

Rizza, M. G., & Morrison, W. F. (2003). Uncovering stereotypes and identifying characteristics of gifted students and students with emotional/behavioral disabilities. *Roeper Review, 25,* 73–77.

Robinson, N. M. (2002a). Introduction. In M. Neihart, S. M. Reis, N. M. Robinson, & S. M. Moon (Eds.), *The social and emotional development of gifted children: What do we know?* (pp. xi–xxiv). Waco, TX: Prufrock Press.

Robinson, N. M. (2002b). Individual differences in gifted students' attributions for academic performances. In M. Neihart, S. M. Reis, N. M. Robinson, & S. M. Moon (Eds.), *The social and emotional development of gifted children: What do we know?* (pp. 61–70). Waco, TX: Prufrock Press.

Ross, A. O. (1979). The gifted child in the family. In N. Colangelo & R. Zaffrann (Eds.), *New voices in counseling the gifted* (pp. 402–407). Dubuque, IA: Kendall/Hunt.

Ruf, D. (2004). Independence and relationship issues in intellectually gifted adolescents. Retrieved April 1, 2008, from http://www.educationaloptions.com/gifted_adolescents.htm

Rysiew, K. J., Shore, B. M., & Leeb, R. T. (1999). Multipotentiality, giftedness, and career choice: A review. *Journal of Counseling and Development, 77,* 423–429.

Sajjadi, S. H. (2000). Counseling gifted students: Past research, future directions. *Gifted Education International, 15,* 111–121.

Santrock, J. W. (1996). *Adolescence.* Chicago: Brown & Benchmar.

Scarborough, J. L., & Gilbride, D. D. (2006). Developing relationships with rehabilitation counselors to meet the transition needs of students with disabilities. *Professional School Counseling, 10,* 25–33.

Schuler, P. (2002). Perfectionism in gifted children and adolescents. In M. Neihart, S. M. Reis, N. M. Robinson, & S. M. Moon (Eds.), *The social and emotional development of gifted children: What do we know?* (pp. 71–79). Waco, TX: Prufrock Press.

Schultz, R. A., & Delisle, J. A. (2003). Gifted adolescents. In N. Colangelo & G. A. Davis (Eds.), *Handbook of gifted education* (3rd ed., pp. 483–492). Needham Heights, MA: Allyn & Bacon.

Silverman, L. K. (1989). Invisible gifts, invisible handicaps. *Roeper Review, 12,* 37–42.

Silverman, L. K. (1993a). A developmental model for counseling the gifted. In L. K. Silverman (Ed.), *Counseling the gifted and talented* (pp. 51–78). Denver, CO: Love.

Silverman, L. K. (1993b). Social development, leadership, and gender issues. In L. K. Silverman (Ed.), *Counseling the gifted and talented* (pp. 291–328). Denver, CO: Love.

Silverman, L. K. (1993c). Techniques for preventive counseling. In. L. K. Silverman (Ed.), *Counseling the gifted and talented* (pp. 81–109). Denver, CO: Love.

Silverman, L. K. (1993d). Career counseling. In L. K. Silverman (Ed.), *Counseling the gifted and talented* (pp. 215–238). Denver, CO: Love.

Silverman, L. K. (2003). Gifted children with learning disabilities. In N. Colangelo & G. A. Davis (Eds.), *Handbook of gifted education* (pp. 533– 543). Boston: Allyn & Bacon.

Speirs Neumeister, K. L. (2004). Factors influencing the development of perfectionism in gifted college students. *Gifted Child Quarterly, 48*, 259–274.

Steele, C. M. (1997). A threat in the air: How stereotypes shape the intellectual identities and performance of women and African Americans. *American Psychologist, 52*, 613–629.

Stormont, M., Stebbins, M. S., & Holliday, G. (2001). Characteristics and educational support needs of underrepresented gifted adolescents. *Psychology in Schools, 38*, 413–423.

Swiatek, M. A. (1995). An empirical investigation of the social coping strategies used by gifted adolescents. *Gifted Child Quarterly, 39*, 154–161.

Swiatek, M. A. (1998). Helping gifted adolescents cope with social stigma. *Gifted Child Today, 21*(2), 42–46.

Swiatek, M. A. (2001). Social coping among gifted high school students and its relationship to self-concept. *Journal of Youth and Adolescence, 30*, 19–29.

Szymanski, E. M., & Corn, A. L. (1989). Enabling gifted students with disabilities: A challenge to rehabilitation counselors. *Journal of Applied Rehabilitation Counseling, 20*(1), 8–12.

Townsend, B. L., & Patton, J. M. (1995). *Three "warring souls" of African American high school students.* (ERIC Document Reproduction Service No. ED400250)

VanTassel-Baska, J. (1991). Teachers as counselors for gifted students. In R. M. Milgram (Ed.), *Counseling gifted and talented children: A guide for teachers, counselors, and parents* (pp. 37–52). Norwood, NJ: Ablex.

VanTassel-Baska, J. (1993). Academic counseling for the gifted. In L. K. Silverman (Ed.), *Counseling the gifted and talented* (pp. 201–214). Denver, CO: Love.

VanTassel-Baska, J. (1998a). Counseling talented learners. In J. VanTassel-Baska, (Ed.). *Excellence in educating gifted and talented learners* (pp. 489–509). Denver, CO: Love.

VanTassel-Baska, J. (1998b). Appropriate curriculum for the talented learner. In J. Van-Tassel-Baska (Ed.), *Excellence in educating gifted and talented learners* (pp. 339–361). Denver, CO: Love.

VanTassel-Baska, J., & Baska, L. (1993). The roles of educational personnel in counseling the gifted. In L. K. Silverman (Ed.), *Counseling the gifted and talented* (pp. 181–200). Denver, CO: Love.

Vespi, L., & Yewchuk, C. (1992). A phenomenological study of the social/emotional characteristics of gifted learning disabled children. *Journal for the Education of the Gifted, 16*, 55–72

Vialle, W. J., & Paterson, J. (1998). Deafening silence: The educational experiences of gifted deaf people. *Gifted Education International, 13*(1), 13–22.

Whitmore, J. R. (1981). Gifted children with handicapping conditions: A new frontier. *Exceptional Children, 48*, 106–114.

Zentall, S. S., Moon, S., Hall, A. M., & Grskovic, J. A. (2001). Learning and motivational characteristics of boys with AD/HD and/or giftedness. *Exceptional Children, 67*, 499–519.

Zimmerman, E. (1995). Factors influencing the art education of artistically gifted girls. *Journal of Secondary Gifted Education, 6*, 103–112.

Chapter 3

Exploring Issues and Opportunities in Gifted Students' Transitions to College and Career

BY

SUSANNAH
WOOD

AND

M. KATHERINE
GAVIN

"The gifted seek careers that will enable them to create meaningful lives and contribute to the whole. In future generations, service and social responsibility may become the entire focus of career counseling programs" (Silverman, 1993, p. 234).

Current Concerns

OF THE MANY QUESTIONS REGARDING IDENTITY that gifted adolescents must answer, a very important one is how they will use their talent. For many gifted adolescents, the choice of careers is the answer to "Who am I?" (Greene, 2002), yet decisions regarding future education, training, money, and the application of talent are complex and not easily determined. Choosing a career path is not solely a one-time decision, although many gifted adolescents feel that it must be. Careers are part of a developmental process, intertwined with cognitive, social, and emotional developmental areas (Greene, 2002).

Career decision-making and college choices typically arise during the secondary school experience and stem from gifted students' academic needs and performance. Because of their advanced abilities, gifted students often are perceived as having the necessary capabilities and skills to make appropriate decisions as to "what to do with the rest of [their] lives," even though these students need just as much, if not more, guidance and support when wrestling with these issues (Frederickson, 1986). Gifted adolescents can be trapped in a career path, or adrift on the many paths of careers, and left feeling unsatisfied, unhappy, and confused as the result of multipotentiality, poor decision-making, and inadequate course preparation (Kerr, 1990). By not providing the necessary skills, information, and support for gifted adolescents as they embark on the developmental journey of career exploration, talent can be wasted (Fredrickson, 1986).

Expectations

However, the issue of who owns the particular talent and how it will be applied is a struggle all gifted adolescents will face. Once identified, gifted adolescents may feel the implicit pressure of society's expectations. The need to choose the "right" or "perfect" career path can become even more burdensome for gifted students who want to please significant figures in their lives (Greene, 2002). Parents want the best for their adolescents; ensuring the talent or the gift is not "wasted" may mean that the choice made regarding their child's college or career fits more with their ideas of what is good or right (Colangelo, 2003) than the child's wishes. Families have different ideas concerning the prestige, rigor, status, or high earning power of particular colleges or career paths, which can conflict with the values of peers and teachers (Silverman, 1993). Expectations are informed by family norms, education, traditions, and religious and cultural beliefs (Greene, 2002), all of which must be considered by gifted adolescents. Adolescents may opt not to pursue their own dreams and goals in order not to disappoint family members or teachers, or to forfeit these adults' love and respect (Greene, 2003).

The struggle over the "right" or "perfect" career path also can be influenced by gender role expectations (Kerr, 1991, 1994; Kerr & Cohn, 2001). Parental opinions are highly important to gifted women (Reis, 2002), who may put off making decisions or attaining postsecondary education in order to reduce the dissonance between family expectations and career goals (Greene, 2003). When searching for careers, some gifted girls seem to choose altruistic paths or want careers that will make the world a better place (Kerr & Nicpon, 2003). However, gifted girls also seem to be less rigid in their sex role identification and currently are identifying college majors and career paths that have been considered nontraditional (Kerr & Colangelo, 1988; Kerr & Nicpon, 2003).

Gifted young women continue to struggle with the integration of career and family, and encounter the perceived forced-choice between family and career (Kerr & Nicpon, 2003). Young gifted women also may believe that by behaving "smart" or acting on their gifts, they risk future intimate relationships with possible mates who may feel threatened by the displayed talent, thereby changing their behaviors so as not to be perceived as "competing" with young men (Kerr, 1994). Women who do marry or partner may feel as if they have to compromise their dreams and goals if their significant others do not support them (Kerr & Nicpon, 2003). Career guidance, as part of talent development, and adult support should explore the realities and possibilities of this synthesis for gifted girls (Greene, 2003).

Gifted young men, however, may choose career paths for different reasons. Even if their talent and passion lie in the arts or humanities, gifted men may feel compelled to cease their pursuit for careers in these fields in favor of careers with more earning potential or those labeled as more "masculine," such as medicine, law, business, or engineering (Colangelo & Kerr, 1991). In pursuing wealth, status, and power, gifted men risk overworking and losing time spent with family (Kerr & Nicpon, 2003).

Multipotentiality

In the discussion of gifted students' career choices, the concept of multipotentiality usually arises. There have been several definitions of multipotentiality, including: (1) "children who give evidence of high performance and capability in a variety of intellectual and creative areas" (U.S. Commissioner of Education, 1972, as cited in Rysiew, Shore, & Leeb, 1999, p. 423); (2) those who have the ability to "select and develop any number of competencies to a high level" (Frederickson & Rothney, 1972, as cited in Rysiew et al., 1999, p. 424); and (3) "individuals who have diverse talents (and interests also) and who could succeed at a high level in a number of different fields" (Colangelo, 2003, p. 377).

Multipotentiality is linked to talent areas, abilities, interests, or a combination of these concepts (Rysiew et al., 1999). These definitions refer to gifted students who have an "embarrassment of riches" (Gowan, 1980, p. 67) or who are experiencing the "overchoice syndrome," when interest, ability, motivation, and opportunity all are plentiful (Rysiew et al., 1999, p. 424). However, there has been a lack of empirical studies to support the idea of multipotentiality (Colangelo, 2003; Greene, 2003; Rysiew et al., 1999), and Greene (p. 68) advocated for the use of the word *multidimensional* in order to capture the diverse aspects of students' strengths, weaknesses, predispositions, and preferences for subject areas. Regardless of the term used, gifted students still encounter difficulties in narrowing a single career from several feasible options, in perfectionism, in the pressure of expectations of others, and in making commitments in the face of doubts about choices made (Rysiew et al., 1999).

Decision-Making

Students who not only have multiple abilities, but also multiple interests, motivation, and opportunity, may have difficulty in decision-making (Rysiew, Shore, & Carson, 1994, as cited in Greene, 2003). While students typically are asked to make decisions regarding areas of specialization required by some career paths, these decisions are hampered by a lack of experiences or opportunities in postsecondary settings in which students can explore majors, fields, and other areas of interest (Greene, 2002). Students who must choose among jobs that do not allow for flexibility in talents or interests may waiver between options, or delay the decision while experiencing confusion and anxiety (Pask-McCartney & Salomone, 1988, as cited in Rysiew et al., 1999). However, gifted students who make late decisions risk falling behind their same-age peers in career progress and even social development (Rysiew et al., 1999). One reason that some gifted students stave off the decision-making process is that they simply lack the knowledge of how the process works even though adults and educators assume that they know the process well (Greene, 2002). These late-deciding students so often are preoccupied with maintaining high levels of performance during high school that they can delay their career planning (Frederickson, 1986).

Some gifted adolescents conceptualize career decision-making as an existential question and as an extension of the quest for identity (Greene, 2002). Although some adolescents feel "called" to one path or occupation that suits them completely, others risk being "locked" into one choice (Silverman, 1993). Because gifted adolescents demonstrate earlier career maturity, they also may demonstrate certainty about particular careers (Kelly & Colangelo, 1990), hence limiting explorations even in postsecondary settings that offer more choices (Frederickson, 1986; Greene, 2002; Kerr, 1990, 1991). Gifted students who foreclose early in the career decision-making process also run the risk of finding themselves at a college they did not select, majoring in an area that they do not like, and having no plan as to where to go in the future (Greene, 2002). In addition, these students may not understand the degree of perseverance, passion, and long-term planning entailed if it means higher education or extensive training before they can do what they dream (Greene, 2002). Money, time, training, education, and family planning are all interconnected in the decision-making process, and some gifted students may find themselves committed to the pursuit of a career even though they have doubts about it (Colangelo, 2003; Rysiew et al., 1999).

Decision-making also is affected by the degree of perfectionism or fear of failure that may be experienced by the gifted student. Changing majors, delays, and indecision can be the result of unhealthy perfectionism, and a fear of disappointing significant others (Frederickson, 1986; Greene, 2003; Silverman, 1993). Because many gifted students have a strong sense of social justice and moral concern (Lovecky, 1993), these students may choose service-orientated occupations in order to improve the lives of others (Hansen & Hall, 1997; Passow, 1988, as cited in Greene, 2003). Although these careers can be satisfying to the gifted student, they may not meet the expectations of others who value more lucrative or status-oriented occupations.

Reflection, self-examination, and exploration of interests and values pertaining to the world of work also are critical needs of gifted students that begin in elementary school (Greene, 2002). In essence, because gifted students can conceptualize faster and more abstractly, and will begin self-exploration earlier than their average age peers, guides and mentors need to be in place so that this exploration into values and interests can be facilitated (Rysiew et al., 1999). Parents, teachers, and school counselors all play vital roles in helping gifted adolescents choose a career path that is satisfying and productive.

School-to-Work Opportunities and Practices

To begin, career exploration should be seen as an extension of talent development, and as a lifelong process rather than a series of discreet jobs (Colangelo, 2003; Greene, 2002). Individualized counseling and services are important in the career exploration of the gifted student because not all gifted students are alike or share the same goals, values, identity, or background (Greene, 2003). Within the family unit, enrichment, resources, and support can be provided for gifted students to investigate and explore their abilities and talents (Greene, 2002; Silverman, 1993). Parents and guardians can help gifted students identify family traditions, values, dreams, and expectations, as well as teach and guide the decision-making process. Collaboration between families and schools allows for a well-rounded picture of the gifted student's talents, skills, values, interests, and ideas (Greene, 2003).

Academic ability also is an important consideration and one variable of career development (Greene, 2003). Within the context of the school, teachers can relate subjects and concepts to careers, and are in a prime position to observe the student's abilities and personality (Greene, 2002). The professional school counselor can facilitate, individually or collaboratively with teachers, and can establish small groups for gifted students to discuss careers, colleges, dreams, and expectations in a safe place. School counselors can provide ability-appropriate tests, advanced career inventories and assessments, and, through the use of flexible academic blueprints (VanTassel-Baska, 1993, 1998), help the gifted student choose the optimal academic path with reference to classes (Greene, 2002).

Job Shadowing/Apprenticeships/Internships/Dual-Credit Opportunities

Apprenticeships and internships allow students to experience the world of work, possibly gain academic credit, learn from role models, and gain information on careers (Kelly & Cobb, 1991; Silverman, 1993). Benefits include meeting the superior ability needs of gifted students, career exploration and development, development of potential, psychosocial advancement, connections with the larger world, shared rewards, and community and school collaboration (Clasen & Clasen, 2003).

Students who engage in job shadowing typically follow or "shadow" a professional for a week or more in order to conceptualize what a particular career entails (Silverman, 1993). Prior to this engagement, educators should assess their local resources and help students narrow down what types of careers they may wish to shadow, keeping in mind that students can engage in more than one of these during their secondary experience (Silverman, 1993). Educators can request that students complement this experience with daily journaling and evaluation of the shadowing process, interviews with professionals, and exploration of training and education costs, salaries, future trends and related careers—components similar to "Job Studies" as suggested by Willings (1986, as cited in Silverman, 1993).

Apprenticeships and internships generally require the student to work as a professional-in-training for one semester or more while still receiving high school credit. Typically, gifted students work as an assistant to a professional in upper level management of the career field of choice (Silverman, 1993). There are several different types of programs and structures that can facilitate internship and apprenticeship opportunities for gifted students.

One conceptualization of an internship program could be modeled after a program promoted by the now nonoperational National School-to-Work program and operating in Pinellas County (FL) schools as the Executive Internship program. Senior students earn high school elective and junior college course credit while actively working with personnel for 10 to 15 hours a week in a variety of work settings and professional fields. Students attend meetings; gather, analyze, and interpret data; and engage in professional presentations. This particular program meets the needs of gifted students specifically by focusing on critical thinking skills, analytical thinking, theory to practice, evaluation skills, and goal-setting, which are built into both work experiences and curriculum. Students are responsible for weekly summary logs, answering log questions, résumé and cover letters, goal-setting activities, using T-Charts (communication charts used by employers), an ethics study, a list of career options, job studies, vocabulary studies, journal article reviews, an essay on their experience, a leadership development project, and presentations of their products. Coordinators recruit students, direct and plan the experience, generate and structure policies, monitor academic credit policy, provide site visits, and review intern progress. For more information, visit http://it.pinellas.k12.fl.us/schools/eip/What_is_EIP.html.

Programs like the career or partnership academies provide internships as part of a triadic structure that features a school-within-school structure, college preparation curriculum with a career theme, and partnerships with community employers (Winthrop, 2001). These academies are not geared toward specific job preparation; rather, they focus on exposing students to fields and industries and facilitate the acquisition of workplace skills that are necessary across most jobs. Junior and senior students in the academies attend one career-related and two or three academic classes, taught by a team of academic and technical teachers who partner to coordinate the program (Winthrop, 2001). Hence, students in Career Academies also gain awareness of how academic skills, such as research, writing, public speaking, technology skills, organization, and responsibility are relevant to the workplace (Winthrop, 2001). Educator/coordinator duties entail identifying employer partners, promoting the program, recruiting students, structuring program policies, monitoring and evaluating student progress, and program evaluation (Winthrop, 2001). Student responsibilities include time commitment, application and selection processes, transportation, educational and work performance expectations, and evaluation of performance (Winthrop, 2001). For more information, visit http://casn.berkeley.edu/resources/internship.pdf.

Mentorships

Mentorships, apprenticeships, internships, and shadowing opportunities have been suggested as ways of meeting the needs of gifted students and have been recommended for all gifted students, especially gifted students from disadvantaged backgrounds, underachieving gifted students, and gifted girls who need female mentors (Clasen & Clasen, 2003; Silverman, 1993). The opportunity to meet and work with adults who are already succeeding in the student's field of interest or talent provides the gifted adolescent with the needed role model who can speak knowledgeably about the world of work in that field, and offers paths toward entrance into that field, including education and training. Mentorships provide the link between knowledge and skills gained in school to the student's life after school (Casey & Shore, 2000), explore issues pertaining to the student's development and outlook on life (Cox & Daniel, 1983; Freedman, 1993), and facilitate the understanding of critical issues pertaining to career and professional socialization (Clasen & Clasen, 2003). Mentors act as teachers, experts, guides, advisors, friends, and role models (Clasen & Clasen, 2003).

In fact, a mentorship can have different meanings for different people. Some describe it as a special bond, a role-model situation, a teaching/learning experience, and a supportive relationship fostering encouragement and praise. All definitions have in common the fact that a mentorship is a unique relationship between two people that should enrich the lives of both individuals involved. In terms of the gifted and talented field, Torrance (1984) talked about this mentor-mentee relationship as an individualized relationship developed over time that is characterized by mutual respect and commitment. In this relationship, students work with their mentors to develop their scholarly interest into research directions. In Torrance's classic 22-year longitudinal study, he found that mentors do make a difference for both men and women. In fact, both groups who had a mentoring experience attained relatively high levels of education. Also, the presence or absence of a mentor made a statistically significant difference in the quality of adult creative achievement and number of recognized creative achievements (Torrance, 1984).

A personal connection generally is involved in establishing a mentorship. In particular, for gifted students at the secondary level, mentorships often are arranged individually through guidance counselors or personal connections with experts in local universities, businesses, and industries. However, there are a few university enrichment programs in place that specifically focus on academic mentorships. Additionally, there are many summer or enrichment programs at the university level for talented students that focus on academic coursework. Many of these programs offer opportunities for students to spend time on a one-to-one basis with university professors. However, mentorships are not the focus of these programs and they are not included here.

An example of a mentorship program focused on secondary students is the UConn Mentor Connection. This experience is an annual 3-week summer program at the University of Connecticut for academically talented secondary students. Established in 1997, this residential program provides approximately 85 students opportunities to participate in creative projects and research investigations under the supervision of university mentors. The mission of the program is reflected in four goals: (1) to recruit highly motivated, academically talented students from throughout the nation; (2) to allow students to achieve their highest potential by participating in cutting-edge research projects in all areas of arts and sciences that provide direct, apprentice-based involvement with faculty members and advanced graduate students who are conducting research; (3) to increase students' awareness about their career opportunities; and (4) to demonstrate that high-level potential can be found and developed across cultural, ethnic, and socioeconomic groups. For more information, visit http://www.gifted.uconn.edu/mentor.

A similar program is offered at the National Security Agency (NSA). NSA's High School Work Study Program is designed for high school students to work 32 hours per week in a paid position during the summer following their junior or senior year with a mentor on projects related to their areas of interest and aptitude in computer science and engineering. For more information, visit http://www.nsa.gov/careers/students_3.cfm

The University of Texas Health Center at San Antonio offers the Student Internship Program for talented high school students. This is a year-round program designed to provide an intensive, hands-on, creative and interdisciplinary research experience. In this experience, students are paired with senior investigators who serve as mentors and role models on the research project. For more information, visit http://www.uthscsa.edu/outreach/summer.asp.

The Research Science Institute sponsored by the Center for Excellence in Education in collaboration with the Massachusetts Institute of Technology hosts a free 6-week summer institute for approximately 75 rising high school seniors who are interested and talented in mathematics and science. As part of this program, students complete hands-on research investigations with top mentors at corporations, universities, and research organizations. For more information, visit http://www.cee.org/rsi.

Mentorships provide many benefits to students: new knowledge and skills used by practicing professionals, socialization, exposure to career fields and opportunities, and personal support, praise, and encouragement. Gifted high school students often do not find appropriately challenging options in their high school's typical curriculum, and mentorships, either during the school year or in the summer, can provide these enriching opportunities.

Suggested Best Practices

Below is a list of synthesized strategies that all educators can employ to support students in their career exploration (Colangelo, 2003; Greene, 2002; Silverman, 1993; VanTassel-Baska, 1998):

- Approach career exploration and *career counseling as a developmental process* with extensions of identity exploration and talent development (Greene, 2002). A career is a lifestyle, not just a job or specific position (Colangelo, 2003). Careers can be concurrent or serial, and students should consider that they probably will switch both jobs and careers several times in their lifetime (Silverman, 1993). Discussion of life themes, societal trends, values, and personality types are components of career counseling.

- *Provide multiple venues for career counseling* including small groups, classroom activities, and individual discussions. Include both gifted students with similar concerns to normalize their experience and multiple significant persons from the student's life in these meetings (Colangelo, 2003; Greene, 2002; Silverman, 1993).

- *Provide support for parents and guardians* through parent workshops that touch on topics including family activities that develop student interests, holding high expectations for students of both sexes, identifying critical periods in talent development, finding experts in students' fields of interest who can instruct and mentor, planning for college, and finding scholarships and financial aid (Silverman, 1993).

- *Teach decision-making* and identify early and late decision makers (Silverman, 1993).

- Consider Advanced Placement, acceleration, enrichment, or other alternative education opportunities to meet student ability level, and extend these opportunities by discussing careers within subject areas (Greene, 2002; Silverman, 1993).

- Expose students to *role models and mentors* (Clasen & Clasen, 2003; Silverman, 1993).

- *Explore hobbies and leisure activities* as possible avocations and as ways of developing more and different abilities and interest areas (Colangelo, 2003).

- Facilitate *student ownership of career planning* (Greene, 2002).

- *Use biographies* as teaching tools and include discussions of societal norms, expectations of self and others, and gender roles and stereotypes (Silverman, 1993).

- *Use the Internet* to explore careers and colleges.

- *Use the Internet* to create online portfolios to display student talent and work.

- *Discuss expectations* of self and others.

- *Use interest, values, and ability inventories.* Consider the appropriate off-level tests, or tests at the adult level depending on the student's cognitive

WOOD AND GAVIN

ability. For students who exhibit multipotentiality, consider using forced-choice tests for better discernment of interests (Greene, 2002).

- *Provide shadowing, internships, and apprenticeship opportunities* especially in jobs that combine interests and abilities in multiple fields (Silverman, 1993).
- Model and provide opportunities for *community service and volunteering* (Silverman, 1993).
- Discuss gender roles, socialization, and expectations.

A partnership effort to provide gifted adolescents information on colleges and occupations, and to discuss the results of inventories and assessments, will equip these students with knowledge, but parents, extended family, community members, teachers, and counselors also must help gifted students make sense of the information, and teach them skills to decrease anxiety when the choices seem vast and overwhelming. Gifted adolescents need "appropriate and interconnected counseling services, including career counseling that emphasizes personal responsibility for decision-making and continual adjustment and adaptation to changes in career and in life" (Greene, 2002, p. 232). Partnerships among parents, communities, and schools are critical in order for gifted students to learn the appropriate skills to identify the best fit among their multiple talents, values, and interests. Further, an understanding of all of these factors helps students make authentic choices to further their talent development amid multiple and typically competing expectations. Without the appropriate guidance, society stands to lose talent and ability, and gifted adolescents stand to lose a sense of identity, worth, and life satisfaction.

Suggested Readings

Fredrickson, R. H. (1986). Preparing gifted and talented students for the world of work. *Journal of Counseling and Development, 64,* 556–557.

Greene, M. J. (2002). Career counseling for gifted and talented students. In M. Neihart, S. M. Reis, N. M. Robinson, & S. M. Moon (Eds.), *The social and emotional development of gifted children: What do we know?* (pp. 223–236). Waco, TX: Prufrock Press.

Greene, M. J. (2003). Career adrift? Career counseling of the gifted and talented. *Roeper Review, 25,* 66–73.

National School-to-Work Opportunities Office. (1998). *Gifted education/school-to-work models: Best practices and unique approaches.* Washington, DC: U.S. Department of Education.

Silverman, L. K. (1993). Career counseling. In L. K. Silverman (Ed.), *Counseling the gifted and talented* (pp. 215–238). Denver, CO: Love.

Winthrop, J. (2001). *Internship handbook for career academies.* Berkeley, CA: University of California. (ERIC Document Reproduction Service No. ED455446)

Suggested Web Sites

Kid Source Online—http://www.kidsource.com/kidsource/content/career_planning.html

National Research Center on the Gifted and Talented—http://www.gifted.uconn.edu/nrcgt/newsletter/spring02/sprng022.html

Hoagies' Gifted Education Page—http://www.hoagiesgifted.org/counseling.htm

Center for Excellence in Education—http://www.cee.org/rsi

University of Texas Health Center at San Antonio—http://www.uthscsa.edu/outreach/summer.asp

National Security Agency: http://www.nsa.gov/careers/students_3.cfm

University of Connecticut Mentorship Program: http://www.gifted.uconn.edu/mentor

References

Casey, K. M., & Shore, B. M. (2000). Mentors' contributions of gifted adolescents' affective, social, and vocational development. *Roeper Review, 22,* 227–230.

Clasen, D. R., & Clasen, R. E. (2003). Mentoring the gifted and talented. In N. Colangelo & G. A. Davis (Eds.), *Handbook of gifted education* (3rd ed., pp. 254–267). Needham Heights, MA: Allyn & Bacon.

Colangelo, N. (2003). Counseling gifted students. In N. Colangelo & G. A. Davis (Eds.), *Handbook of gifted education* (3rd ed., pp. 373–387). Needham Heights, MA: Allyn & Bacon.

Colangelo, N., & Kerr, B. A. (1991). Extreme academic talent: Profiles of perfect scores. *Journal of Educational Psychology, 82,* 404–410.

Cox, J., & Daniel, N. (1983, September/October). The role of the mentor. *Gifted Child Today,* 54–61.

Fredrickson, R. H. (1986). Preparing gifted and talented students for the world of work. *Journal of Counseling and Development, 64,* 556–557.

Greene, M. J. (2002). Career counseling for gifted and talented students. In M. Neihart, S. M. Reis, N. M. Robinson, & S. M. Moon (Eds.), *The social and emotional development of gifted children: What do we know?* (pp. 223–236). Waco, TX: Prufrock Press.

Greene, M. J. (2003). Career adrift? Career counseling of the gifted and talented. *Roeper Review, 25,* 66–73.

Gowan, J. C. (1980). Issues on the guidance of gifted and creative children. In J. C. Gowan, G. D. Demos, & C. J. Kokasha (Eds.), *The guidance of exceptional children: A book of readings* (2nd ed., pp.66–70). New York: Longman.

Hansen, J. B., & Hall, E. G. (1997). Gifted women and marriage. *Gifted Child Quarterly, 41*, 169–180.

Kelly, K. R., & Cobb, S. J. (1991). A profile of the career development characteristics of young gifted adolescents: Examining gender and multicultural differences. *Roeper Review, 13*, 202–206.

Kelly, K. R., & Colangelo, N. (1990). Effects of academic ability and gender on career development. *Journal for the Education of the Gifted, 13*, 168–175.

Kerr, B. A. (1990). *Counseling gifted students* (Monograph for the Leadership Accessing Program*)*. Indianapolis: Indiana Department of Education. (ERIC Document Reproduction Service No. ED323688)

Kerr, B. A. (1991). Educating gifted girls. In N. Colangelo & G. A. Davis (Eds.), *Handbook of gifted education* (pp. 402–415). Needham Heights, MA: Allyn & Bacon.

Kerr, B. A. (1994). *Smart girls: A new psychology of girls, women and giftedness.* Dayton: Ohio Psychology Press.

Kerr, B. A., & Cohn, S. (2001). *Smart boys: Talent, manhood, and the search for meaning.* Scottsdale, AZ: Gifted Psychology Press.

Kerr, B. A., & Colangelo, N. (1988). The college plans of academically talented students. *Journal of Counseling and Development, 67*, 42–49.

Kerr, B. A., & Nicpon, M. F. (2003). Gender and giftedness. In N. Colangelo & G. A. Davis (Eds.), *Handbook of gifted education* (3rd ed., pp. 373–387). Needham Heights, MA: Allyn & Bacon.

Lovecky, D. V. (1993). The quest for meaning: Counseling issues with gifted children and adolescents. In L. Silverman (Ed.), *Counseling the gifted and talented* (pp. 29–50). Denver, CO: Love.

Reis, S. (2002). Gifted females in elementary and secondary school. In M. Neihart, S. M. Reis, N. M. Robinson, & S. M. Moon (Eds.), *The social and emotional development of gifted children: What do we know?* (pp. 125–136). Waco, TX: Prufrock Press.

Rysiew, K. J., Shore, B. M., & Leeb, R. T. (1999). Multipotentiality, giftedness, and career choice: A review. *Journal of Counseling and Development, 77*, 423–429.

Silverman, L. (1993). Career counseling. In L. Silverman (Ed.), *Counseling the gifted and talented* (pp. 215–238). Denver, CO: Love.

Torrance, E. P. (1984). *Mentor relationships: How they aid creative achievement, endure, change, and die.* Buffalo, NY: Bearly Limited.

VanTassel-Baska, J. (1993). Academic counseling of the gifted. In. L. Silverman (Ed.), *Counseling the gifted and talented* (pp. 201–214). Denver, CO: Love.

VanTassel-Baska, J. (1998). Counseling talented learners. In J. VanTassel-Baska (Ed.), *Excellence in educating gifted and talented learners* (pp. 489–509). Denver, CO: Love.

Winthrop, J. (2001). *Internship handbook for career academies.* Berkeley: University of California. (ERIC Document Reproduction Service No. ED455446)

Current State of Education for Gifted Secondary Students

PRESIDENT **GEORGE W. BUSH'S** plan for high schools included encouraging the growth of Advanced Placement (AP) and International Baccalaureate (IB) programs, and training teachers in low-income schools to teach these courses. Another stated goal was to enhance math and science achievement for high school graduates, along with bolstering the level of teaching these subjects in middle and high schools (Dixon & Moon, 2006). Further, The National Governors Association (NGA), in their plan called *Ready? Set? Go!* (Warner, n.d.) has established 10 steps toward a new approach to high schools geared to challenging students. Three of the steps are to define a rigorous college and work preparatory curriculum for high school students; provide financial incentives for disadvantaged students to take rigorous AP exams and college-preparatory and college-level courses; and expand college-level learning opportunities in high school for minorities, English language learners, low-income students, and youth with disabilities. The NGA desires to raise the level of rigor and increase the opportunities for high school graduates to be successful as they transition into postsecondary life (Roberts, 2006).

Exactly what services that directly benefit gifted secondary students are federally funded? The only specifically designated funding supporting gifted students is the Jacob K. Javits

Gifted and Talented Students Education Act (Javits). The Javits program funds research and demonstration programs through The National Research Center on the Gifted and Talented and through competitive grants; it is not a program or service funding source for school districts. Although the research developed under the Javits Act contributes to best practices for working with gifted students, funding for the program is frequently in jeopardy (National Association for Gifted Children [NAGC], 2008).

Because many secondary schools regard AP and IB as their gifted secondary programs, gifted students benefit from the current focus on them. In fact, federal funding for both Advanced Placement and International Baccalaureate, although targeted primarily at minority and lower socioeconomic students, impacts gifted adolescents in all groups as well. They benefit from trained teachers and from increased course offerings that are direct outcomes of the increased funding efforts. Both of these programs receive federal funding for teacher training as well as for fee reduction for the examinations for students. For fiscal year 2008, Congress allotted $43.5 million for IB and AP programs, especially those focused on mathematics, science, and foreign languages (U.S. Department of Education, 2008). The White House requested $70 million for these programs for fiscal year 2009, which, if approved, would make even more resources available for advanced learning.

Although Advanced Placement began in 1955 with a statement concerning curriculum for gifted and talented, it now is focused on all students, and targets instruction for preparation to take the AP exam (Dixon, 2006). More information about both Advanced Placement and International Baccalaureate is presented in Chapter 7 of this volume. Readers should note that although there are advanced learning opportunities available, and some are receiving federal support, no federal funding is available specifically to design and implement secondary programs and services for gifted students. This is a call to action for all concerned with gifted adolescents.

Part II begins with three chapters that focus on the current programs that affect gifted secondary students. In Chapter 4, Gallagher analyzes NAEP data and how they impact gifted secondary adolescents and their programs. She offers a short history and follows it with essential information that informs our understanding of how gifted adolescents are both helped and shortchanged by the program. Chapter 5 reviews five issues that are relevant in the reform efforts for secondary students. Gentry, Peters, and Jeffrey review the following: *The State of the States Report*; high school restructuring efforts and gifted education; career and technical education and talent development; reform efforts in testing at the secondary level; and finally reform efforts that affect highly qualified teachers. In Chapter 6, Gavin reviews the monographs addressing secondary education currently available from The National Research Center on the Gifted and Talented and describes the focus and outcomes for each. In addition, she describes projects funded under the Javits Act that have focused specifically on secondary issues.

We continue Part II with a focus on the current available programming options for gifted secondary students. In Chapter 7, Gallagher describes AP and

IB programming. In Chapter 8, Olszewski-Kubilius and Dixon focus on special schools, magnet schools, and school options (honors classes, seminars, and extracurricular activities) for gifted adolescents. In Chapter 9, Olszewski-Kubilius discusses early entrance to college as a current option, while in Chapter 10 she reviews the popular talent search possibilities. In Chapter 11, Limburg-Weber writes about study abroad opportunities as viable options for secondary students. We conclude Part II with Chapter 12, in which Olszewski-Kubilius reviews the current emphasis on distance education, focusing on how it currently serves gifted secondary students. In sum, Part II of this monograph covers what is currently happening for gifted secondary students. We try to present these openly and fairly, as options that occur today. The final section of the monograph, Part III, focuses on the Task Force on Gifted Secondary Education's view of what should happen for gifted secondary students in the future.

References

Dixon, F. A., & Moon, S. M. (2006). *The handbook of secondary gifted education.* Waco, TX: Prufrock Press.

National Association for Gifted Children. (2008). *Legislative update.* Retrieved April 14, 2008, from http://www.nagc.org/index2.aspx?id=585&al.

Roberts, J. L. (2006). Teachers of secondary gifted students: What makes them effective. In F. Dixon & S. M. Moon (Eds.), *The handbook of secondary gifted education* (pp. 567–580). Waco, TX: Prufrock Press.

U.S. Department of Education. (2008). *Department of Education budget tables.* Retrieved April 14, 2008, from http://www.ed.gov/about/overview/budget/budget09/summary/appendix4.pdf.

Warner, M. R. (n.d.). *Ready? Set? Go!: Redesigning the American high school.* Retrieved June 6, 2008, from http://www.nga.org/cda/files/04chairmantopten.pdf

Current Programs Affecting Secondary Students

Chapter 4

The National Assessment of Educational Progress (NAEP)

BY

SHELAGH A. GALLAGHER

What the NAEP Can—and Can't— Report About Gifted Students

ACCOUNTABILITY IS UNDOUBTEDLY a centerpiece of modern education. As states struggle to find meaningful ways to assess student growth for No Child Left Behind (NCLB; 2001), the overall health of educational achievement is assessed through the National Assessment of Educational Progress (NAEP). Christened "The Nation's Report Card," the NAEP remains the only "continuing and nationally representative measure of achievement in various subjects over time" (Lee & Weiss, 2007, p. 1). The NAEP seems a reasonable place to consult when seeking information about high-performing students, or gifted students, or both. In fact, the NAEP contains little information about the former and virtually none about the latter. To understand this more fully, first it is necessary to understand some basic information about NAEP construction, administration, and scoring.

NAEP101: The Basics of Test Construction, Administration, and Scoring

The first NAEP assessment was administered by the National Center on Educational Statistics (NCES) in 1969.

By the 1980s, it was firmly established (Olson, 2002) with assessments in grades 4, 8, and 12 in subjects including mathematics, science, reading, writing, civics, geography, U.S. history, and art. In 2003, the assessment mandate of the NAEP tightened to align more closely with the NCLB legislation. Currently, the NAEP must be administered in math and reading every 2 years in both the fourth and eighth grades. Assessments of 12th-grade students in mathematics and reading must take place "at regularly scheduled intervals," currently interpreted as every 4 years. The remaining subjects are now assessed as time and budget permit.

NAEP tests are constructed using frameworks for each subject designed by teams of content experts, teachers, and other educators. The frameworks provide a general guide to selecting content and skills that are representative of specific subjects at the appropriate grades.

Samples and Demographic Variables. NAEP administrators attempt to identify a representative sample of students nationwide for each assessment. States must participate to receive Title I money, so motivation to cooperate is high. Demographic variables are gathered about the students, their schools, and their teachers to provide context for data analysis. The 2005 mathematics assessment database includes more than 220 demographic variables.

Score Levels. Test results on the NAEP assessment are converted into scaled scores. Mathematics and science scales range from 0–300; in reading and history, they range from 0–500. Student scores also are categorized into three levels:

> *Basic.* . . . partial mastery of prerequisite knowledge and skills that are fundamental for proficient work at each grade assessed.
> *Proficient.* . . . solid academic performance for each grade assessed. Students reaching this level have demonstrated competency over challenging subject matter, including subject-matter knowledge, application of such knowledge to real-world situations, and analytical skills appropriate to the subject matter.
> *Advanced.* . . . superior performance at each grade assessed. (Grigg, Donahue, & Dion, 2007, p. 3)

Although Basic, Proficient, and Advanced are the official categories, discussion of scores that are "Below Basic" has been frequent enough to make it a *de facto* fourth category. The lines of demarcation separating one level from the next are different for each subject. For instance, a scaled score of 346 out of a possible 500 is the dividing line between Proficient and Advanced in reading; in history, the line was set at a scaled score of 276 in the 2006 administration.

An ongoing debate has ensued over the operational definition of the three achievement levels and the ambiguity and inconsistency of the dividing lines. This debate finally culminated in a strongly worded position statement from the National Academy of Sciences (NAS) that, although they may be useful for tracking students over time, many aspects of the process of creating and assigning the achievement levels are flawed (Pellegrino, Jones, & Mitchell, 1998). The NAS and the NCES came to consensus that "achievement levels should continue to be used on a trial basis and should continue to be interpreted and used with caution" ("Status of Achievement Levels," ¶ 3). The levels continue to be used, however, since the panel also came to consensus that ". . . tracking changes in the percentages of students performing at or above those cut scores (or, in fact, any selected cut scores) can be of use in describing changes in student performance over time," (Pellegrino et al., 1998, p. 176) and there is no indication that an improved approach will be substituted in the near future.

Data Reporting. The NCES publishes a report of results and technical information for each assessment. The NAEP database is so large, however, that reports only provide information about a highly important, but relatively small, portion of the data. To encourage secondary analysis of the NAEP data, a database is available in the public domain: the NAEP Data Explorer (NDE) at http://nces.ed.gov/nationsreportcard/naepdata. This data repository contains many of the demographic variables and scores for NAEP assessments in most content areas from 1994 to the present, and was instrumental in this exploration of what the NAEP can and cannot tell us about advanced students.

Students in the "Advanced" Range

Students who score at the Advanced level on the NAEP are in extremely short supply. Approximately 2% of students who participated in the 2005 NAEP mathematics assessment scored at the Advanced level (Grigg et al., 2007), an average of one student per every two schools in the sample. Advanced-level students in other subjects are similarly sparse: In reading, 4.6% of the 12th-grade sample achieved the Advanced level (Grigg et al., 2007), and only 2.81% did in science (Grigg, Lauko, & Brockway, 2006). The NAEP U.S. history assessment had the lowest numbers of Advanced-level students, 1% of the 11,300 sampled students scored at the Advanced level (Lee & Weiss, 2007). This is not solely a current phenomena; the number of Advanced level students has always been fewer than 6% in most subjects. Table 1 provides a summary of students at each level in mathematics, science, U.S. history, and reading from 1992 to the present. These miniscule numbers give rise to three questions: (1) Why do so few students reach the Advanced level? (2) What do we know about the NAEP performance of gifted and/or high-achieving students generally? and (3) Why has there been so little attention to high-achieving students in NAEP reports?

Why Do So Few Students Reach the Advanced Level?

The NAEP designations of Basic, Proficient, and Advanced are controversial. Among the criticisms leveled at the NAEP designers is that the line between

TABLE 1

Percent of 12th-Grade Students Scoring in Each NAEP Score Category in History, Science, Mathematics, and Reading

Subject	Year	Sample Size	Below Basic	SE	Basic	SE	Proficient	SE	Advanced	SE
History	1994[1]	n/a	57.21%	1.106	32.26%	0.866	9.69%	0.609	0.84%	0.174
	2001	29,000	57.45%	1.214	31.59%	0.868	9.71%	0.718	1.25%	0.309
	2006	11,700	53.12%	1.052	33.95%	0.847	11.84%	0.661	1.09%	0.155
Science	1996	n/a	43.10%	1.025	35.47%	0.841	18.62%	0.725	2.81%	0.307
	2000	n/a	47.88%	1.200	33.85%	0.846	16.11%	0.756	2.16%	0.306
	2005	14,300	46.21%	0.759	35.33%	0.475	16.52%	0.579	1.94%	0.179
Mathematics*	2005	9300	39.37%	0.764	37.65%	0.624	20.80%	0.629	2.18%	0.222
Reading	1992[1]	n/a	20.31%	0.599	39.48%	0.663	36.28%	0.797	3.95%	0.278
	1994[1]	n/a	25.49%	0.726	38.22%	0.714	32.08%	0.913	4.21%	0.537
	1998	n/a	23.67%	0.699	36.22%	0.551	34.53%	0.816	5.58%	0.364
	2002	n/a	26.33%	0.754	37.68%	0.612	31.48%	0.804	4.50%	0.271
	2005	12,100	27.47%	0.763	37.15%	0.877	30.75%	0.532	4.63%	0.347

[1] Accommodations were not permitted for this assessment.

Note. Observed differences are not necessarily statistically significant. Detail may not sum to totals because of rounding. Data from National Assessment of Educational Progress (NAEP) 1992, 1994, 1998, 2002, 2005 Reading Assessments; 1994, 2001, 2006 History Assessments; 1996, 2000, and 2005 Science Assessments; and 2005 Mathematics Assessment.

* The Mathematics framework was redesigned for the 2005 assessment, resulting in significant changes. The new framework is considered sufficiently different as to prohibit comparisons with previous years.

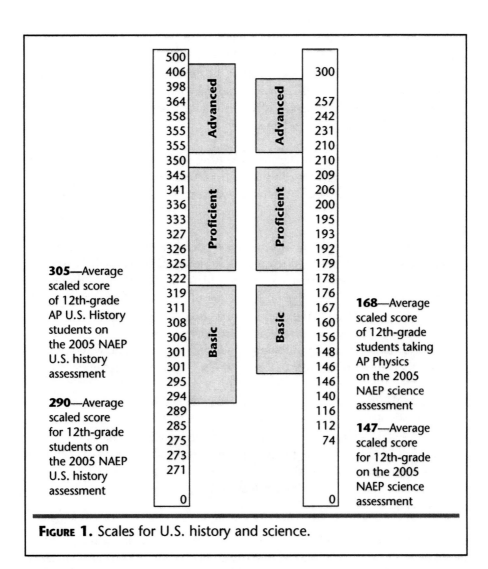

FIGURE 1. Scales for U.S. history and science.

Proficient and Advanced is too high, making an Advanced score all but inaccessible. To provide context, Figure 1 shows the scales for U.S. history and for science, along with the divisions designating Basic, Proficient, and Advanced performance. A scaled score of 355 out of 500 is the lower end of the Advanced level on the NAEP U.S. history assessment; 210 is the lower end of Advanced level for the science assessment. Students taking AP Physics received an average score of 168.

Is it reasonable to expect advanced 12th-grade students to achieve scores above 168 on the NAEP Science assessment or is the standard simply too high? Rothstein, Jacobsen, and Wilder (2006) provided an interesting point of comparison by estimating how many students from other nations would be likely to achieve this level on the NAEP. According to their estimates, only 8% of Chinese students and 6% of Taiwanese students would score at the NAEP Advanced level. China and Taiwan both scored well above the U.S. on the TIMSS, and Rothstein et al. argued that the low estimates for students in these countries give evidence that the standard is much too high. However, these authors fail to point out that if their estimates are correct, Chinese students would still score at the Advanced level at three times the rate of American students, and Taiwanese students at two times the American rate. Regardless of whether the bar is too high, the numbers of U.S. students scoring at the Advanced level should not be considered acceptable.

How Hard Is It? The argument that the Advanced level is too high to reach might make some sense statistically, but it is less compelling from other points of view. The descriptions of what "Advanced" work represents from the frameworks seem reasonable:

> Students performing at the *Advanced* level demonstrate the knowledge and reasoning abilities required for a solid understanding of the Earth, physical, and life sciences at a level appropriate to grade 12. In addition, they demonstrate knowledge of the themes of science (models, systems, and patterns of change) required for integrating knowledge of scientific principles from Earth, physical, and life sciences. Students can design investigations that answer questions about real-world situations and use their reasoning abilities to make predictions. (Grigg et al., 2006, p. 36)

Sample NAEP items also are released to the public through an Internet-based repository. The items are coded according to year, subject, and item difficulty. Figure 2 provides examples of items considered cognitively difficult in mathematics, science, and history. Each of these items is considered appropriately complex 12th-grade content according to their respective content frameworks. These items should not be out of reach of 12th-grade students, yet very few students answered them correctly.

The AP Conundrum. Of all of the students who participate in the NAEP, it would be most reasonable to expect Advanced Placement (AP) students to be at the Advanced level. To some extent, this statement is supported: NAEP participants who also are enrolled in an AP course are better represented at the Advanced level. However, this is only part of a complicated picture, and does not describe performance of AP students as a whole. The benefit of criterion-referenced tests is that they create an established standard independent of group comparisons; AP students may do significantly better than others on the NAEP, but that may be of only modest value if their achievement is still far below an established standard of knowledge and understanding—and it is. Using AP Physics as an example, 12.87% of students enrolled in AP Physics B or C scored at the Advanced level of the NAEP science test, a rate six times higher than the overall 1.94%. However, it also is true that the average scaled score for the same AP Physics students was 168.04, placing the group average at the upper end of the Basic range. Content gaps across science disciplines might be a credible explanation for why AP science students had such

---

2005 Mathematics Assessment

The remainder when a number n is divided by 7 is 2. Which of the following is the remainder when $2n + 1$ is divided by 7 ?
A. 1
B. 2
C. 3
D. 4
E. 5

Correct: 25%

2006 U.S. History Assessment

What was the main issue in the debates between Abraham Lincoln and Stephen A. Douglas in 1858?
A. Is slavery morally wrong?
B. Should slavery be allowed to expand to new territories?
C. Do Southern states have the constitutional right to leave the Union?
D. Are free African Americans citizens of the United States?

Correct: 28%

2005 Science Assessment

A radio transmitter broadcasts a signal at a given frequency. If the broadcast frequency is increased, what happens to the speed and the wavelength of the radio waves?

Speed	*Wavelength*
A. Increases	Decreases
B. Increases	Increases
C. Remains the same	Decreases
D. Remains the same	Increases

Correct: 15%

FIGURE 2. Sample Challenging items from the 12th-grade NAEP.

a low average score; however, this seems less likely given that the same pattern emerges when looking at the performance of students in AP U.S. History on the NAEP U.S. history assessment. The average scaled scores for students in AP U.S. History was 305 on a scale of 0–500, in the middle of the Basic range. This is true even though 3.73% of AP U.S. History students scored at the Advanced level, nearly four times the rate of other students. Given the increasing national investment in the Advanced Placement program (see Chapter 7, this volume), this should be of concern in circles far beyond gifted education advocates. Taken together, the data suggest that, even if the NAEP sets the bar high at the Advanced level, more gifted students should be able to reach it. Although some items are challenging, they are not beyond the grasp of well-educated students in advanced classes. Topics covered are part of the standard curriculum, and the thinking required is "typical" higher order thinking. Even so, average scores of students in Advanced Placement courses are far below the expected performance of "advanced" students. Another question raised by the low numbers at the Advanced level is the relative status of identified gifted students on the NAEP.

What Do We Know About the NAEP Performance of Gifted and/or High-Achieving Students?

NAEP gathers fairly comprehensive demographic data about students and schools. Students are asked to report gender, race, income, and whether they are ESL or disabled—but not if they are gifted. The NAEP background questionnaire that teachers complete for students on IEPs includes specific instructions not to fill out the questionnaire if a child is gifted. Initially, the NAEP school demographic data included a question about the percent of students who participated in the school's gifted program, but that variable was dropped for 12th grade between 1998 and 2002 in every subject assessed. In truth, this question may have been of little use in 12th grade because many high schools do not offer formal gifted education programs. Currently, there are no items that ask either about gifted students or gifted programs on the 12th-grade NAEP. The item that asked if students were assigned to 12th-grade classes by ability level was omitted from all subject assessments by the year 2000.

If the performance of gifted students cannot be assessed directly, proxy variables might provide a reasonable substitute. Unfortunately, even proxies are hard to find. Enrollment in Advanced Placement or International Baccalaureate (IB) is a shaky proxy, because not all gifted students enroll in AP courses, and not all who enroll in AP courses are gifted. Potentially more interesting is a question asking whether the student is above, at, or below the median age for his or her grade level, as this might give hints as to the efficacy of either wholesale or subject-based grade skipping. An item catalogued under School Organization asks if the school has a special focus on mathematics, science, or the arts; specialized schools of this sort often draw large numbers of gifted students, but again, this is an imprecise measure. Closer to the mark would be the question that asks what proportion of the student body is enrolled in AP, IB, or honors courses. Schools with between 75% and 90% of student enrollment in AP or IB might reasonably be considered a magnet for motivated and achieving, if not gifted, students. When all is considered, however, all these gyrations will only result in approximate, inadequate numbers. As currently configured, the NAEP cannot provide a report card on the nation's brightest students.

Information about teachers of gifted students is similarly difficult to find. The only question addressing specialized certification lumps gifted certification along with other areas of special education. With more than 20 states still without a mandate for services or teacher licensure in gifted education, a national database would provide invaluable information about the efficacy of each.

Why Has There Been so Little Attention to High-Achieving Students in NAEP Reports?

Few students score at the Advanced level of the NAEP and there's no telling how identified gifted students fare. Recent summary reports in mathematics, reading, science, and history barely mention the Advanced-level statistics. To be fair, the NAEP database is huge and it would be impossible to create a report that does justice to every interesting aspect of the data. The number of students at the Advanced level is so small that it does not communicate about the broad health of the educational system. However, even within this small set of students, there are data worthy of some attention, especially in the sciences where the small proportion of Advanced-level students had decreased by half since 1996, with a more precipitous drop among males. If these numbers are indeed representative, then the shrinking numbers may indicate a return to pre-Sputnik complacency, an odd turn of events in the Information Age. In 1996, 2.81% of students scored at the Advanced level in science; in 2000 that proportion dropped to 2.16% and to 1.94% in 2005. The drop among males is more precipitous: decreasing from 4.12% in 1996 to 2.65% in 2005; females at the Advanced level dropped from 1.56% in 1996 to 1.27% in 2005. The proportion of girls who scored at the Advanced level in reading also dropped significantly between 1996 and 2005. It is perplexing why this is not headline news; however, there may be two reasons.

Following the Money. The NAEP simply may be assessing where the federal investment is greatest. In FY 2007, $37 million was spent by the federal government on Advanced Placement incentives and teacher training, more than five times the rate of federal funding for the Javits Gifted and Talented Act ($7.6 million; U.S. Department of Education, 2007). It is reasonable that the government would want to determine the return on its investment, but disappointing that the data are not described more comprehensively.

Incorporating Gifted Students Increases Overall Test Scores. Analysis of NAEP data without considering student ability may mask important differences between typical and gifted students, resulting in an overall inflation of American students' average performance. If gifted students were separated out of the analysis, scores for typically developing students might well be much lower.

Summary of Key Points

- As currently configured, it is impossible to discern achievement levels of gifted students on 12th-grade NAEP assessments.
- Between 2% and 6% of students who participate in the various national NAEP assessments achieve scores at the Advanced level. A normal distribution of ability would suggest that the proportion should be much higher.
- Advanced-level students are disproportionately White, male, and middle to upper class.
- Few in number to begin with, the proportion of students at the Advanced level is shrinking. The lack of attention paid to what seems to be a serious deficit in sophisticated knowledge as measured by the NAEP is a matter of concern to anyone who works with gifted students.
- Students who take Advanced Placement classes do not score at the Advanced level in the numbers that one might reasonably expect. Given the increasing encouragement that schools and parents receive to have students enrolled in Advanced Placement classes, investigation of these data seems imperative.
- A cursory look at the Advanced items would suggest that that performance levels should be higher. Although there clearly are challenging items to be found on the NAEP, they should not be out of reach for well-trained gifted students
- The hyper-vigilant focus on lower achievement and/or the overzealous emphasis on accountability tests may be eroding the pool from which innovative thinking can emerge.
- Gifted education is controversial; ambiguity sustains controversy.
- Advocacy to reinstate items asking about students identified as gifted, teacher preparation in gifted education, and the nature of gifted programs is essential. These data would provide an important resource to support evidence-based judgments regarding the efficacy of gifted education.

References

Grigg, W., Donahue, P., & Dion, G. (2007). *The Nation's Report Card: 12th-grade reading and mathematics 2005* (NCES 2007-468). Washington, DC: U.S. Department of Education, National Center for Education Statistics.

Grigg, W. S., Lauko, M. A., & Brockway, D.M. (2006). *The Nation's Report Card: Science 2005* (NCES 2006–466). Washington, DC: U.S. Government Printing Office.

Lee, J., & Weiss, A. (2007). *The nation's report card: U.S. history 2006* (NCES 2007–474). Washington, DC: U.S. Government Printing Office.

No Child Left Behind Act, 20 U.S.C. §6301 (2001).

Olson, L. (2002, March 13). A NAEP primer. *Education Week,* pp. 10–11.

Pellegrino, J. W., Jones, L. R., & Mitchell, K. J. (Eds.). (1998). *Grading the nation's report card: Evaluating NAEP and transforming the assessment of educational progress.* Washington, DC: National Academies Press.

Rothstein, R., Jacobsen, R., & Wilder, T. (2006, November). *"Proficiency for all"—An oxymoron.* Paper prepared for the Symposium, "Examining America's Commitment to Closing the Achievement Gap: NCLB and Its Alternatives," sponsored by the Campaign for Educational Equity, Teachers College, Columbia University.

Status of achievement levels. (n.d.). Retrieved May 15, 2008, from http://nces.ed.gov/nationsreportcard/nde/help/qs/index.asp#Status_of_Achievement_Levels.asp

U.S. Department of Education. (2007). *Department of Education fiscal year 2008 congressional action.* Retrieved May 29, 2008, from http://www.ed.gov/about/overview/budget/budget08/08action.pdf

Chapter 5

Reform Efforts

BY

MARCIA
GENTRY,

AND

SCOTT
PETERS

Issue I: A Summary of Trends in Current National Practices in Secondary Schools as Described in the *2006–2007 State of the States* Report

THE *STATE OF THE STATES REPORT 2006–2007* is a compilation of data regarding gifted education practices occurring around the country. The 2007 publication is a collaboration between the National Association for Gifted Children (NAGC) and the Council of State Directors of Programs for the Gifted. The biennial document is the only national report on gifted education in the United States. In this most recent report, 43 state agencies completed the 149-item survey. Of these 43 states, only 27 have mandated services for gifted and talented learners.

In order to gain a better understanding of what pedagogical practices were most common at the high school level, states were asked to identify their top instructional delivery methods from a list of possible practices. Twenty-nine state agencies responded to this question with Advanced Placement (26) identified as the most common instructional method for gifted and talented high school students. This response was followed by dual enrollment in college courses (16), gifted and talented delivery methods within the regular classroom

(10), and specific self-contained gifted and talented classrooms (10). Special magnet schools (5), International Baccalaureate (IB) programs (4), independent study programs (4), resource rooms (1), self-paced learning (1), mentorships (1), and virtual learning (1) were less frequently reported practices. States were allowed to select more than one service method, and 14 were unable to estimate their top service methods. It is not surprising that Advanced Placement (AP) was the most widely reported method, given its prevalence in American high schools and its ready-made advanced content. However, AP courses do not meet the needs of all gifted students, especially those who are identified in leadership, artistic, or creative areas. The response "regular classroom" is an ambiguous category because it is unknown what strategies are taking place in these classrooms. It is likely that services are left to the individual classroom teacher. Only one state each reported mentorship or independent study as part of its top methods. Telescoping received no responses. The minimal use of these methods is surprising given the positive research findings concerning their use with secondary students. Cluster grouping was not included in the survey options, as it is an elementary program, but was reported in the "other" category for one state.

The *State of the States* report surveyed state education agencies to determine which states had specific funding for gifted and talented services as well as what schools received that funding. Thirty-one states reported some kind of funding for gifted and talented services from the state. Of these, the largest number (24) received funding based on formula or other allocation, while seven receive funding from grants. The largest number of states (12) reported that their funding is distributed through local education agencies as part of their general state funding. Ten states dispersed funds to local agencies via an application system, six distributed funds through governor's schools or summer programs, and six states had a competitive grant system. Five states distributed funds to local education agencies via a state mandate, three to virtual schools, three to residential schools, and seven disbursed funds through "other" means, such as through administrative units, through state directors, or directly to districts upon hiring of qualified personnel.

State and local institutional practices play an important role in the quality of education that gifted and talented students receive. Local educational agencies were surveyed concerning other related gifted and talented practices. Although most states require students to be age 5 by September before entering school, nine states allow for early entrance to kindergarten. Eight states leave it to the local education agency to determine early entrance policies, and 14 have no stated policies, thereby leaving it up to the local agency as well. Conversely, 12 states specifically prohibit early entrance to kindergarten. In a similar fashion to early entrance, 26 states do not offer any kind of alternative high school diploma without also completing the traditional high school curriculum. Seventeen states leave this decision up to the local education agencies.

Dual or concurrent enrollment in community college or university courses constitutes an educational practice that allows students to participate in advanced courses. A major question pertains to whether the state allows for dual or concurrent enrollment. Of those responding, 31 states reported policies allowing for dual or concurrent enrollment programs. Seven specifically leave the decision up to the local education agencies, whereas five do so by default since they do not have a stated policy. Nine states allow for middle school students to be concurrently enrolled in high school courses, five specifically prohibit this, and 13 have no stated policy, thereby leaving it up to local school districts.

The opportunity for a student to be promoted based on proficiency in a curricular subject is a form of acceleration that meets the academic needs of many gifted students. This form of acceleration allows students to enroll in advanced classes that provide new material and greater challenge. Thirteen states had policies that specifically permitted proficiency-based promotion, whereas eight states forbid such practice. Most states (22) were neutral on the practice, leaving the policy to local educational agencies. Similarly, most states (29) leave it to the local agencies to determine what types of services to provide to students who have demonstrated proficiency. Common options are grade or subject advancement (15), individual instruction (13), and independent study (13). Some states allow for high school credit based on proficiency. Eleven states reported having policies that permitted the practice, whereas two states had policies denying credit toward high school graduation based on demonstrated proficiency. The remaining states (30) allowed local educational agencies to decide whether to grant credit for proficiency.

State policy on gifted and talented teacher education and training is a cornerstone for effective programs and services. Mandated education for preservice teachers who worked within specialized programs for gifted students was required in 5 of the 43 states. Eighteen of 42 responding states require certification or endorsement. Most states (37 of 43 reporting) do not require regular classroom teachers to have any training in gifted education.

Synthesis of Findings and Recommended Considerations From These Data

Perhaps the main realizations yielded by the *2006–2007 State of the States* report are that services, funding, policies, support, and teacher preparation for gifted secondary education are inconsistent and limited. Effective programs and service delivery methods have been developed for gifted secondary students, but these programs and service delivery methods have yet to be enacted in any large-scale fashion in secondary schools. Often, services, if they exist, are unidimensional, such as the use of Advanced Placement without other services. The report effectively highlights areas for growth in gifted secondary education, especially in areas concerning funding, policy, and teacher training. Currently, little funding is provided to local educational agencies to encourage programming, and only a few states fund special programs and schools for gifted secondary students. Policies exist in some states that directly benefit gifted students, and in other states contrary policy exists to their detriment. In the absence of consistent funding, teachers with knowledge of the nature and needs of gifted students might be able to offer differentiated curriculum and instruction to these students, as the regular classroom is the most frequently cited locale where gifted students' needs are addressed at all grade levels. However, precious few states require in-service or preservice teachers to complete any coursework or professional development concerning gifted students and their education. This might be the best place to begin with the magnitude of work that lies ahead.

In the *2004–2005 State of the States* report (NAGC, 2005a), 48 states responded as compared to 43 respondents for the 2006–2007 report. It is logical to conclude that programming in the nonresponding states might not be prevalent at the same levels as in the states from which the Council of State Directors received responses. At the very least, this disinterest in participation serves as an indicator concerning the tenor of gifted education in these states.

Issue 2: High School Restructuring Efforts and Gifted Education

In February 2005, Microsoft Corporation chairman Bill Gates said, "Our high schools were designed 50 years ago to meet the needs of another generation. Until we design them to meet the needs of this century, we will keep limiting, even ruining, the lives of millions of Americans each year" (Feller, 2005, ¶ 2). Modifying the structure of traditional high schools is a fundamental component of the educational reform movement. Several recent high school restructuring efforts have the potential to usher in advancements for gifted and talented students. However, high school restructuring is a continuous effort, and the potential benefits for gifted and talented students remain unclear. Current high school reform trends that hold promise for gifted students include increasing academic rigor, decreasing the number of dropouts, providing students with smaller and more individualized learning environments, providing minority students greater access to college, and increasing emphasis on career academies (Bill & Melinda Gates Foundation, 2005; Conley, 2002; Cushman, 1997; Funk & Bailey, 1999).

Smaller Learning Communities

One of the most prevalent restructuring modifications in secondary schools involves creating smaller learning communities (SLC). In 2005, the U.S. Department of Education began a 5-year program awarding grants to local educational agencies utilizing the SLC model (U.S. Department of Education, Office of Elementary and Secondary Education, 2006). These communities break large school populations into smaller subgroups, allowing students to build strong connections with teachers and fellow students. Small autonomous groups within the larger school often are referred to as "schools-within-schools." The focus of the subgroups varies from school to school. Common groupings include house programs in which students take courses with fellow house students, magnet programs that emphasize a specialized curricular focus, and career academies (Cotton, 2001). Academic and career programs allow students to build on their strengths and interests, a typical focus of gifted education programming (Renzulli, Gentry, & Reis, 2003). They also allow for greater student choice in determining their educational environment and curriculum; again, characteristics that often distinguish gifted programs.

One important aspect of SLCs is their capacity to address the affective needs of students. Overexcitabilities, perfectionism, difficulties obtaining affiliations, and unrealistic goals are a few of the affective challenges facing gifted children (Piechowski, 2006). Students within SLCs develop relationships with their teachers that extend beyond the classroom (Darling-Hammond, Ancess, & Ort, 2002). The ability to address the affective needs of students is beneficial for all students, including gifted and talented students (NAGC, 1995).

Small learning communities provide students the opportunity to engage in specialized curriculum at deeper levels than in traditional high schools. In their study of the Coalition Campus Schools Project, Darling-Hammond et al. (2002) reported that teachers utilized multiple instructional methods to meet the diverse needs of students. These differentiated strategies ranged from small-group discussions and guided inquiry to independent research and performance assessment. Instruction grounded in real-world applications was another defining feature of the classrooms. For more than two decades, experts in the field of gifted and talented education have recommended many of these same curricular modifications (e.g., Reis, 2004; Renzulli, 1988; VanTassel-Baska, 1998).

Buchanan and Woerner (2002) investigated innovative high schools from around the nation and found that gifted students benefited when student choice was a central element within the school. Career academies, which function as SLCs, can effectively meet the needs of both traditional and nontraditional gifted and talented students. Recent work has investigated the role of career and technical education (CTE) in identifying and meeting the needs of talented secondary students, and concluded that CTE provides an important means of addressing the academic needs of a wider array of talented secondary students (Gentry, Hu, Peters, & Rizza, 2008).

Competency-Based Promotion

Competency-based promotion is a second high school restructuring movement that holds promise for gifted students. This reform allows students to progress through school at a level and pace commensurate with their ability. Students who demonstrate proficiency can progress at a rapid pace, leading to early graduation or the ability to take more in-depth or advanced courses (Plucker, Zapf, & Spradlin, 2004). In 2001, Oregon created the Proficiency-Based Admission Standards System or PASS. According to the PASS model, student proficiency in math, English, science, and social science are assessed by state university and community college faculty. In 2006–2007, 13 states reported having policies permitting proficiency-based promotion, whereas 8 states prohibited this practice and 22 states did not have a specified policy, leaving such decisions to local educational agencies (NAGC & Council of State Directors, 2007).

Early College High Schools

Colangelo, Assouline, and Gross (2004) in *A Nation Deceived* described an accelerated high school reform called Early College High Schools (ECHS). These schools provide students with an alternate pathway toward graduation and early college entrance. Students in these programs, traditionally at-risk students, enroll in participating universities after completing only 2 years of high school. This model results in students who graduate from high school with 2 years of college credit completed. Such schools have the benefit of making college more accessible to students who would not normally consider attending college. It also effectively reduces the number of years spent in college, thus minimizing the amount of money spent on tuition. Students also avoid the duplication of advanced high school courses and beginning college core courses. While the majority of ECHS focus on at-risk students, many gifted and talented students who are at risk go unnoticed due to the factors that place them at risk. Thus, ECHS offer a means by which students with gifts and talents from at-risk situations might be recognized and nurtured. Such efforts might provide similar opportunities for other students who may not be at risk, but who could benefit from and handle the college-level work.

Middle College High Schools

Similar to the ECHS is the Middle College High Schools (MCHS) model. Such venues are another new school restructuring configuration that incorporate the inclusion and structure of college (Cavalluzzo, Jordan, & Corallo, 2002). High school students attend courses at a local college. They become involved in campus life, sharing educational resources with college faculty and students. Career education and community service are common requirements of MCHS participating schools.

Providing Appropriate Challenge

Increasing academic rigor is a common goal in high school restructuring. Often, plans to improve academic rigor merely result in increasing graduation standards (Plucker et al., 2004). Promoting Advanced Placement (AP) and International Baccalaureate (IB) programs are a few positive ways in which secondary schools are strengthening their curricular programs (Nugent & Karnes, 2002). The American Competitiveness Initiative allocated close to $250 million to support AP and IB programs as well as science, technology, engineering, and math (STEM) programs (Zapf, Spradlin, & Plucker, 2006). Establishing new graduation criteria alone doesn't lead to curriculum that is more in-depth, complex, and abstract. Creating interest-based, student driven, real-world learning experiences requires more than stricter standards; it requires a greater commitment to staff development (Reis & Gentry, 1998).

Summary and Suggested Considerations for Potentially Promising Practices

Borman, Hewes, Overman, and Brown (2003) conducted a meta-analysis of comprehensive school reform efforts. They analyzed 232 models and identified 3 as having strong evidence of effectiveness: Direct Instruction (Association for Direct Instruction, 2005), The School Development Program (Comer School Development Program, 2006), and Success for All (Success for All Foundation, 2006). Of these models, The School Development Program was the only program to show strong evidence of effectiveness with high school students. The program was created by James Comer from Yale University and has the goal of providing holistic development by mobilizing adults and caretakers in the community. Several other programs in this meta-analysis were evaluated as "highly promising," including two models pertinent to secondary students: Expeditionary Learning Schools Outward Bound and Modern Red Schoolhouse. Expeditionary Learning Schools Outward Bound (2006) involves an exploratory curriculum that is predicated on self-discovery, collaboration, community service, and reflection. Modern Red Schoolhouse (2006) is a kindergarten through 12th-grade program that combines the virtues of traditional American education with modern innovations to create a curriculum of rigor and values. All of the aforementioned programs may contain some elements beneficial for gifted students; however, further study is warranted.

Issue 3: Reform Efforts in Career Technical Education and Talent Development for General and Talented Students

The integration of gifted education and talent development with career and technical education (CTE) has been slow in coming for several reasons. However, perhaps the largest obstacle to this worthy and important part of the American education system is the fact that it still carries with it the stigma that it is meant only for those students who cannot be successful in traditional classes and/or who are not college bound (Greenan, Wu, & Broering, 1995). This stereotype has likely developed because students with higher degrees of spatial intelligence and interest are traditionally drawn to the more hands-on applications such as those afforded by CTE programs (Mann, 2001). These same students might struggle in traditional courses because of their all-too-often abstract nature or the focus on skill and drill.

The Association for Career and Technical Education (ACTE) released a position paper entitled *Reinventing the American High School for the 21st Century* (2006).

This paper outlined the role that CTE can play in high-school-wide reform efforts and the many benefits that can be afforded all students. By far, the largest reform on the part of the CTE community is the emphasis that CTE programs should not be on the other side of the artificial line from traditional academic coursework. Rather, the ACTE issued eight recommendations for reform focusing on how CTE programs can further the goal of preparing every student for full participation in a spectrum of college opportunities, meaningful work, and career advancement.

In addition to simply allowing for a wider range of student interests that are not addressed in traditional courses, CTE programs also facilitate the application of advanced academic topics. Based on the belief that CTE topics do not exist in isolation from the traditional math, science, English, and other general courses, this reform posits that students learn and apply traditional academic knowledge to enhance learning and to better increase motivation and engagement (Plank, 2001). The idea of contextualized learning is common in educational discourse, and CTE reforms focus integrated curriculum, application of knowledge and skills, and development of individual interests (Gentry, Peters, & Mann, 2007).

Another major reform effort is based on research that has shown that even a part-time focus on CTE courses can help prevent students from dropping out of school (Plank, 2001). This, in and of itself, should be reason enough to include CTE in the general high school setting, as the current national graduation rate is approximately 70%. In summary, the reform efforts are twofold: increase CTE participation for all students as a means to apply and work with previous and traditional academic material, and increase CTE participation as a means for students to engage in interest-centered learning for career exploration and personal motivation.

Gifted education and CTE programs do not often go together as can be understood in the context of the current stereotypes of how education progresses. CTE has been seen as directed toward the non-college-bound student and certainly not for the gifted student (Greenan et al., 1995). One result of this disconnect has been that, historically, gifted students have been counseled away from CTE courses and programs (Bachtold, 1978; Brenneman, Justice, & Curtis, 1980; Ellis, 1976; Herr, 1976; Pulvino, Colangelo, & Zaffrann, 1976; Zaffrann & Colangelo, 1977). However, the national reconceptualization of giftedness to include all areas of human endeavor provides a rationale to connect gifted education and CTE (U.S. Department of Education, 1993). Recent research has explored gifted and talented students' experiences in CTE programs, and has included both traditionally identified gifted students and the nontraditionally talented students (Gentry et al., 2008; Gentry, Rizza, Peters, & Hu, 2005). Opening CTE programs to gifted and talented students and encouraging them to explore their options outside of the traditional academic areas provide another avenue for students to develop their potentials.

CTE programs can provide effective educational experiences for students who are succeeding in school as well as for those who are not (Gentry et al., 2007, 2008; Plank, 2001). Such education provides opportunities for students to work with others of similar interests, provides chances for students to express creativity and leadership ability, and provides situations in which students can demonstrate otherwise unmanifested skills and talents (Gentry et al., 2007; Stone & Alfeld, 2004). In an era of educational accountability, CTE allows for a much wider net to be cast in reaching all types of student learners and in addressing a wide variety of students' interests.

Although Milne (1982), Dayton and Feldhusen (1989), and Greenan (1988) all researched vocationally gifted students in the 1970s and 1980s, the idea has made little progress. Only recently have researchers examined part-time CTE settings for their effects on talented students and how those students view their CTE experience and their traditional high school experience (Gentry et al., 2007, 2008). This research has explored the idea that gifted and talented students enjoy and even prefer the hands-on and autonomous work that occurs in CTE settings. Gentry and her colleagues have called for research into the effects of CTE on potential gifted and talented dropouts.

Summary and Suggested Considerations

Dayton and Feldhusen (1989) as well as Greenan et al. (1995) emphasized that having skilled people from CTE areas is just as important as having people skilled in traditional academic areas. Nurturing high school students' talents and interests is the first, and perhaps most crucial, step in preparing tomorrow's workforce. Career and technical education has recently become a topic in gifted education, and with its extensive use of technology and cutting-edge integrated sciences, along with its emphasis on applied learning, it holds promise as an important option for talented secondary students. With the current focus placed on differentiation, enriched learning, and leaving no child behind, reform efforts are moving toward widening the availability of CTE programs to all students and encouraging these students to pursue such courses and programs as viable options for their future (ACTE, 2006).

Issue 4: Reform Efforts in Testing at the Secondary Level

High-stakes tests affect secondary students across the country and include middle school proficiency exams and high school exit exams. Perhaps the most visible result of the No Child Left Behind Act (NCLB; 2001) has been the implementation of new testing mandates in grades K–8. Current legislation proposes extending these accountability measures into high schools. The stated intent of the federal law was to "close the achievement gap with accountability, flexibility, and choice so that no child is left behind" (NCLB, 2001, p. 1). While this seems fair enough on paper, the fact of the matter is that schools in a country as ethnically, racially, socioeconomically, and politically diverse as the United States do not fit nicely into what Ohanian (1999) titled her book as the *one-size-fits-few* style of education. Ohanian described the folly of educational standards as trying to develop a one-size-fits-all approach to education and to testing. Perhaps the greatest problem with current practices in large-scale educational testing involves the amount of time it will take for the effects of these efforts to be known. Only recently have the results of empirical studies that address the effects of testing on teachers, students, and the educational system been published.

The largest studies to date, based on the results of high-stakes testing, were conducted by the Educational Policy Studies Laboratory at Arizona State University. Amrein and Berliner (2002) found results that were not encouraging. This study investigated the performance of schools and students in states that had high-stakes tests required throughout school, but they focused most specifically on high school exit exams. Results indicated that approximately 66% of schools with recently implemented high school graduation exams experienced negative effects in their graduation rates, dropout rates, and/or in the average age of their students return-ing to earn a GED. The authors also found that in states such as Massachusetts and Texas, students were being held back at increasing rates in the grade prior to the high-stakes assessment in order to keep them from failing the test and lower-ing the schools' percentage of passing students. The removal of low-performing students from secondary schools for this same reason was commonly found.

In a second and more recent study, Nichols, Glass, and Berliner (2005) created a Pressure Rating Index (PRI) and correlated the results on this assessment with those on the National Assessment for Educational Progress scores from 1990–2003 in 25 states. They found that the increased pressure from high-stakes testing nega-tively influenced students at many levels. In fact, increased PRI scores were cor-related with a decrease in the likelihood of 10th-grade students moving on to 12th grade and were ineffective in raising reading scores at the 4th- and 8th-grade levels. The overall findings suggest that the pressure of high-stakes testing mandated by NCLB does not lead to any benefit or increase in student achievement.

The increased emphasis on testing currently drives the content that students are taught (Amrein & Berliner, 2002). The focus on preparing for testing has resulted in a narrowed curriculum and a reduction in the number and diversity of courses and electives offered to students (Eisner, 2001; Gentry, 2006a). Further evidence exists that teaching to the test does not equate to quality learning (Mayer, Mul-lens, & Moore, 2000), with other evidence suggesting that increased standardized test results measure shallow thinking, and are correlated with low-level learning (Amrein & Berliner, 2002; Kohn, 2000; Moon, Callahan, & Tomlinson, 2003). One result of the emphasis on testing has been the increased devotion of time to test-specific preparation. Moon et al. found that teachers in schools with 30% or more poverty tended to spend significantly more time teaching to the test. Teachers also reported additional pressure from administrators to improve scores, even to the extent that a greater percentage of these teachers feared the loss of their jobs over high-stakes test scores. The constant fear is keeping teachers from practicing the art of teaching and forcing them instead to teach only what is tested and only up to the level that is tested (Eisner, 2001; Gentry, 2006a).

Perhaps one of the populations that receives the most disservice by high-stakes testing consists of students with gifts and talents (Gallagher, 2004; Gentry, 2006a; Golden, 2004). With the emphasis on minimal proficiency, little attention or effort has been paid to those performing or with the potential to perform at much higher levels than their peers. With teachers and administrators scared of losing their jobs, the blame cannot be placed on them (Amrein & Berliner, 2002). Several authors (e.g., Gallagher, 2004; Gentry, 2006a; Golden, 2004; Kaplan, 2004; Tomlinson, 2002) have discussed the consequences that gifted and talented students face as the result of No Child Left Behind high-stakes testing. Gentry (2006a) stated "proficiency is not enough, yet with NCLB proficiency is the goal and the focus, leaving many students who can exceed proficiency in educational deprival" (p. 24). Gentry (2006a) also argued that an increased number of dropouts; teachers afraid to teach; cheating, lying, and fuzzy math involving high-stakes test statistics; and teaching to the test result from the NCLB implicated high-stakes assessments. Addressing the needs of low-achieving students has left high-achieving and high-potential students with little to do in post-NCLB classrooms.

Summary and Suggested Considerations

Tomlinson (2002) pointed out the irony of NCLB and the American education system in general. The two bedrock values of equity and excellence seem to have been forgotten in this era of accountability, reform, and high-stakes testing. She notes that a lack of funding creates little incentive to develop student skills beyond proficiency, thus placing at risk the needs of gifted secondary students. In summary, for secondary students to achieve at high levels, instruction and assessment must reach beyond the current proficiency testing mentality. Secondary students risk, in the current climate, judgment of "why they are what they score," rather than learning to love the act of learning (Gentry, 2006b; Pope, 2003).

Issue 5: Highly Qualified Teachers' Reform and Gifted Education

Gifted secondary students require depth, complexity, and access to advanced content (Tomlinson et al., 2002). Further, they need opportunities to explore content areas at a pace commensurate with their abilities and interests (VanTassel-Baska & Sher, 2003). Instruction by teachers who have deep content knowledge and who understand the unique learning needs of gifted students would create an ideal learning environment for these students. Does the "Highly Qualified Teachers" phrase from current law meet this need?

The No Child Left Behind Act of 2001(NCLB) placed a major emphasis on teacher quality (title 1, section 1119). "Highly qualified" is the term the federal government uses to describe competent and effective teachers. The Department of Education defined highly qualified teachers as those who have a bachelor's degree, a state teaching certification, and proof of content knowledge in the subject areas they teach. The definition of highly qualified in these terms represents a teacher's educational preparation but not his or her actual teaching skill level. For more than a decade, researchers have studied the connection between teacher instructional ability and student achievement (Peske & Haycock, 2006). Teachers' academic skills, mastery of content, experience, and pedagogical skills all have been shown as factors that affect gains in student learning (Darling-Hammond & Youngs, 2002; Ehrenberg, 1994; Goldhaber & Brewer, 1996; Wayne & Youngs, 2003).

An important objective of the NCLB's highly qualified teacher classification was to remedy the inequitable distribution of qualified teachers. Specifically, high-poverty schools typically have difficulty recruiting and retaining expert teachers. The issue of improving teacher quality, especially among those who work with low socioeconomic and ethnically diverse student populations, is a concern for educators in gifted and talented education. The field of gifted education has prioritized developing the talents of impoverished and underrepresented minority students, as witnessed by recent Javits grant recipients (Moore, Ford, & Milner, 2005; NAGC, 2005b).

While educators of gifted and talented children and policymakers of NCLB may share some common philosophical goals, the approaches to achieving those outcomes are different. The NCLB Act defines highly qualified in terms of minimum teacher preparation standards. Gifted education, with its emphasis on rigorous and meaningful instruction, focuses on highly qualified teaching practices and knowledge of gifted children. These practices include grouping strategies, accelerated learning, higher order thinking, conceptual understanding, and authentic assessment (Colangelo et al., 2004; Rittle-Johnson, Siegler, & Alibali, 2001). Knowledge of gifted children includes understanding the unique social and emotional needs of gifted students, such as affiliation versus achievement, multipotentiality, and perfectionism (Colangelo, 2002; Piechowski, 2006). These methods and ideas have been recently updated in the Teacher Knowledge and Skill Standards for Gifted and Talented Education by NAGC and the Council for Exceptional Children (2006). A highly qualified teacher, therefore, would be one who could integrate deep content knowledge, pedagogy, and student affective needs (Southeast Center for Teaching Quality, 2004).

The major effect of NCLB's highly qualified teacher classification on gifted and talented education is that it ignores the gifted and talented student population. The act's mandates that all teachers be highly qualified pertain specifically to K–12 teachers who provide direct instruction in core subjects, and this content expertise can benefit gifted secondary students. However, the federal government's insistence on highly qualified educational preparation and certification stops short of applying these standards to gifted education. Special education teachers and teachers of the gifted and talented are required to be certified in their subject area, not in their area of specialization (e.g., gifted and talented). As a result of the lack of federal legislation requiring special certification, few states mandate that teachers of gifted and talented students complete coursework or training concerning this population of learners and their unique needs. The *State of the States Report* (NAGC & Council of State Directors, 2007) related that only 18 states required teachers who work with gifted and talented youth in special programs to have a certificate or endorsement in gifted education.

NCLB's silence regarding gifted and talented education stands in stark contrast to the federally commissioned report, *National Excellence: A Case for Developing America's Talent* (U.S. Department of Education, 1993). The report detailed how America is squandering the talent of its brightest students. The report noted that gifted elementary students knew 35–50% of the curriculum before they started the school year and that schools need to emphasize teacher education on instructional methods to better meet the needs of gifted and talented students.

Some educators have called NCLB an unfunded mandate; yet, technically this is not accurate (Heritage Foundation, 2003). Each year the federal government allocates funding for NCLB. President Bush's 2007 proposed budget for NCLB was $24.4 billion (U.S. Department of Education, 2006). Local educational agencies have spending discretion and may direct funding to gifted and talented programs at the elementary and secondary level. They are eligible for funds received under Title I: Improving the Academic Achievement of the Disadvantaged, Title II: Preparing Training and Recruiting High Quality Teachers and Principals, and from block grants in Title V: Innovative Programs. Although districts may use these funds for gifted and talented programs, it remains unclear whether any of these federal dollars actually matriculate to gifted programs, particularly when local educational agencies are focused on at-risk students and academic failure.

Summary and Suggested Considerations

The requirement that teachers hold degrees or certifications specific to the subject that they teach could have positive effects on gifted students enrolled in advanced courses, especially in math and science. Gifted secondary students require advanced and sophisticated curriculum and instruction. They also need access to current and advanced knowledge in higher level areas of study. Thus, an increase in the overall content knowledge among secondary teachers would greatly benefit gifted and talented students by providing them with content-expert teachers. Rich content expertise can result in appropriate depth and complexity for talented secondary students. Conversely, content-specific credential requirements could eliminate "block" interdisciplinary instructional situations in which a teacher integrates two disciplines, such as English and history (Keller, 2005). Teachers would be required to hold certifications in both subject areas. Thus, under NCLB's highly qualified teacher requirements, integration of two content areas in secondary education will become both less likely and less common.

No Child Left Behind's highly qualified teacher status centers on teacher content knowledge requirements as the method of achieving teacher equity within schools. Although standardized content requirements hold potential for gifted and talented students who enroll in advanced courses and who need teachers with expertise in the content areas, the absence of standards for pedagogical and socioemotional knowledge poses serious concerns for gifted and talented children. Therefore, a highly qualified teacher needs training and support in meeting the needs of all students, including gifted and talented students.

References

Amrein, A., & Berliner, D. (2002). *An analysis of some unintended and negative consequences of high-stakes testing*. Tempe: Arizona State University, Educational Policy Studies Laboratory.

Association for Career and Technical Education. (2006). *Reinventing the American high school for the 21st century.* Retrieved April 8, 2008, from http://www.acteonline.org/policy/legislative_issues/upload/ACTEHSReform_Full.pdf

Association for Direct Instruction. (2005). *What is direct instruction?* Eugene, OR: Author. Retrieved April 8, 2008, from http://adihome.org/articles/DIN_05_01_01.pdf

Bachtold, L. M. (1978). Reflections of gifted learners. *Gifted Child Quarterly, 22,* 116–124.

Bill & Melinda Gates Foundation. (2005). *Rigor, relevance, and results: The quality of teacher assignments and student work in new and conventional high schools*. Seattle, WA: Author.

Borman, G. D., Hewes, G. M., Overman, L. T., & Brown, S. (2003) Comprehensive school reform and achievement: A meta-analysis. *Review of Educational Research, 73,* 125–230.

Brenneman, C. J., Justice, F. L., & Curtis, S. M. (1980). Gifted and talented students in vocational education: Review of the literature. *The Journal of Vocational Education Research, 1*(3), 55–65.

Buchanan, N. K., & Woerner, B. (2002). Meeting the needs of gifted learners through innovative high school programs. *Roeper Review, 24,* 213–219.

Cavalluzzo, L., Jordan, W., & Corallo, C. (2002). *Case studies of high schools on college campuses: An alternative to the traditional high school program*. Charleston, WV: Appalachian Regional Education Laboratory.

Colangelo, N. (2002). *Counseling gifted and talented students* (Research Monograph No. 02150). Storrs: University of Connecticut, The National Research Center on the Gifted and Talented.

Colangelo, N., Assouline, S. G., & Gross, M. U. M. (2004) *A nation deceived: How schools hold back America's brightest students* (Vol. 1). Iowa City: The University of Iowa, The Connie Belin & Jacqueline N. Blank International Center for Gifted Education and Talent Development.

Comer School Development Program. (2006). *Overview of the school development program*. Retrieved April 8, 2008, from http://www.med.yale.edu/comer/about/overview.html

Conley, D. T. (2002). Preparing students for life after high school. *Educational Leadership, 59*(7), 60–63.

Cotton, K. (2001). *New small learning communities: Findings from recent literature.* Portland, OR: Northwest Regional Education Lab.

Cushman, K. (1997). Why small schools are essential. *Horace, 13*(3). Retrieved April 8, 2008, from http://www.essentialschools.org/cs/resources/view/ces_res/18

Darling-Hammond, L. D., Ancess, J., & Ort, S. W. (2002). Reinventing high school: Outcomes of the Coalition Campus School Project. *American Educational Research Journal, 39,* 639–673.

Darling-Hammond, L., & Youngs, P. (2002). Defining "highly qualified teachers": What does "scientifically-based research" actually tell us? *Educational Researcher, 31*(9), 13–25.

Dayton, J. D., & Feldhusen, J. F. (1989). Characteristics and needs of vocationally talented high school students. *Career Development Quarterly, 37,* 355–364.

Ehrenberg, R. G. (Ed.). (1994). *Choices and consequences: Contemporary policy issues in education.* Ithaca, NY: ILR Press.

Eisner, E. (2001). What does it mean to say a school is doing well? *Phi Delta Kappan, 82,* 367–372.

Ellis, J. R. (1976). *A final report: An exploratory study of professional opinions and current practices regarding career education for exceptionally gifted and talented students.* Dekalb: Northern Illinois University.

Expeditionary Learning Schools Outward Bound. (2006). *Design principles.* Retrieved April 8, 2008, from http://www.elob.org/aboutus/principles.html

Feller, B. (2005, February 27). Calling high schools obsolete, Microsoft chief urges restructuring. *The Boston Globe.* Retrieved April 8, 2008, from http://www.boston.com/news/education/k_12/articles/2005/02/27/calling_high_schools_obsolete_microsoft_chief_urges_restructuring

Funk, P. E., & Bailey, J. (1999). Small schools, big results: Nebraska high school completion and postsecondary enrollment rates by size of district. Walthill, NE: Nebraska Alliance for Rural Education. (ERIC Document Reproduction Service No. ED441633)

Gallagher, J. (2004). No child left behind and gifted education. *Roeper Review, 26,* 121–123.

Gentry, M. (2006a). No child left behind: Neglecting excellence. *Roeper Review, 29,* 24–27.

Gentry, M. (2006b). No child left behind: Gifted children and school counselors. *Journal of Professional School Counseling, 10,* 73–81

Gentry, M., Hu, S., Peters, S., & Rizza, M. (2008). Talented students in an exemplary career and technical education school: A qualitative inquiry. *Gifted Child Quarterly, 52,* 183–198.

Gentry, M., Peters, S., & Mann, R. (2007). Differences between general and talented students' perceptions of their career and technical education experiences compared to their traditional high school experiences. *Journal of Advanced Academics, 18,* 372–402.

Gentry, M., Rizza, M., Peters, S., & Hu, S. (2005). Professionalism, sense of community, and reason to learn: Lessons from an exemplary career and technical education center. *Career and Technical Education Research, 30,* 47–85.

Golden, D. (2004, December 19). Initiative to leave no child behind leaves out gifted: Educators divert resources from classes for smartest to focus on basic literacy. *The Wall Street Journal,* p. A1.

Goldhaber, D. D., & Brewer, D. J. (1996). Evaluating the effect of teacher degree level on educational performance. *Developments in School Finance*. Retrieved April 8, 2008, from http://nces.ed.gov/pubs97/97535/97535l.asp

Greenan J. P. (1988). Talented students in career, vocational, and technical programs. *Educational Forum, 59*, 409–422.

Greenan, J., Wu, M., & Broering, K. (1995). Talented students in career, vocational, and technical education programs. *The Educational Forum, 59*, 409–421.

Heritage Foundation. (2003). *What unfunded mandates? CBO study reveals Washington not at fault for state budget crises*. Retrieved April 8, 2008, from http://www.heritage.org/Research/Budget/wm283.cfm

Herr, E. L. (1976). Career education for the gifted and talented: Some observations. *Peabody Journal of Education, 53*, 102–103.

Kaplan, S. (2004). Where we stand determines the answers to the questions: Can No Child Left Behind legislation be beneficial to gifted students? *Roeper Review, 26*, 124–125.

Keller, B. (2005, December 14). Actual measure of "highly qualified" teachers just beginning to come to light across nation. *Education Week*, pp. S6–9.

Kohn, A. (2000). *The case against standardized testing: Raising the scores, ruining the schools*. Portsmouth, NH: Heinemann.

Mann, R. L. (2001). Eye to eye: Connecting with gifted visual-spatial learners. *Gifted Child Today, 24*(4), 54–57.

Mayer, D., Mullens, J., & Moore, M. (2000). *Monitoring school quality: An indicators report*. Washington, DC: U.S. Department of Education, National Center for Educational Statistics.

Milne, B. (1982). *Vocational education for gifted and talented students*. Columbus: Ohio State University Center on Education.

Modern Red Schoolhouse. (2006). *Our mission*. Retrieved April 8, 2008, from http://www.mrsh.org/about_us/mission.php

Moon, T., Callahan, C., & Tomlinson, C. (2003, April 28). Effects of state testing programs on elementary schools with high concentrations of student poverty—good news or bad news? [Electronic version]. *Current Issues in Education, 6*(8). Retrieved June 3, 2008, from http://cie.asu.edu/volume6/number8/index.html

Moore, J. L., III, Ford, D. Y., & Milner, H. R. (2005). Recruiting is not enough: Retaining African American students in gifted education. *Gifted Child Quarterly, 49*, 49–65.

National Association for Gifted Children. (1995). *Position statement: Addressing affective needs of gifted children*. Retrieved April 8, 2008, from http://www.nagc.org/index.aspx?id=384

National Association for Gifted Children. (2005a). *State of the states 2004–2005*. Washington DC: Author.

National Association for Gifted Children. (2005b). *2005 Javits Grants*. Retrieved April 8, 2008, from http://www.nagc.org/index.aspx?id=1050

National Association for Gifted Children, & Council for Exceptional Children. (2006). NAGC–CEC *Teacher knowledge & skill standards for gifted and talented education*. Washington, DC: Author. Retrieved April 8, 2008, from http://www.nagc.org/uploadedFiles/Information_and_Resources/NCATE_standards/final%20standards%20(2006).pdf

National Association for Gifted Children, & Council of State Directors of Programs for the Gifted. (2007). *State of the states 2006–2007*. Washington DC: Author.

Nichols, S., Glass, G., & Berliner, D. (2005). *High-stakes testing and student achievement: Problems for the No Child Left Behind Act.* Tempe: Arizona State University, Educational Policy Studies Laboratory.

No Child Left Behind Act, 20 U.S.C. § 6301 (2001).

Nugent, S. A., & Karnes, F. A. (2002) The Advanced Placement program and the International Baccalaureate programme: A history and update. *Gifted Child Today, 25*(1), 30–39.

Ohanian, S. (1999). *One size fits few: The folly of educational standards.* Portsmouth, NH: Heinemann.

Peske, H. G., & Haycock, K. (2006). *Teacher inequality: How poor and minority students are shortchanged on teacher quality.* Washington, DC: Education Trust.

Piechowski, M. M. (2006). *"Mellow out," they say. If I only could: Intensities and sensitivities of the young and bright.* Madison, WI: Yunasa Books.

Plank, S. (2001). A question of balance: CTE, academic courses, high school persistence, and student achievement. *Journal of Vocational Education Research, 26,* 279–327.

Plucker, J. A., Zapf, J. S., & Spradlin, T. E. (2004). *Redesigning high schools to prepare students for the future.* Bloomington: Indiana University, Center for Evaluation and Policy.

Pope, D. C. (2003). *Doing school: How we are creating a generation of stressed out, materialistic, and miseducated students.* New Haven, CT: Yale University Press.

Pulvino, C. J., Colangelo, N., & Zaffrann, R. T. (1976). *Laboratory counseling programs.* Madison, WI: Research and Guidance Laboratory.

Reis, S. M. (2004). *Essential readings in gifted education.* Thousand Oaks, CA: Corwin Press.

Reis, S. M., & Gentry, M. (1998). The application of enrichment clusters to teachers' classroom practices. *Journal for the Education of the Gifted, 21,* 310–334.

Renzulli, J. S., (1988). The Multiple Menu Model for developing differentiated curriculum for the gifted and talented. *Gifted Child Quarterly, 32,* 298–309.

Renzulli, J. S., Gentry, M., & Reis, S. M., (2003). *Enrichment clusters: A practical plan for real-world, student-driven learning.* Mansfield, CT: Creative Learning Press.

Rittle-Johnson, B., Siegler, R. S., & Alibali, M. W. (2001). Developing conceptual understanding and procedural skill in mathematics: An iterative process. *Journal of Educational Psychology, 93,* 346–362.

Southeast Center for Teaching Quality. (2004). *Unfulfilled promise: Ensuring high quality teachers for our nation's students.* Retrieved April 8, 2008, from http://www.teachingquality.org/pdfs/NCLB_PublishedReport.pdf

Stone, J., & Alfeld, C. (2004). Keeping kids in school: The power of CTE. *Techniques.* Retrieved September 25, 2006, from http://www.acteonline.org/members/techniques/apr04_feature3.cfm

Success for All Foundation. (2006). *About SFAF.* Baltimore: Author. Retrieved April 8, 2008, from http://successforall.com/about/index.htm

Tomlinson, C. (2002, November 6). Proficiency is not enough. *Education Week,* pp. 36–38.

Tomlinson, C. A., Kaplan, S. A., Renzulli, J. S., Purcell, J., Leppien, J., & Burns, D. (2002). *The parallel curriculum: A design to develop high potential and challenge high-ability learners.* Thousand Oaks, CA: Corwin Press.

U.S. Department of Education. (1993). *National excellence: A case for developing America's talent.* Washington, DC: U.S. Government Printing Office.

U.S. Department of Education. (2006). *Fiscal year 2007 budget request advances NCLB implementation and pinpoints competitiveness.* Retrieved April 8, 2008, from http://www.ed.gov/news/pressreleases/2006/02/02062006.html

U.S. Department of Education, Office of Elementary and Secondary Education. (2006). *Smaller learning communities program.* Retrieved October 30, 2006, from http://www.ed.gov/programs/slcp/applicant.html

VanTassel-Baska, J. (1998). *Excellence in educating gifted and talented learners.* Denver, CO: Love.

VanTassel-Baska, J., & Sher, B. (2003). Accelerating learning experiences in core content areas. In J. VanTassel-Baska & C. A. Little (Eds.), *Content-based curriculum for high-ability learners* (pp. 27–46). Waco, TX: Prufrock Press.

Wayne, A. J., & Youngs, P. (2003). Teacher characteristics and student achievement gains: A review. *Review of Educational Research, 73*(1), 89–122.

Zaffrann, R. T., & Colangelo, N. (1977). Counseling with gifted and talented students. *Gifted Child Quarterly, 21*, 305–321.

Zapf, J. S., Spradlin, T. E., & Plucker, J. A. (2006) *Redesigning high schools to prepare students for the future: Update.* Bloomington: Indiana University Center for Evaluation and Policy.

Authors' Note

The authors gratefully acknowledge the contribution of Todd Jeffrey on earlier versions of this chapter.

Chapter 6

Research Monographs and Javits Grant Projects Focused on Gifted Secondary Education

BY

M. Katherine Gavin

Monographs

TO DATE THERE ARE NINE MONOGRAPHS with a focus on secondary education, written by experts in the field, and commissioned by the National Research Center on the Gifted and Talented (NRC/GT) at the University of Connecticut. Because the research center is funded under the Jacob K. Javits Gifted and Talented Students Education Act, the emphasis of these reports is on developing talents in at-risk populations who have been traditionally underserved. The following descriptions help in focusing understanding on these relevant topics.

Culturally Diverse Students

In *Teaching Thinking to Culturally Diverse, High Ability, High School Students: A Triarchic Approach*, Coates, Perkins, Vietze, Cruz, and Park (2003) presented five projects using an intervention to improve the thinking abilities of high-ability, ethnic minority, high school students at an urban magnet school. This intervention was based on Robert J. Sternberg's triarchic theory, which suggests that intelligence has three components: analytical, creative, and practical. There is an added focus on language background, language use, and writing abilities. Findings indicated that college-based intensive and supportive intervention activities improved analytical and creative thinking skills, but did not improve practical skills. Despite language background and usage differences among the different ethnic groups, there was no difference in student writing performance. Confidence in using English was related to writing performance measures rather than a preference for using language. Finally, students with higher grade point averages tended to be more hierarchical thinkers.

Developing the Talents and Abilities of Linguistically Gifted Bilingual Students: Guidelines for Developing Curriculum at the High School Level (Angelelli, Enright, & Valdés, 2002) contains general suggestions for implementing a curriculum in interpretation and translation. The authors also provided basic lesson suggestions that can be followed in teaching beginning courses in interpretation and translation at the high school level for bilingual students who are experienced interpreters for their families. Recommendations include broadening identification procedures to include linguistically talented students with the recognition that this is not a simple task. Moreover, students with a unique type of linguistic giftedness, needed for translating and interpreting, should be identified among immigrant children. The implementation of a Translation/Interpretation Program encourages collaboration among teachers of existing classes, motivates students because they see the long-term relevance of their learning, and holds students accountable for their learning in many other language-oriented classes.

Reis, Hébert, Díaz, Maxfield, and Ratley (1995) conducted a case study of 35 high school students with diverse backgrounds in a large urban high school. The monograph, *Case Studies of Talented Students Who Achieve and Underachieve in an Urban High School*, seeks to answer the research question, "Why do some academically talented students fail in school when others succeed?" Using qualitative research methods, the researchers compared both achieving and underachieving students with similar high abilities. The findings indicate that achievement and underachievement were not disparate concepts, and a student who once was an achiever could become an underachiever. No relationship was found between poverty and underachievement, between parental divorce and underachievement, or between family size and underachievement. Students who achieved in school acknowledged the importance of being grouped in advanced classes; received support and encouragement from each other and from their teachers, guidance counselors, and mentors; and took part in multiple extracurricular activities.

Programming and Academic Issues for Gifted Secondary Students

In *The Case for Weighting Grades and Waiving Classes for Gifted and Talented High School Students*, Cognard (1996) conducted research to gather data on the use of weighted grades in high schools and the practice of waiving classes, using questionnaires, interviews, and a review of published literature. Findings revealed that the majority of high schools in the study reported that they use some form of weighted grades. There is no consistency among schools as to which classes or grades are weighted, how much each grade is weighted, and/or how labeling on transcripts occurs. Weighted grades appear to benefit students in most cases. Regarding waiving classes, there is no consistency among schools on how classes are waived, but generally no class is waived unless students show mastery of material. When students are allowed to waive lower level classes, they usually receive no credit for the course, and often they must take more advanced classes in the same academic discipline.

Callahan (2003) conducted a review of Advanced Placement (AP) and International Baccalaureate (IB) programs for talented students in American high schools with a focus on science and mathematics. This review included the general historical background, overriding philosophies, procedures, perceived advantages and disadvantages, and a discussion of the growth of and research on the AP and IB programs. Results showed that steadily increasing enrollment in AP and IB programs is attributed to a number of factors. These include an increase in available courses, a lack of other rigorous and challenging options, government financial support, a national trend toward increased time to complete the baccalaureate degree, and recommendations to gifted learners. In addition, beliefs about advantages in the college admission process and the use of AB and IB programs as indicators of school quality encourage students to enroll in these courses. Finally, the quality of curriculum, the level of challenge, and the learning environment in AP and IB programs draw students into the programs. The AP program seems to fit with the idea that giftedness is characterized functionally rather than by test scores. However, there are equity concerns in these programs. There are also possible disadvantages to AP programs. They may fail to develop understanding of concepts and key ideas because of focusing on covering a vast amount of material through lecture. For the same reason, they may fail to develop metacognitive skills, leaving students unprepared for upper level college courses. Finally, they may discourage students from taking rigorous non-AP courses.

Renzulli and Park (2002) conducted two studies on high school dropouts using the National Education Longitudinal Study of 1988 (NELS: 88) database, and reported on them in the monograph, *Giftedness and High School Dropouts: Personal, Family, and School-Related Factors*. The results of the first study, an analysis of the dropout questionnaire, indicated many of the gifted male students left school because they were failing, got a job, could not keep up with their schoolwork, and/or did not like school. Gifted female students left school because they did not like school, were pregnant, became a parent, or were failing. Many parents whose child dropped out of school tried to persuade him or her to stay in school, but many did not offer counseling services to their child. In the second study, findings indicated that of the total gifted population, 5% dropped out of school. Almost half of the gifted dropout students were in the lowest quartile socioeconomic level, while only 3.6% of these dropouts were in the highest quartile. More Hispanics and Native Americans dropped out of school than White and Asian Americans. A high percentage of gifted dropouts had parents who had not finished high school.

The fourth monograph on academic issues is a handbook designed to assist economically disadvantaged and first generation college attendees. In this monograph, Wright and Olszewski-Kubilius (1993) offer the gifted student a framework for the college search process. Some recommendations urge students to examine strengths, weaknesses, and career goals to find the right college match; take challenging courses at all levels; take part in extracurricular activities: follow directions on applications and watch deadlines; use essays and interviews to give insight into personality; and weigh college acceptances carefully.

Students in Special School Settings

In *Undiscovered Edisons: Fostering the Talents of Vocational-Technical Students*, Taylor (1995) adapted the Enrichment Triad Model to include an integrated career development model, Focus On. The author proposed a broadened implementation process that takes into account the needs of students as they travel through the stages of career development. Identification of talent also needs to be broadened to reflect the population that is being targeted for services. Vocational identities can be influenced by involvement in gifted and talented programming that encourages creative productivity. The process involves an interaction of abilities, creative potential, and commitment to a problem that is of interest to the learner.

Students With Cerebral Palsy

In *Recognizing Talent: Cross-Case Study of Two High Potential Students With Cerebral Palsy*, Willard-Holt (1994) explored the experiences of an elementary and a high school student who had cerebral palsy and were not able to communicate with speech. Findings revealed that identifying students with physical handicaps can be problematic. Scores on traditional tests and inventories may be lower because of conditions like limited speech, difficulties with hand manipulation ability, or fewer life experiences based on impaired mobility. Programming and instruction has to be sensitive to a student's mode of communication to facilitate the expression of cognitive abilities. Finally, a relaxed, positive classroom atmosphere that centers on respect for the student has a positive effect on intellectual development.

Web Site

The National Research Center on the Gifted and Talented has made the abstracts and findings from the complete reports described above available online at the following Web address: http://www.gifted.uconn.edu/nrcgt/resource.html. The monographs also can be ordered online at this Web site and are listed as the references below.

U.S. Department of Education Javits Grants Focused on Secondary Students

The Jacob K. Javits Gifted and Talented Students Education Act funds grants to carry out a coordinated program of scientifically based research, demonstration projects, innovative strategies, and similar activities designed to build upon and enhance the ability of elementary and secondary schools to meet the educational needs of gifted and talented students. The major emphasis of the program is on serving students traditionally underrepresented in gifted and talented programs, particularly economically disadvantaged, limited English proficient (LEP), and disabled students. The goal is to help reduce the serious gap in achievement among certain groups of students at the highest levels of achievement.

In keeping with this goal, one of the specific objectives is to establish and operate innovative projects for serving gifted and talented students whose needs may not be met by more traditional gifted programs. These projects include summer programs, mentoring programs, service learning activities, and projects connected to business and industry. Other projects include providing challenging coursework that is disseminated through technologies, such as distance learning for students in schools and/or districts that do not have the resources to provide these opportunities.

A review of projects funded since 1996 found the vast majority focused on elementary students and schools. In fact, only nine projects that were funded since that year had a major focus on secondary education. All projects focused on traditionally underserved and disadvantaged populations, including low-income urban high school students and low-income rural middle and high school students. Two projects specifically targeted Native American students. A description of these projects follows in Table 1.

Web Site

For further information about these grant awards, please visit http://www.ed.gov/programs/javits/awards.html.

Summary and Suggested Practices in Using these Materials

These monographs and Javits Grant Reports are highly useful for developing programs and strategies at the local and district levels; interested professionals should use the relevant results to inform practice and institute change in schools. These reports add to the materials that are currently available to practitioners who seek evidence of useful and successful programs.

TABLE 1

Secondary School Projects Funded by Javits Grants

Project Name	Place and Year	Focus	Outcome
Problem-Based Learning in Social Studies	University of North Carolina—1996 for 3 years.	Problem-based learning that involves solving real-world problems, self-directed learning, and exploring content through immersion in current and historical episodes with relevance to the targeted student population.	Rigorous and relevant social studies curriculum units for economically disadvantaged high school students.
Project Scientists-in-the-Schools (SIS)	Lamar University—2002 for 5 years.	Field testing of inquiry model developed by the San Francisco Exploratorium Institute for Inquiry; professional development provided for teachers and scientists.	Content-rich and challenging science education in weekend and summer science academies at Lamar university for disadvantaged middle and high school students.
Project Gate	Ball State University—1996 for 3 years.	Professional development for teachers in five Indianapolis high schools in differentiation in math, science, and technology, including writing tiered lessons.	A CD containing information about the implementation of Project Gate with clips of some of the differentiated lessons.
Project LOGgED On: Learning Opportunities for the Gifted Economically Disadvantaged—Online	University of Virginia—2002 for 5 years.	Online professional development for teachers; learning opportunities in the science area for students in middle and high school.	Case-based online advanced courses in environmental science and physics are being developed for high school students.
CHAMPS Project	Mississippi School for Science and Mathematics—2002 for 5 years.	Identification of and services to students in grades 5–10 who are highly capable in mathematics and science.	Advanced coursework opportunities for identified students through a 2-week residential summer institute and distance learning seminars.
The Urban Scholars Program	University of Massachusetts-Boston—1996 for 3 years.	Implementation of an integrated system of rigorous standards and assessments tied to curriculum and professional development.	Models for effective talent identification and development; Models to address the need to improve the quality of education for all students at target schools.
Project Aspire: Creating Opportunities for Rural, Low-Income Students	Indiana Academy for Science, Mathematics and Humanities—2002 for 3 years.	Development and implementation of a sustainable Advanced Placement preparatory curriculum with concurrent instructional strategies and assessment appropriate to each course.	Online distance learning provides Advanced Placement courses to 10 project schools. Academic and counseling support services are provided to students.

Project Name	Place and Year	Focus	Outcome
Project LOGIC: Leadership Opportunities for Gifted Indian Children	University of Oklahoma American Indian Institute—1997 for 3 years	Development of alternative identification criteria for talented secondary American Indian students; professional development for teachers	Summer leadership institutes and weekend leadership seminars for American Indian youth and their educators to conduct field testing of materials.
Project LEAP (Leadership Excellence Achievement and/or Performance)	Osage County (OK) Interlocal Cooperative—1996 for 3 years	Development of academic, artistic, and/or leadership abilities in secondary students in northeastern Oklahoma, most of whom are American Indians. Components include identification, curriculum, parental awareness, and professional development.	Dissemination of materials including the development of study units incorporating the students' culture.

Conclusion

What are the current options for secondary students? How can these students plan and then implement a well-designed plan that gives them options in their education? These are the questions that guide the second section of Part II of this volume. Again, the focus is on current practices and options available to secondary students. A well-informed educator, administrator, counselor, or parent is aware of these options in pursuit of helping these students reach their potential as effectively and efficiently as possible.

References

Angelelli, C., Enright, K., & Valdés, G. (2002). *Developing the talents and abilities of linguistically gifted bilingual students: Guidelines for developing curriculum at the high school level* (Research Monograph No. 02156). Storrs: University of Connecticut, The National Research Center on the Gifted and Talented.

Callahan, C. M. (2003) *Advanced Placement and International Baccalaureate programs for talented students in American high schools: A focus on science and mathematics* (Research Monograph No. 03176). Storrs: University of Connecticut, The National Research Center on the Gifted and Talented.

Coates, D. L., Perkins, T., Vietze P., Cruz, M. R., & Park, S. J. (2003) *Teaching thinking to culturally diverse, high ability, high school students: A triarchic approach* (Research Monograph No. 03174) Storrs: University of Connecticut, The National Research Center on the Gifted and Talented.

Cognard, A. M. (1996). *The case for weighting grades and waiving classes for gifted and talented high school students* (Research Monograph No. 96226). Storrs: University of Connecticut, The National Research Center on the Gifted and Talented.

Reis, S. M., Hébert, T. P., Díaz, E. I., Maxfield, L. R., & Ratley, M. E. (1995). *Case studies of talented students who achieve and underachieve in an urban high school* (Research Monograph No. 95120). Storrs: University of Connecticut, The National Research Center on the Gifted and Talented.

Renzulli, J. S., & Park, S. (2002). *Giftedness and high school dropouts: Personal, family, and school-related factors* (Research Monograph No. 02168). Storrs: University of Connecticut, The National Research Center on the Gifted and Talented.

Taylor, L. A. (1995). *Undiscovered Edisons: Fostering the talents of vocational-technical students* (Research Monograph No. 95214). Storrs: University of Connecticut, The National Research Center on the Gifted and Talented.

Willard-Holt, C. (1994). *Recognizing talent: Cross-case study of two high potential students with cerebral palsy* (CRS94308). Storrs: University of Connecticut, The National Research Center on the Gifted and Talented.

Wright, A. L., & Olszewski-Kubilius, P. (1993) *Helping gifted children and their families prepare for college: A handbook designed to assist economically disadvantaged and first generation college attendees* (Research Monograph No. 93201). Storrs: University of Connecticut, The National Research Center on the Gifted and Talented.

Program Options for Secondary Students

Chapter 7

Evolving Relationships With AP and IB

BY

SHELAGH A. GALLAGHER

FOR **2** WEEKS IN **MAY 1954,** a small group of gifted high school students took experimental college-level tests in five subjects. For 2 weeks in May 2006, another group of high school students did the same thing, only there were 1.34 million students and the tests covered 37 subjects. Much about the Advanced Placement (AP) Program has changed since representatives from prestigious Northeastern universities gathered and agreed that: ". . . the advancement of American education demands the strengthening of secondary schools, especially in those divisions in which the ablest students are enrolled . . ." (Rothschild, 1999, p. 178).

From the 1950s to the late 1980s, the program grew in numbers of courses and numbers of students—and, parents might add, in numbers of dollars—but AP maintained its focus on gifted students. More recently, that focus has shifted. Literature from the College Board now claims that: "The AP Program isn't just for the top students or those headed for college. The only requirements to take an AP course are a strong curiosity about the subject you plan to study and the willingness to work hard" (College Board, 2006, p 4). This statement emphasizes the question concerning the match between gifted students and Advanced Placement.

Proving the power of serendipity, Europeans developed the International Baccalaureate (IB) Diploma Programme at the same time the Americans developed Advanced Placement. The goal of the IB program was to establish a curriculum rigorous enough to serve an internationally recognized standard. As a result, IB was designed as an entire scope and sequence, unlike the course-by-course AP development process. Having a diploma from the IB program denoted overall advanced achievement, providing students with increased latitude to cross national boundaries to attend university. Other differences between AP and IB include the increased international emphasis of the IB program, the IB core course on epistemology called the Theory of Knowledge, and a slightly more holistic attention to both content and pedagogy in IB. Dissemination of the two programs also differs: while AP can be "purchased" course by course, schools have to invest in the entire IB curriculum, and commit to intensive training. The two programs share an emphasis on advanced, accelerated content, qualifying exit examinations, a propensity to draw gifted students, and new ventures to reach broader constituencies (Poelzer & Feldhusen, 1997).

Some raise concerns that as AP and IB classes get larger and more heterogeneous, they could become less appropriate for gifted students (Callahan, 2003; Lichten, 2000; Winebrenner, 2006). Others note that gifted students have reaped huge benefits from Advanced Placement, and still could (Nugent & Karnes, 2002; VanTassel-Baska, 2000). One reason it is hard to establish a position with regards to AP and IB is that the functions they are called to serve are constantly shifting. In order to understand the relationship between gifted secondary education and AP or IB, it is first necessary to understand the nature and implications of these shifts.

AP and IB as Sources of Opportunity for Gifted Students

From the beginning, gifted students welcomed AP and IB as refreshing additions to high school curriculum. Early reports suggest that the rigorous college format, not the promise of college credit, drew gifted students to AP classroom doors. These were students motivated to take on a challenge; many were former talent search students (Brody & Mills, 2005; see Chapter 10, this volume, for information on talent searches.). From the 1980s onward, 75–80% of talent search students were taking an average of two to three AP courses (Lubinski, 2004). AP students—at least those who were also in the Talent Search—consistently reported liking AP courses, and thought better of the academic environment of their school when AP was offered (Lubinski, Webb, Morelock, & Benbow, 2001). This finding is not entirely consistent, however. For example, in one study of college students, those who had been in AP English did not rate their high school experiences more favorably than same-ability classmates, although they did prefer their AP class over other coursework (Thompson & Rust, 2007). Early AP students saw the AP exam as a representative challenge that allowed them to test their ability as college students; they often matriculated into college without requesting credit for their AP classes (Rothschild, 1999).

AP gained status as a prestigious course when principals began to offer weighted grades. The rationale behind weighted grades was to encourage students who were concerned with risking their class standing by taking a highly rigorous course. The small shift in grading policy had sizable consequences, for the weighted grades also changed the class rank scale. The change motivated students to enroll not only to benefit from faster paced learning, but also to hold on to their class rank. Becoming valedictorian was not likely without AP in a school with weighted grades.

Soon other benefits of AP began to emerge. Young gifted students considering early college admission could safely test the waters of college-level coursework while in high school (Olszewski-Kubilius, 1995). Because of the convenient content-based outline of the curriculum, AP courses easily could be packaged for delivery by mail and in computer-based formats, and eventually by means of distance education (Olszewski-Kubilius & Lee, 2003). Gifted students seemed motivated to take AP classes regardless of age or delivery format (Ravaglia, Suppes, Stillinger, & Alper, 1995).

The early years were not without controversy. From the beginning, concerns were raised about the structure of the AP curriculum, about the cost of the test, and about the disparities in participation by gender and cultural group. On the other hand, AP had all of the benefits of acceleration: It was easy to administer, relatively inexpensive, required few adjustments in overall curriculum, and embodied the added promise of a tangible reward in return for hard work (Colangelo, Assouline, & Gross, 2004). Given the sizable benefits and belief that the challenges could be overcome, soon AP became an institution in gifted education (Gallagher, 2004); moreover, it became the nation's name brand for high achievement.

AP and IB as College Gatekeepers

Initially, AP and IB programs provided opportunity: the opportunity to place out of a few college classes. A significant change in the function of AP and IB occurred when college admissions officers realized that AP and IB tests could be used for more than placement decisions; they also could be used as part of an admissions formula. Sometime around the mid-1980s, college admissions officers began to take a closer look at the number of AP and IB courses students completed in addition to the scores on AP and IB tests as a part of the admissions process; AP and IB have become increasingly entwined with college admissions ever since. In an analysis of admissions policies of more than 1,600 public and private universities, Breland, Maxey, Gernand, Cumming, and Trapani (2002) found that the number of Advanced Placement courses, AP class grades, and exam scores were among the top 10 admissions criteria, ranking fifth, sixth, and ninth respectively.

Espanshade, Hale, and Chung (2005) examined more closely the effect of AP coursework on admission to elite universities. After analyzing the admissions patterns of 45,000 applications from three top-tier universities, they reported that students with one AP class on their high school transcript were 30% more likely to be accepted into a college or university than students with no AP courses. The authors emphasized that, "the admissions advantage is statistically significant and cumulative the more AP examinations a student has taken" (p. 276). Given the increasingly competitive environment of college admissions for gifted students (Davies & Hammack, 2005), it is clear why students and parents may be tempted to load a transcript with AP or IB courses. However, this may not always work to the student's advantage. Espanshade et al. (2005) also noted an inverse effect for schools that offer numerous courses:

> A student has the best odds of being accepted by an elite college if he or she comes from a high school where no AP tests are taken (and, presumably, where no AP courses are offered). These odds steadily deteriorate as a high school's academic climate improves. If a student with the same academic credentials applies from a high school where the average number of AP tests per senior is between 0.4 and 0.8, the odds of admission are 36 percent lower. And at the most competitive high schools—those with more than 1.5 AP tests per senior—the same applicant has 53 percent lower odds of admission. (p. 279)

Naturally, this does not suggest that having numerous AP courses actually causes students to be rejected from elite universities. According to Espanshade and colleagues (2005), a more reasonable interpretation is that elite universities use proportional models where only a few students from a given high school or region are admitted. When academic standards at a high school increase, so do the number of applications to elite colleges. If colleges do not adjust the proportion of students accepted, then the ratio of accepted applications decrease.

Advanced Placement's shift in purpose from allowing college credit to allowing college entrance had a profound effect: AP and IB became less of an opportunity and more of a requirement as they became the gatekeepers to college admissions. Linking AP and IB to college admissions had two dramatic and somewhat opposing effects. The first effect was to increase the pressure on gifted students to take not one or two but numerous AP courses in order to compete for spots in elite college programs. Some gifted students began taking AP classes in ninth grade in order to have a respectable list for their college applications. In 2004–2005, 164,178 ninth and tenth graders took AP tests nationally (Texas Education Agency, 2006). Approximately 10,000 students took six or more AP exams during the 2006 testing weeks (College Board, 2006), a college course load that outpaces most college freshmen.

The second, much broader, effect was to place pressure on *all* college bound students to enroll in AP and IB. As college admissions became more competitive in the 1990s, it became increasingly more important to have an AP class, prefer-ably several, or to have the IB certificate on every student's high school transcript. In other words, AP and IB were becoming essential to general education as well as gifted education.

AP and IB as High School Standard Bearers

The synergy between rigorous coursework and gifted minds helped AP build its reputation as a program with consistent, objective, and high—but accessible—standards, just as the nation was engaged in a hunt for a reliably rigorous cur-riculum standard. The AP test seemed like a rock of Gibraltar to states struggling with the design and implementation of accountability assessments. With colleges increasingly attentive to the number of AP or IB courses on a student's transcript, and with pressure to increase "relevance and rigor" in the curriculum, high school principals began to expand the number of AP courses offered, the number of stu-dents enrolled, and the number of passing AP or IB test scores in order to make their programs seem strong. As they did, the purpose of AP and IB began to shift again, from being a standard for college admissions to being a cornerstone of American high school reform.

The idea to use AP and IB as a centerpiece of reform caught on quickly. Schools received compelling monetary encouragement to commit to AP and IB; unparal-leled investment continues to be poured into the programs to encourage their use. The federal government provided $32.2 million in 2006 for the Advanced Place-ment Incentive Program and Test Fee Program. This is an impressive sum compared to the 2006 funding of $9.6 million for the Javits Gifted and Talented Students Education Act. Other federal agencies supported an increased emphasis on the AP/IB movement as well. The Committee on Prospering in the Global Economy (2007), a group commissioned by the National Academies, recommended that by 2010 at least 1.5 million students should be taking at least one AP or IB test in mathematics or science, an increase of nearly 20%.

Increasing numbers of states specifically mention AP, and to a lesser extent, IB in their state policies. According to the Education Commission of the States (ECS; 2006), 13 states require that either every district or every high school offer at least one AP course or the IB program, with West Virginia requiring every high school to offer four AP courses or the IB program beginning in 2008–2009. Addition-ally, 29 states mention AP in their state statutes; 12 states mention IB. Schools are rewarded for having more AP courses, more students enrolled, and more passing scores. Because so many states have embraced these programs, the ECS has actu-ally published guidelines on how to include AP in state education plans to help ensure the comprehensiveness of state policies. To its credit, much of this effort is to ensure equal access to AP courses regardless of racial, economic, or regional differences (ECS, 2006).

AP and IB as Opportunities?

In the mid-1970s, Sidney Marland, former U.S. Commissioner of Education (1970–1973), first proposed that AP could be "an effective instrument for serving gifted but socially disadvantaged students" (Rothschild, 1999, p. 190). Thirty years later, sizable disparities still exist between mainstream students and the poor and culturally diverse, both in AP/IB course taking and in exam performance (Anthony, 2007). Because they are gatekeepers to college, access to AP or IB is critical to capable low-income and culturally different students. In their new role as standard bearers, having more low-income and culturally different students in AP or IB classes has become a national goal. Despite federal and state policies supporting increasing access to these students, three barriers stand in the way of effective use of AP as a means of equalizing opportunities for disadvantaged groups: putting programs in schools, ensuring that culturally diverse and low-income students enroll prepared to succeed, and providing appropriate supports necessary to encourage success in this population.

The first barrier is simply getting the program to schools. Ubiquitous as they may seem, there were no AP courses in 43% of U.S. high schools in 2001 (Commission on the Future of the Advanced Placement Program, 2001). Expansion to create equal opportunity for disadvantaged gifted students is completely consonant with current priorities in gifted education (Anthony, 2007); however, it requires more than a grant to achieve equitable success. Analyzing the aggressive AP expansion in Texas during the 1990s, Klopfenstein (2004) found that established programs expanded at a much faster rate than new programs. The net effect was that schools serving at-risk students actually fell behind in AP access. The second barrier is getting traditionally underserved students enrolled. This seems more likely if there is a cohort of similar students in the class, and if the class is held in an environment that is comfortable to the students (Griffith & Walter, 2006). Equally important, however, is that students enter AP classes prepared. Even students with the most potential are not likely to perform well in a fast-paced 11th-grade class if they have never before been exposed to rigorous content. A growing body of research indicates that for students to be successful in AP classes, they must first be successful students. The College Board has proactively addressed this issue with its pre-AP initiative and structure for vertical teaming; other forms of vertical alignment are also effective. The third barrier to successful participation in AP by disadvantaged students is lack of adequate classroom supports. Studies consistently point to a common set of requirements that AP courses must meet to succeed with low-income or culturally disadvantaged populations, including extra teacher preparation, extra student support, and particular attention to classroom climate. Numerous studies document that even when AP courses are available to disadvantaged students, they tend to be taught by less-experienced teachers (Burton, Yepes-Baraya, Cline, & Myung-in Kim, 2002; Geiser & Santelices, 2004) even though teacher experience is a factor that contributes to success in AP (Furry & Hesch, 2001; Geiser & Santelices, 2004).

AP and IB as . . . What?

Opportunity to enroll in AP and IB was expanding to ever broader populations as the programs moved from opportunity providers to college gatekeepers and then to standard bearers. The number of students in AP courses has more than doubled since the inception of federal incentive grants; in Dallas alone, the number of students who took AP exams went from 379 to 1,130 in the first year incentives were offered (Committee on Prospering in the Global Economy of the 21st Century, 2007). As classes become more heterogeneous, concerns grow that the pace will slow and the rigor diminish in order to accommodate more typically developing students. This, in turn, raises the question of what meaningful results occur for gifted students when they participate in AP or IB.

The call for broader distribution of AP classes and increased participation from more students is made in the face of inconsistent evidence of program efficacy. Research on the effectiveness of AP provides an interesting perspective from which to view the rush to support AP and IB as either programs for gifted students or programs for all.

AP and IB Students in College

The AP program was built on the premise that at least some capable students could accelerate their college experience; a similar assumption lies behind the move to include AP in college admissions decisions. Most studies demonstrate that AP students are successful in college; the real question is whether they are more successful in a meaningful way than non-AP students. Some studies do indicate that the AP students fare better, taking more challenging college courses, selecting double majors, and graduating with honors in comparison to like-ability nonparticipants (Curry, MacDonald, & Morgan, 1999). Participation in Advanced Placement classes also was found to predict GPA and honors status among talent search students in all subjects except science (Brody, Assouline, & Stanley, 1990). Interestingly, other studies of Advanced Placement and college performance in science suggest that AP course taking has minimal, if any, effect on college grades in science (Sadler & Tai, 2001), although AP exam scores do seem to have predictive value.

Although these findings are interesting, it is important to note that none of the above studies control for possible intervening variables. As Brody and Mills (2005) pointed out, many early AP students were also Talent Search students—that is, they were extremely capable and already achievement oriented. Failing to take ability and motivation into account in prediction models could falsely inflate study results. Geiser and Santelices (2004) found that the number of AP courses does not predict college success or college persistence in freshman and sophomore years when background factors such as parent education and high school rigor are taken into account. They also found that AP exam scores do predict college success, even after accounting for ability and motivation. Klopfenstein and Thomas

(2006) found that the predictive value of AP coursework diminished when other non-AP coursework, especially math and science achievement, were included in regression models. In short, AP exam scores clearly seem to have some predictive value related to college performance, but the effect of sheer course participation is unclear, and is probably modest.

Equally important is the quality of thinking that AP students bring into college classrooms. Henderson (1995), reporting on experiences of former AP English students in college English composition classes, reported that students who took AP English consistently focused on low-level interpretations of class assignments, attending more to technical aspects of assignments than to expression of ideas.

AP and IB High School Achievement

The equivocal results of studies of the predictive power of AP raise the question of what AP students in high school know beyond what a typical student knows. This is a hard question to answer without access to raw data from AP tests; however, a general sense of achievement can be gleaned from AP students who participated in other large achievement studies. An early international study reported by Callahan (1994) compared advanced students in the U.S. with international advanced students. On the common test of science skills, advanced U.S. students, all of whom were enrolled in AP courses in the target subject, ranked last in biology and close to last in physics and chemistry (Callahan, 1994). Similarly, a 1998 report of the Trends in International Mathematics and Science Study (TIMSS) presented data showing that advanced U.S. students scored poorly in mathematics and physics compared to similarly able international students (Gonzalez, Smith, & Sibberns, 1998). Concerned that AP students might be misrepresented in these findings, the College Board sponsored a separate study with the same lead researcher, this time ensuring that AP students were from reputable, established programs. In the second study, average scores for AP Calculus and Physics students were the highest of all groups, regardless of nationality. In contrast, non-AP calculus and physics students in the U.S. had the poorest average scores (Gonzalez, O'Conner, & Miles, 2001). However, the proportion of AP students in the new sample who scored 3 or above on the AP test was disproportionately high when compared to national AP statistics (College Board, 2007a), suggesting potentially skewed results and continued ambiguity regarding the international competitiveness of AP students.

Another view of achievement is available through the National Assessment of Educational Progress (NAEP), which gathers AP enrollment information in its background questionnaire. The NAEP Data Analysis tool makes it possible to compare AP participants and nonparticipants in a given subject. U.S. history serves as a good example because all high school students take U.S. history, but only a fraction take AP U.S. History. Table 1 presents the 2006 NAEP U.S. History scaled scores of 12th-grade AP U.S. History students and 12th graders who did not take AP U.S. History. Clearly, the AP students scored higher than their non-AP counterparts; to this extent, the course seems successful—without controlling for

TABLE 1

Average Scaled Scores for NAEP U.S. History, Grade 12 Question "Are You Currently Enrolled in or Have You Taken an Advanced Placement Course in U.S. History?"

Reporting Group	Average Scale Score			
	Mean	SE	Standard Deviation	SE
All students	290.27	0.75	30.91	0.35
Yes (22%; approx 249)	305.03	1.19	33.49	0.64
No (78%; approx 880)	286.41	0.72	28.80	0.37

Note. The NAEP U.S. History scale ranges from 0 to 500. Data from National Assessment of Educational Progress (NAEP) 2006 U.S. History Assessment. Accommodations were not permitted for this assessment.

influential background variables. Taken from a different perspective, the data tell a different story. A score of 305 puts the average AP U.S. History student in the Basic level of the NAEP score levels, the lowest official category.

Table 2 presents the proportion of AP U.S. History students at each of the three achievement levels and unofficial "Below Basic" category (see Gallagher, Chapter 4, this volume). Although the data again show the overwhelming majority of students at the Advanced level of the NAEP are AP U.S. History students, they also reveal that only 3.73% of AP U.S. History students reach the NAEP Advanced level. On the other hand, a third of AP U.S. History students score in the Below Basic range, the lowest NAEP level. The 33% of AP U.S. History students in the Below Basic range is substantially lower than the 58% of other students scoring Below Basic, which on a relative scale makes the AP U.S. History students much better performers. However, the fact that one third of the students in a rigorous history course are in the bottom achievement range is disquieting. After all, the NAEP is designed to assess typical 12th-grade achievement. Even acknowledging the possibility that the cutoff scores for the NAEP levels are too high (Shepard, Glaser, & Linn, 1993), having one third of students in the bottom category doesn't seem all that advanced. Indeed, as Callahan (1994) noted, many of the items at the Advanced level of the NAEP are not all that hard. Rogers' (2004) meta-analysis also suggests that AP does not stand out as superior to other forms of acceleration. According to Rogers, Advanced Placement yielded an effect size of .27—far from negligible, but second to lowest of the forms of acceleration studied, and equivalent to 3 months additional learning.

Overall, the results seem to suggest that these AP students are more knowledgeable than non-AP students, but perhaps not as knowledgeable as expected for a student receiving advanced instruction, and certainly not if there were initial

TABLE 2

Percentages of Students at Each Achievement Level for NAEP U.S. History, Grade 12, "Are You Currently Enrolled in or Have You Taken an Advanced Placement Course in U.S. History?" (Student Reported)

Responding Group	Below Basic		At Basic		At Proficient		Advanced	
	Percent	SE	Percent	SE	Percent	SE	Percent	SE
All Students	57.21%	1.106	32.26%	0.866	9.69%	0.609	0.84%	0.174
Yes	33.11%	1.517	36.18%	1.472	26.98%	1.619	3.73%	0.557
No	58.35%	1.039	33.58%	0.867	7.71%	0.541	0.36%	0.103

Note. Observed differences are not necessarily statistically significant. Detail may not sum to totals because of rounding. Data from National Assessment of Educational Progress (NAEP) 2006 U.S. History Assessment. Accommodations were not permitted for this assessment.

ability differences between the two groups. More disquieting, comparisons using the NAEP do not assess differences in quality of thought. Gifted students can and should be doing so much more than practicing content acquisition and text interpretation. True value is added to a gifted child's repertoire when rigorous content is combined with equally challenging thinking.

AP and IB in the Classroom

From the beginning, responsibility for AP courses was divided in two: the College Board took responsibility for curriculum and classroom teachers were responsible for delivery. Even the best curriculum can seem inadequate if it is poorly delivered. Only a few studies attempt to pinpoint the qualities of an effective AP classroom. Furry and Hesch (2001) surveyed 360 California AP teachers in five different subject areas. Responses of teachers with high-scoring students were compared to teachers with low-scoring students. They concluded that successful AP classrooms had the following dimensions: (1) experienced AP teachers, (2) ongoing contact with feeder schools (vertical alignment), (3) well-prepared students, and (4) school administrators who communicated expectations for success on the AP test. The authors particularly noted that 40% of the teachers surveyed felt that their AP students were unprepared and that 60% had large gaps in their background knowledge.

Furry and Hesch (2001) also reported that teachers, feeling stuck between college syllabi and standardized AP tests, tended to rely on didactic instruction to ensure student success; others have found this to be true as well (Burton et al.,

2002; Callahan, 2003; Herr, 1991; Hertberg-Davis, Callahan, & Kyburg, 2006). Hertberg-Davis and colleagues (2006) conducted perhaps the largest qualitative study of AP and IB classrooms to date. Their interviews and observations of AP and IB teachers found teaching to the test was fast-paced and fact-based. Students in these classrooms felt pressured to achieve—sometimes to an unhealthy level—but felt the sacrifice would be worth the effort in their preparation they received. As a group, they preferred these classes over their other schoolwork, although nontraditional AP students tended to report a poorer "fit" with the classroom environment. Smaller classroom-based research studies of AP classes also are revealing. Vanderbrook (2006) studied five students in AP or IB classes and found that while students acknowledged the courses were challenging, the challenge came from memorization rather than intellectual understanding.

Ironically, the few studies that investigate AP and instructional style suggest that higher levels of engagement, inquiry-oriented instruction, and conceptual organization lead to higher levels of student success. Husic, Linn, and Sloane (1989) investigated differences in instructional style in regular and AP Computer Science classes over the course of a year. Students in the regular computer science class were significantly more likely to report emphasis on basic information and guided instruction, while students in the AP Computer Science class reported more open-ended, problem-solving instructional styles. While the authors suggest that the cognitive demand of the AP class required adjustment in instructional style, it is equally possible that the adjustment in instructional style was necessary because the students in the class were gifted. Henderson, Winitzky, and Kauchak (1996) analyzed the instructional practice of effective AP U.S. History teachers. Among the characteristics associated with success were more frequent questioning, better distributed questions, higher levels of student engagement, and more assignments and feedback. They also found that successful AP teachers had more organized knowledge structures and used them to present course content more efficiently. Well-organized knowledge structures are a result of content expertise. These findings suggest that effective AP teachers have deep content knowledge supporting their conceptual frameworks.

This is one area in which IB can be distinguished from AP, perhaps because of the pervasive influence of the Theory of Knowledge course on the overall IB curriculum. For example, Taylor and Porath (2006) found graduates of IB programs were likely to list intellectual stimulation as an advantage.

Some Promising Trends

AP is firmly woven into the fabric of American high schools. The debate over whether all students can succeed in AP will inevitably continue for some time, despite the fact that a majority of research to date has been conducted primarily with gifted learners, and that research suggests that AP could improve.

Fortunately, there is strong encouragement in policy trends for AP to retain high standards and orientation toward rigor while making necessary improvements. In the report *Access to Excellence*, the Commission on the Future of the Advanced Placement Program (2001) called for AP to make aggressive efforts to provide services to underserved schools but to do so with all necessary supports and without sacrificing standards. Encouragingly, they embraced the importance of AP teachers and instruction, and called for articulated quality standards, increased teacher support, and more rigorous research.

The Center for Education in the National Academy of Sciences also commissioned a series of reports under the umbrella title of *Learning and Understanding: Improving Advanced Study of Mathematics and Science in U.S. High Schools* (National Research Council [NRC], 2002) that center on AP and IB mathematics and science. Emphasizing the role of appropriate instruction, these reports recommend that both programs come into closer alignment with current research on learning by enhancing conceptual and interdisciplinary content, decreasing the emphasis on content to make room for deeper exploration, better guidance on appropriate pedagogy, and more attention to the technical merits of culminating examinations (NRC, 2002). Ambitious, forward thinking, and evidence based, these reports call for sizable paradigm shifts for programs that originally only aspired to deliver traditional college courses to high school students.

Researchers who have invested substantial effort in identifying strengths and challenges in AP and IB also provide evidence-based recommendations. Although the themes sound similar to recommended practices for K–8 gifted programs, they are worth acknowledging: access should be open, but multiple, flexible criteria for enrollment should be used to ensure that the students who enroll are capable of succeeding; quality standards should be articulated; clear communications among teacher, parent, administrator, and school counselor should be established to engage support for high-quality standards; and teachers should use incentives and then supports to prepare, attract, and sustain traditionally underrepresented students (Callahan, 2003; Geiser & Santelices, 2004; Klopfenstein, 2003) Also attending to equity issues, Geiser and Santelices (2004) suggested encouraging colleges and universities to award college credit only for AP test scores of 4 and 5. This counterintuitive recommendation would seem to actually increase disparity in the number of college credits awarded for AP test scores, because more minority and disadvantaged students receive scores of 3 than 4 or 5 on AP tests. Geiser and Santelices pointed out, however, that over 90% of credits awarded for AP courses at the University of California are for scores of 3, and that minority and disadvantaged students are still significantly outnumbered by White and Asian students at this level. A smaller proportion of all students, regardless of race, score 4 or 5 on AP tests, so limiting college credits to this level of performance automatically reduces racial disparity.

In a tacit acknowledgement that there are still changes needed in AP, the College Board instituted a nationwide course audit. Beginning in 2006 and continuing indefinitely, course syllabi must be approved by the College Board before a school can designate it as "AP" (College Board, 2008). An enormous undertaking, this is a commendable move on the part of the College Board. However, it is equally true that teachers are likely to continue to adapt and stray from the written syllabus as long as they feel the need to respond to a wide range of abilities.

A second College Board initiative supports recognizing differences between learners who invest and achieve differentially in the AP program. Scholar Awards tier the accomplishments of AP students and recognize a small group of students with impressive achievements (College Board, 2007b). Conceptually, this seems to be the equivalent of awarding distinguished AP students with academic letters. However, several features of the awards are problematic. First, students are accorded the title of AP Scholars if they receive a score of 3 or higher on three or more exams. According to the College Board, a 3 is equivalent to a C, a fairly low level for a "scholar." Second, the awards are only available to students who take three or more exams. A student whose passion is art and takes only the two AP art courses would not qualify for an award, even if he or she scored 5 on both exams. Third, students climb to higher tiers of distinction by taking more tests. The criteria for National Scholar include scoring 4 or higher on eight exams. This reemphasizes a test-driven, more-is-better orientation, rather than true scholarship. The focus on number of tests also limits the top awards to students who are either affluent enough to pay for eight exams or to students whose school system has enough funding to subsidize eight exams per student. Finally, given the competitive nature of both gifted students and college admissions, providing an award for taking more courses and tests is like giving drugs to an addict.

AP, IB, and the Gifted: Then and Now

From the outset, Advanced Placement and International Baccalaureate filled a spot in the enormous gap in programming for gifted secondary students. Without a doubt, the programs have done some good regardless of whether they predict anything about college performance. AP and IB classes have successfully kept gifted high school students engaged in learning when very few alternatives were available. This and the link between AP test scores and performance in similar college content are two consistent, positive findings from the early years.

It is a new era. Although many have urged AP to retain its high standards as it expands, evidence continues to mount from multiple sources that quality may be threatened. Currently, no one knows why; research is needed to unravel the extent to which vacillations in scores are related to or caused by heterogeneous grouping, rapid expansion, test fatigue, instructional quality, or other factors. Determining the nature and extent of the impact of expanding AP and IB courses to a wider range of students requires much more research.

In the meantime, knowledge about learning and gifted students also has grown, changing expectations of acceleration (Colangelo et al., 2004) and expanding options for gifted secondary programming generally (Dixon & Moon, 2006). Although in the past AP may have been the only option, we now have the tools to make it an optimal option. In its current form, AP, and to a lesser extent IB, are not really designed to meet the full cognitive needs of gifted students (Gallagher, Chapter 1, this volume). However, with adjustment, they could be. Research demonstrates that gifted students fare well when the deep content base in AP is delivered using inquiry-oriented, constructivist approaches (Burton et al., 2002; Henderson et al., 1996; Husic et al., 1989). Evidence also suggests that, in some subjects at least, students can succeed on the test without taking a formal AP class—again, supporting the notion that variations in content and instructional style are possible (Texas Education Agency, 2006). The great advantage here is that there are proven methods for adjusting content to incorporate additional dimensions of scholarship without sacrificing core learning.

The early success of AP and IB was built on a synergy of rigorous curriculum and gifted minds. Evidence suggesting that vertical alignment, student screening, and strong student background all contribute to success in AP and IB classes suggest that they are still appropriate for students who have natural ability, intrinsic motivation, and/or systematic high-level preparation. At the same time, it may be necessary to consider the extent to which we want one or two models dominating secondary options for gifted learners. A side effect of mandating multiple AP courses is that it limits students to a single form of curriculum and currently to a limited style of pedagogy. IB tends to be more constructivist in its orientation, but is still somewhat conscribed.

Are AP and IB Appropriate for Gifted Students?

Perhaps this is a question best left open for now. With so much shifting still going on in AP and IB, it is hard to say what population they will best serve in the future. In the meantime, we can embrace them as strong programs that are potentially suitable for gifted students, without allowing them to dominate secondary options for gifted students. A considered agenda for gifted secondary educators will work to make AP as good as it can be for gifted learners and support additional options that add different dimensions to gifted adolescents' experiences.

Program Recommendations:
Ensuring High AP/IB Standards

- AP is successful when students have the necessary background knowledge and skills. Any student should be allowed to participate in screening for AP classes; however, screening should precede AP enrollment. Screening using multiple indicators of talent is best (Clark, 2006; Gallagher & Gallagher, 1994; Richert, 1987).

- AP is successful when vertical alignment is strong. Using either pre-AP or other approaches, districts seeking to increase AP enrollment should start with strong preparation strands in middle school and even elementary school (Furry & Hesch, 2001).
- AP is successful when taught by experienced teachers. AP teaching positions should be protected and rewarded. Schools must provide incentives for culturally diverse instructors to teach AP classes. Professional development should include content, pedagogy, and the characteristics of gifted learners.
- AP test scores predict some aspects of college success; AP course taking alone, does not. Schools must encourage students to take the AP test, but only when students are screened prior to enrollment.

Program Recommendations: Ensuring a Healthy, Diverse, Advanced Secondary Program

- Advanced Placement should not be a proxy for early college admissions. Administrators should create a per year or per semester cap on the number of AP courses a student can take. Schools must ensure the policy is flexible enough to allow highly gifted students who are very young or unable to take advantage of early college enrollment to take additional AP courses.
- Schools should engage in comprehensive parent education regarding the variable benefits of AP, including the following: (1) many colleges award credit when students receive scores of 3 on AP (or the equivalent on IB) tests, but some don't; (2) at many colleges and universities, individual departments make decisions about the AP or IB score required to receive credit, and policies may vary across departments; and (3) some colleges limit the number of courses waived, placing a cap on the tuition savings.
- Schools should require college counseling for students who have completed four AP courses, and encourage students to research the AP/IB award policies of their target colleges or universities.
- Schools should support other options for gifted students, including highly rigorous, creative, original courses; dual enrollment with local colleges; and/or online college courses.
- Schools should support efforts of specialized schools such as the public residential schools of the National Consortium of Secondary Schools Specializing in Mathematics, Science, and Technology (NCSSSMST) in efforts to document and disseminate their curricula in order to broaden the scope of advanced high school studies.

Policy Recommendations

- Schools must support the expansion of AP and IB into locations that do not have these options, so that all capable students have access to at least one kind of advanced accelerated option. They must monitor expansion efforts to ensure equitable access to all racial groups and income levels.
- Schools should discourage oversaturation of AP or IB, or exclusive use of AP or IB as the singular option for gifted students.
- Schools should encourage local colleges to give credit for highly rigorous, locally developed courses.
- Schools should encourage the College Board to be more specific in its communications to parents about variations awarding college credit, especially for scores of 3 on AP exams, across and within colleges or universities.
- Schools should encourage a revision of the Scholars Award to focus on quality of performance (as indicated by exam scores) over quantity of exams completed.
- Schools should advocate for policy changes that broaden the scope of federal efforts to support highly rigorous secondary courses beyond AP and IB.

Research Recommendations

All interested groups should advocate for access to AP test data to support independent item analyses. Also needed are more independent research investigations of the viability of AP for gifted students in a variety of settings, including:

- Comparisons of AP and IB classrooms to clarify similarities and differences.
- Comparisons of AP and IB students in college with students of equivalent ability who took honors classes, attended magnet schools, or attended other types of schools, to determine the relative merits of Advanced Placement as compared to other curriculum models recommended for gifted adolescents.
- Comparisons of AP test scores of students who enroll in traditional AP classes with scores of students who learn similar advanced content in different venues.
- Comparisons across AP and IB classes to determine the relative effectiveness of inquiry-based or didactic approaches to the curriculum.
- Comparisons of performance of students taking different numbers of AP classes to determine if there is a threshold of effectiveness for students of different ability levels.
- Investigations into the reasons why some students fail to complete AP/IB classes (Callahan, 2007).

References

Anthony, T. S. (2007). Advanced Placement. In J. VanTassel-Baska & T. Stambaugh (Eds.), *Overlooked Gems: A national perspective on low-income promising learners* (pp. 75–77). Washington, DC: National Association for Gifted Children.

Beatty, A. S., Reese, C. M., Persky, H. R., & Carr, P. (1996). *NAEP 1994 history report card.* Washington, DC: Office of Educational Research and Improvement, U.S. Department of Education.

Breland, H., Maxey, J., Gernand, R., Cumming, T., & Trapani, C. (2002). *Trends in college admissions: A report of a survey of undergraduate admissions policies, practices, and procedures.* Tallahassee, FL: Association for Institutional Research.

Brody, L. E., Assouline, S., & Stanley, J. (1990). Five years of early entrants: Predicting successful achievement in college. *Gifted Child Quarterly, 34,* 138–142.

Brody, L., & Mills, C. (2005). Talent search research: What have we learned? *High Ability Studies, 16*(1), 97–111.

Burton, N. W., Yepes-Baraya, M., Cline, F., & Myung-in Kim, R. (2002). *Minority student success: The role of teachers in Advanced Placement courses.* New York: College Entrance Examination Board.

Callahan, C. M. (1994). The performance of high ability students in the United States on national and international tests. In P. O'Connell-Ross (Ed.), *National excellence: A case for developing America's talent: An anthology of readings* (pp. 5–26). Washington, DC: Office of Educational Research and Improvement.

Callahan, C. M. (2003). *Advanced Placement and International Baccalaureate programs for talented students in American high schools: A focus on science and mathematics* (Research Monograph No. 03176). Storrs: University of Connecticut, The National Research Center on the Gifted and Talented.

Callahan, C. M. (2007, March). *Social and emotional effects of academic acceleration.* Paper presented at the North Carolina Association for Gifted and Talented conference on academic acceleration, Winston-Salem, NC.

Clark, B. (2006). *Growing up gifted: Developing the potential of children at home and at school* (7th ed.). Columbus, OH: Merrill/Prentice Hall.

Colangelo, N., Assouline, S. G., & Gross., M.U. M. (2004). *A nation deceived: How schools hold back America's brightest students* (Vol. 1). Iowa City: The University of Iowa, The Connie Belin and Jacqueline N. Blank International Center for Gifted Education and Talent Development.

College Board. (2006). *Bulletin for AP students and parents 2006–2007.* New York: Author.

College Board. (2007a). *Advanced Placement report to the nation 2007.* New York: Author.

College Board. (2007b). *AP Central: Scholar awards.* Retrieved April 17, 2008, from http://apcentral.collegeboard.com/apc/public/program/initiatives/2057.html

College Board. (2008). *About the AP audit.* Retrieved April 17, 2008, from http://www.collegeboard.com/about/news_info/ap/courseledger/about.html

Commission on the Future of the Advanced Placement Program. (2001). *Access to excellence: A report of the Commission on the Future of the Advanced Placement Program.* New York: College Entrance Examination Board.

Committee on Prospering in the Global Economy of the 21st Century: An Agenda for American Science and Technology, National Academy of Sciences, National Academy of Engineering, Institute of Medicine. (2007). *Rising above the gathering storm: Energizing and employing America for a brighter economic future.* Washington, DC: National Academies Press.

Curry, W., MacDonald, W., & Morgan, R. (1999). The Advanced Placement program: Access to excellence. *Journal of Secondary Gifted Education, 11,* 17–23.

Davies, S., & Hammack, F. M. (2005). The channeling of student competition in higher education: Comparing Canada and the U.S. *The Journal of Higher Education, 76,* 89–106.

Dixon, F. A., & Moon, S. M. (Eds.). (2006). *The handbook of secondary gifted education.* Waco, TX: Prufrock Press.

Education Commission of the States. (2006). *Advanced Placement courses and examinations: State-level policies.* Denver, CO: Author.

Espenshade, T., Hale, L., & Chung, C. (2005). The frog pond revisited: High school academic context, class rank, and elite college admission. *Sociology of Education, 78,* 269–293.

Furry, W. S., & Hecsh, J. (2001). *Characteristics and performance of Advanced Placement classes in California.* Sacramento: California State University Institute for Education Reform.

Gallagher, J. J. (2004). Public policy and acceleration of gifted students. In N. Colangelo, S. G. Assouline, & M. U. M. Gross (Eds.), *A nation deceived: How schools hold back America's brightest students* (Vol. 2, pp. 39–46). Iowa City: The University of Iowa, The Connie Belin and Jacqueline N. Blank International Center for Gifted Education and Talent Development.

Gallagher, J. J., & Gallagher, S. A. (1994). *Teaching the gifted child.* Boston: Allyn & Bacon.

Geiser, S., & Santelices, V. (2004). *The role of Advanced Placement and honors courses in college admissions.* Retrieved April 17, 2008, from http://repositories.cdlib.org/cshe/CSHE-4-04

Gonzalez, E. J., O'Connor, K. M., & Miles, J. A. (2001). *How well do Advanced Placement students perform on the TIMSS Advanced Mathematics and Physics tests?* Chestnut Hill, MA: Boston College, The International Study Center.

Gonzalez, E. J., Smith, T. A., & Sibberns, H. (1998). *User guide for the TIMSS international database, final year of secondary school, 1995 assessment.* Chestnut Hill, MA: Boston College.

Griffith, K., & Walter, A. (2006). Mo' money, mo' problems? High-achieving Black high school students' experiences with resources, racial climate, and resilience. *Journal of Negro Education, 75,* 478–494.

Henderson, J., Winitzky, N., & Kauchak, D. (1996). Effective teaching in Advanced Placement classrooms. *Journal of Classroom Interaction, 31,* 29–35.

Henderson, S. (1995). Why do I have to be here? The Advanced Placement student in first-year composition: Problems and issues in cognitive development. *Journal of Secondary Gifted Education, 7,* 324–332.

Herr, N. (1991). The influence of program format on the professional development of science teachers: Teacher perceptions of AP and honors science courses. *Science Education, 75,* 619–629.

Hertberg-Davis, H., Callahan, C. M., & Kyburg, R. M. (2006). *Advanced Placement and International Baccalaureate programs: A "fit" for gifted learners?* (Research Monograph

No. 06222). Storrs: University of Connecticut, The National Research Center on the Gifted and Talented.

Husic, F., Linn, M., & Sloane, K. (1989). Adapting instruction to the cognitive demands of learning to program. *Journal of Educational Psychology, 81,* 570–583.

Klopfenstein, K. (2003). Recommendations for maintaining the quality of Advanced Placement programs. *American Secondary Education, 32*(1), 39–48.

Klopfenstein, K. (2004). The Advanced Placement expansion of the 1990s: How did traditionally underserved students fare? *Education Policy Analysis Archives, 12*(68). Retrieved April 17, 2008, from http://epaa.asu.edu/epaa/v12n68

Klopfenstein, K., & Thomas, M. K. (2006). The link between Advanced Placement experience and early college success. Retrieved March 31, 2008, from http://personal.tcu.edu/~kklopfenstei/ap_coll.082206.pdf

Lapp, M. S., Grigg, W. S., & Tay-Lim, B. S.-H. (2002). *The nation's report card: U.S. history 2001* (NCES 2002–483). Washington, DC: Office of Educational Research and Improvement, National Center for Education Statistics, U.S. Department of Education.

Lee, J., & Weiss, A. (2007). *The nation's report card: U.S. History 2006* (NCES 2007–474). Washington, DC: U.S. Government Printing Office.

Lichten, W. (2000). Whither Advanced Placement? *Education Policy Analysis Archives, 8*(29), 1–19.

Lubinski, D. (2004). Long-term effects of educational acceleration. In N. Colangelo, S. G. Assouline, & M. U. M. Gross (Eds.), *A nation deceived: How schools hold back America's brightest students* (Vol. 2, pp. 23–38). Iowa City: The University of Iowa, The Connie Belin and Jacqueline N. Blank International Center for Gifted Education and Talent Development.

Lubinski, D., Webb, R. M., Morelock, M. J., & Benbow, C. P. (2001). Top 1 in 10,000: A 10-year follow-up of the profoundly gifted. *Journal of Applied Psychology, 86,* 718–729.

National Research Council. (2002). *Learning and understanding: Improving advanced study of mathematics and science in U.S. high schools.* Washington, DC: National Academy Press.

Nugent, S., & Karnes, F. (2002) The Advanced Placement program and the International Baccalaureate programme: A history and update. *Gifted Child Today, 25*(1), 30–39.

Olszewski-Kubilius, P. (1995). A summary of the research regarding early entrance to college. *Roeper Review, 18,* 121–125.

Olszewski-Kubilius, P., & Lee, S. (2003). Gifted adolescents' talent development through distance learning. *Journal for the Education of the Gifted, 28,* 7–35.

Poelzer, G., & Feldhusen, J. (1997). The International Baccalaureate: A program for gifted secondary students. *Roeper Review, 19,* 168–171.

Ravaglia, R., Suppes, P., Stillinger, C., & Alper, T. M. (1995). Computer-based mathematics and physics for gifted students. *Gifted Child Quarterly, 39*(1), 7–13.

Richert, E. (1987). Rampant problems and promising practices in the identification of disadvantaged gifted students. *Gifted Child Quarterly, 31,* 149–154.

Rogers, K. (2004). The academic effects of acceleration. In N. Colangelo, S. G. Assouline, & M. U. M. Gross (Eds.), *A nation deceived: How schools hold back America's brightest students* (Vol. 2, pp. 47–58). Iowa City: The University of Iowa, The Connie Belin and Jacqueline N. Blank International Center for Gifted Education and Talent Development.

Rothschild, E. (1999). Four decades of the Advanced Placement program. *The History Teacher, 32*, 175–206.

Sadler, P. M., & Tai, R. H. (2001). Success in introductory college physics: The role of high school preparation. *Science Education, 85*, 111–136.

Shepard, L. A., Glaser, R., & Linn, R. L. (1993). *Setting performance standards for student achievement. A report of the National Academy of Education panel on the evaluation of the NAEP trial state assessment: An evaluation of the 1992 achievement levels.* Stanford, CA: Stanford University, National Academy of Education.

Taylor, M., & Porath, M. (2006). Reflections on the International Baccalaureate program: Graduates' perspectives. *Journal of Secondary Gifted Education, 17*, 149–158.

Texas Education Agency. (2006). *Advanced Placement and International Baccalaureate examination results in Texas, 2004–05* (Document No. GE06 601 10). Austin, TX: Author.

Thompson, T., & Rust, J. (2007). Follow-up of Advanced Placement students in college. *College Student Journal, 41*, 416–422.

Vanderbrook, C. (2006). Intellectually gifted females and their perceptions of lived experience in the AP and IB programs. *Journal of Secondary Gifted Education, 17*, 133–148.

VanTassel-Baska, J. (2000, August). *The role of Advanced Placement in talent development.* Keynote address presented at the Advanced Placement Institute, College of William and Mary, Williamsburg, VA.

Winebrenner, S. (2006). Effective teaching strategies for open enrollment honors and AP classes. *Journal of Secondary Gifted Education, 17*, 159–177.

Chapter 8

Special Schools, Magnet Schools, and Other Options for Secondary Programming

BY

PAULA OLSZEWSKI-KUBILIUS

AND

FELICIA A. DIXON

THERE ARE VARIED TYPES of specialized schools for adolescents who are gifted academically or in the arts. These schools are operated by school districts, universities, state governments, and private entities. Most focus on a particular talent area, such as performing arts, music, or a few related disciplines such as mathematics, science, and technology. Others serve a specialized population, such as gifted children with learning disabilities. Most exist in physical space and real time but some are virtual (e.g., the A. Linwood Holton Governor's School for the Gifted in Southwestern Virginia). There are special schools at both the elementary and secondary level, but some operate across levels, such as combined high school-college programs. Several major categories of specialized schools include state-supported residential high schools (Kolloff, 2003), university-based early college entrance programs (Brody, Muratori, & Stanley, 2004), and magnet high schools.

Magnet schools are typically public schools that are designated for talented students in specialized areas and have selective entrance criteria. Many large school districts have magnet schools and these vary widely in terms of focus, including science and mathematics, foreign language, and the performing arts. Usually, there are selection criteria such as scores on aptitude and achievement tests for schools with a focus on academic areas, and auditions and portfolios for schools with a focus on the arts. Magnet schools typically draw from a wide geographic area, perhaps district wide, and are highly selective and competitive to enter.

Neighborhood schools have been the preference of families for decades. Many magnet schools draw students from the larger district or community, which often necessitates transporting students from different neighborhoods—a practice some-times criticized by those who hold firm to the neighborhood school model. How-ever, this idea is not new. In fact, the oldest magnet school still in operation is Boston Latin School, founded in 1635 (one year before Harvard opened). Offering a classical education, this school focuses on providing rigor for those students who choose to attend. Magnet schools reflect a central academic or vocational theme and stress voluntary participation (Doyle & Levine, 1984). Students come from across the city to attend, and because they choose this particular school, their motivation is likely to be high. Further, the curriculum centers on a central theme and hence, the course of study tends to be much more focused than the general public high school.

Magnet schools are not designed specifically for the gifted; they increase options for students of all abilities and of all interest groups. This stated, they can, however, serve talented students well, especially when the individual desires to concentrate in one particular area (House, 1983). Coleman and Cross (2005) described magnet schools as a variation on the special school concept in which students drawn from a single school, or from an entire school district, report to the magnet school for instruction. They then take special enriched courses, accelerated special classes, seminars, or independent study options in the curricular focus area of the school.

Tannenbaum (2002, as cited in Kay, 2002) stated that

> Magnet schools were originally instituted to stem the flight of inner-city middle-class families to the suburbs by promising intensive concentra-tion in specific disciplines, with each experimental school specializing in its chosen subject area, different from that of other centers. The implied blandishment for middle-class families to remain or resettle in the inner city was that their brightest children would benefit from intensive stud-ies in whatever disciplines they showed signs of precocity. However, the problem with this innovation is that, according to its overarching objec-tives, the need to enrich education for inner-city gifted children did not rest on its own merits, but rather on the success or failure of magnet schools to help achieve inter-class integration in urban communities. (Kay, 2002, p. 3)

Magnet schools can be organized around special programs, or magnets, in each specific building (House, 1983). For example, a single site might emphasize mathematics and science and offer a larger number of advanced courses in these subjects than the neighborhood high school. Teachers in such a school are highly qualified content experts in mathematics and science. Other schools in the district may stress humanities, fine arts, music, or vocational education. Again, students' choice governs the school they attend—not their proximity of residence.

This need for choice is important to gifted students (Gentry, Rizza, & Owen, 2002). Gentry and colleagues reported that gifted children are bored in school and unchallenged, and that little differentiation of curricula and instruction for gifted students occurs in regular classrooms. They advocated for special schools for gifted students because they are more able to meet their needs. Although magnet schools are not specifically for gifted students, the focus of the school and the chance to offer more rigorous and higher level courses often can meet the accelerative needs of high-ability students both at the middle and high school levels.

Von Seggern (1990) stated that gifted and talented students have special educational needs that can be met through special programs. In the past, much of the focus and most of the resources in gifted programming were directed toward the academically gifted; recently more attention has been given to the artistically talented, mostly through magnet schools that may be organized around providing increased learning opportunities in talent areas, interests, or both. The key to success for magnet programs at the secondary level is to offer instruction that is not available in the regular classroom. Teachers at regular schools in the district are then more likely to send their most qualified students to the magnets for accelerated or in-depth learning.

Clark (2008) called for special schools, including magnet schools, as a way to address the needs of highly gifted and profoundly gifted students who need classes in more intensified forms. She advocated for examining the student's level of giftedness, stating that all gifted students need to interact with those who can challenge them and thus, focused courses in these schools would justifiably make up the major part of their educational experience.

Choices and alternatives always have been a hallmark of differentiated instruction. Gifted secondary students need these challenges in order to continue to flourish in their least restrictive environment. Davidson, Davidson, and Vanderkam (2004) wrote,

> Jonathan Kozol, author of *Savage Inequalities: Children in America's Schools*, quotes a New York City resident's observation that academically selective schools such as Bronx Science and Stuyvesant constitute a "citywide skimming policy." Creating magnet schools in cities such as Washington, DC, "is a loser's strategy," Kozol himself says. "Favor the most fortunate among us or they'll leave us too. Then we will have even fewer neighbors who can win political attention for our children." In other words, these false egalitarians believe gifted urban children should be held hostage to others' political needs. (p. 76)

This description illustrates the counter-claim that the magnet school concept evokes in urban policy makers and school planners. The elitism argument that has always surrounded gifted education is often the reason for districts to close magnet schools, raising significant questions concerning equal opportunity, educational effectiveness, and the facilities and prudence of allocating resources necessary for a successful program (Blank, 1984). In addition, Colangelo, Assouline, and Gross (2004) stated that in every state, in every school, in huge cities, and in tiny farm communities, students are ready for much more challenge than the system provides.

Magnet schools do provide an option for a focused education for select students. If a district offers a magnet school, then those who choose to apply may not be a totally gifted population. In this case, teachers must differentiate instruction in the focused courses to meet the needs of high-ability students. This is paramount in any school situation, and magnet schools also must follow these important practices.

In sum, key points to consider about magnet schools include the following:

- These schools may or may not be focused on gifted students.
- These schools are magnets for specific content areas: mathematics, science, and technology; humanities; fine arts; music; or vocational offerings.
- Like other special schools for gifted secondary students, magnet schools often require students to travel to go to school.
- Highly qualified teachers are necessary in order to provide the rigor and challenge along with the advanced courses in a specific focus area.
- Magnet schools are a good option for middle and high school gifted students who seek to specialize in their talent area.

Special Residential Schools

Currently, there are 16 publicly supported residential schools for gifted students chartered by state legislatures. For most of these, students enter after their sophomore year of high school; a few admit students after the completion of ninth grade, such as the Illinois Mathematics and Science Academy. Students typically are admitted based on scores on college entrance exams such as the ACT and SAT, and because state dollars are involved, selection is conducted so that the school population reflects that of the state in terms of race, ethnicity, and geography. These schools have advanced offerings beyond what is available in even the best high schools in the state. They typically also have faculty with exceptionally high levels of content area expertise. In addition, these schools have a select population of students who are more homogeneous with respect to ability levels and interests. Some of these special high schools are located on college campuses, where students are dually enrolled in the special high school and college, taking typical college classes.

Many more special schools for academically gifted students exist around the U.S. More than 100 schools in 29 states are currently listed as members of the National Consortium for Specialized Secondary Schools of Mathematics, Science and Technology (NCSSSMST; 2007). Also, there are schools for students gifted in the performing arts, and these are typically 4-year specialized secondary high schools. These schools may or may not use the word "gifted" in their title, although they may be selective in their admissions and they may call themselves magnet schools or conservatories. Such schools also may have an array of advanced offerings, teachers with advanced training and performance experience in the case of performing arts schools, and a more homogeneous school population in terms of abilities and interests compared to a typical secondary school (see Sayler, 2006, for more information).

Research on the Effects of Special Schools

Specialized schools measure their success in varied ways. Indicators can include the numbers of students who pursue advanced study or careers in the areas in which the schools specialize, as well as the number of awards and honors, contests, and competitions won by students. For example, the Illinois Mathematics and Science Academy (a state-supported school for grades 10–12) tracks the number of students who work with scientists to complete research projects, the number of students who win competitions and awards, the number of students who pursue mathematics and science majors and careers, the number of students who gain admission to prestigious colleges and universities, and the number of students who receive merit-based scholarships for higher education (Office of Research and Evaluation Illinois Mathematics and Science Academy, 2005). Internally, these schools may promote certain values, and thus, track indicators, such as the number of students who do volunteer work or those who experience changes in attitudes and beliefs toward science (K. Hallowell, personal communication, January 12, 2006). State-supported schools often state their mission as to contribute scholars and professionals to the state in key areas or to provide professional development or leadership in the areas of curriculum to schools within their states. Unfortunately, most of the data about success on these and other indicators are contained in reports to state boards and not in journals or other professional outlets. State-supported schools are held accountable by state legislators, but other specialized schools need to demonstrate success on indicators valued by parents to attract students.

Why Choose Special Schools?

Special secondary schools are accelerative programs. Many offer advanced courses including AP classes and college-level classes. Oftentimes, the decision about whether a special secondary school versus an early college entrance program (see Chapter 9, this volume) is more appropriate for a child is made based on access including geography (proximity to home), match to the child's talent domain or interests, the child's maturity for handling living away from home and mingling with older students, and desire for acceleration. One advantage of some special schools is that they have rich curricular offerings that allow students to stay in high school for 4 years.

Specialized schools can offer a more advanced curriculum to students as well as some specialized opportunities that typical secondary schools cannot. These include working in research laboratories or other research experiences, receiving training in how to audition, and acquiring the professional tools, values, and attitudes important to success in a specific field (Subotnik & Jarvin, 2005).

The decision to attend a special school is dependent on many factors, including but not limited to the student's desire and maturity to cope with living away from home, the lack of other alternatives within the student's local community, the degree to which a student has specific, well-identified, and developed areas of talent and interest, the student's motivation to excel and ability to work independently, family support, and the student's need for and availability of a supportive peer group.

Key Points About Special Schools

- Acceleration in curriculum is available at these schools.
- A content focus is often present so that students who desire to concentrate on math and science, or the arts have these options available.
- Most are residential schools, admitting students after the completion of the 10th grade.
- Many of these schools are state supported and, therefore, report to the state legislature.
- Teachers in these schools are content experts, frequently with a Ph.D. in a content area.

Other Options for Secondary Students in Schools

Besides magnet schools, special schools, Advanced Placement (AP) courses, and International Baccalaureate (IB), schools may institute other types of classes especially focused on the needs of gifted students. Such offerings include honors classes, seminars, online courses at universities (see Chapter 12, this volume), dual enrollment, and extracurricular offerings that meet secondary talent needs and interests.

Honors classes may be offered in any of the traditional middle school and high school disciplines, such as algebra, geometry, history, English, foreign languages, chemistry, or biology. VanTassel-Baska (1998) stated that these classes are expected to operate at a higher level of intellectual discourse, to involve more discussion, to require more homework, and to present greater academic challenges to students than general content classes. Further, the curriculum is expected to be differentiated for high-ability students, offering more depth and breadth than typical classes.

Honors classes frequently are offered as classes for gifted students before they take AP classes. For example, students take honors classes in middle school and in

9th and 10th grade before they begin to take AP classes. Because these are more intensive and rigorous classes than the general education offerings, they must be coordinated with each other. A student who takes honors classes in all content areas may be assigned more projects and papers than what the general class would be assigned. The focus of the honors class must be on a qualitatively different type of curriculum, not a quantitatively different one.

A second option, and one that is an excellent offering for secondary students, is the seminar. Seminars are intensive, advanced academic classes in which gifted and talented students are led by teachers in an in-depth study of topics. Dixon (1995) described a seminar in English literature for verbally talented adolescents at the Indiana Academy for Science, Mathematics, and Humanities in which the students read college-level contemporary British literature, studied the political and social events surrounding each piece, and wrote papers that were heavily centered on a synthesis of ideas. Interdisciplinary seminars that incorporate history, literature, and foreign language (e.g., Russian Experience) are excellent offerings for gifted secondary students. These classes can be offered within the context of the regular school. Kolloff and Feldhusen (1986) described the seminar using the following parameters:

- Seminars are organized, regularly scheduled classes.
- Seminars allow much time for discussion, small-group work, and student presentations.
- Seminars focus on a central theme or concept.
- Teachers of seminars have the goal of teaching thinking skills and research skills within the focused content.
- A seminar goal is to foster social-emotional growth and understanding of giftedness among the seminar participants.
- In-depth projects are outcomes of seminars.
- Seminars incorporate career development when appropriate.
- Seminars incorporate art and cultural experiences, and they are often inter-disciplinary.

Dual Enrollment

Dual enrollment programs are very popular because they offer flexibility in that the student is able to take high school and college classes simultaneously (McCarthy, 1999). This option provides another way for high-ability students to experience a higher level of academic challenges. Several state departments of education now require high schools to award academic credit toward high school graduation for college courses that parallel high school courses (Feldhusen, 2003).

Extracurricular Activities

Extracurricular activities are organized student activities not generally considered a part of the regular school curriculum. Calvert and Cleveland (2006) suggested their importance to gifted students, stating, "Unfortunately for gifted teens, school is seldom optimally challenging. Extracurricular activities may provide opportunities for challenge that may be lacking in the regular school curriculum" (p. 529). A variety of activities is available to students, including academic clubs (e.g., math leagues, science clubs that encourage science fair participation, computer clubs, foreign language clubs, debate team, and student government), which further students' skills and enjoyment in the academic area as well as encourage leadership skill development. In addition, music groups such as specialized vocal or instrumental groups (e.g., swing choir; marching band, concert band, chamber orchestra, or jazz band) often fill the need for talent development in the music area for gifted students who are multipotential. Highly talented students may select private lessons or other possibilities out of school to meet their needs.

In addition to influencing academic achievement, participation in extracurricular activities may have social and emotional effects on students. They may find a niche in school with other like-minded students who participate in the same clubs. Some specialized schools encourage students to form their own clubs and seek a sponsor with similar interests. Such is the case at the Indiana Academy, where environmental clubs, service clubs, and diversity groups were formed based on student leadership and initiative.

However, the number of extracurricular possibilities may be limited by the size of the school. Hence, gifted secondary students in rural communities may not have the possibility to participate in a club of their choice based on the lack of other interested students, thereby limiting the available resources. Extracurricular activities often are cited as the most important part of school for some gifted students.

Key Points About Honors Classes, Seminars, and Extracurricular Activities for Gifted Adolescents

- These three options offer choices and opportunities for gifted students at the secondary level.
- Honors classes and seminars are possibilities for public and private schools that focus on differentiation of content, process, and product.
- Extracurricular activities encourage talent development and may be ways of discovering talent among gifted students.
- Specialized schools often encourage students to establish their own clubs according to interest.
- Teachers of seminars have the opportunity to teach a focused topic in their content area that may not be included in the regular curriculum.

Conclusion

In sum, all of these options reflect the current trend in gifted secondary education to offer flexibility in programming. Seemingly, the days of strict scope and sequence are over for now. Instead, schools are making a greater effort to use all available offerings to help meet student needs. When state mandates also can allow for flexibility, the student is able to navigate high school with many attractive choices to meet requirements while blending high school with the collegiate experience.

References

Blank, R. K. (1984). The effects of magnet schools on the quality of education in urban school districts. *Phi Delta Kappan, 66,* 270–272.

Brody, L. E., Muratori, M. C., & Stanley, J. C. (2004). Early entrance to college: Academic, social, and emotional considerations. In N. Colangelo, S. Assouline, & M. U. M. Gross (Eds.), *A nation deceived: How schools hold back America's brightest students* (Vol. 2, pp. 97–107). Iowa City: The University of Iowa.

Calvert, E., & Cleveland, E. (2006). Extracurricular activities. In F. Dixon & S. Moon (Eds.), *The handbook of secondary gifted education* (pp. 527–546). Waco, TX: Prufrock Press.

Clark, B. (2008). *Growing up gifted* (7th ed.). Columbus, OH: Prentice Hall.

Colangelo, N., Assouline, S. G., & Gross, M. U. M. (2004). *A nation deceived: How schools hold back America's brightest students* (Vol. 1). Iowa City: The University of Iowa, The Connie Belin & Jacqueline N. Blank International Center for Gifted Education and Talent Development.

Coleman, L. J., & Cross, T. L. (2005). *Being gifted in school.* Waco, TX: Prufrock Press.

Davidson, J., Davidson, B., & Vanderkam, L. (2004). *Genius denied.* New York: Simon & Schuster.

Dixon, F. A. (1995). The gifted in secondary literature programs. *Understanding Our Gifted, 7*(4), 4–5.

Doyle, D. P., & Levine, M. (1984). Magnet schools: Choice and quality in public education. *Phi Delta Kappan, 66,* 265–270.

Feldhusen, J. F. (2003). Talented youth at the secondary level. In N. Colangelo & G. A. Davis (Eds.), *Handbook of gifted education* (3rd ed., pp. 229–237). Needham Heights, MA: Allyn & Bacon.

Gentry, M., Rizza, M. G., & Owen, S. V. (2002). Examining perceptions of challenge and choice in classrooms: The relationship between teachers and their students and comparisons between gifted students and other students. *Gifted Child Quarterly, 46,* 145–155.

House, P. A. (1983). Alternative educational programs for gifted students in mathematics. *Mathematics Teacher, 76,* 229–233.

Kay, S. I. (2002). An interview with Abraham J. Tannenbaum. *Roeper Review, 24,* 186–191.

Kolloff, P. B. (2003). State-supported residential high schools. In N. Colangelo & G. A. Davis (Eds.), *Handbook of gifted education* (3rd ed., pp. 238–246). Needham Heights, MA: Allyn & Bacon.

Kolloff, P. B., & Feldhusen, J. F. (1986). The seminar: An instructional approach for gifted students. *Gifted Child Today, 9*(5), 2–7.

McCarthy, C. R. (1999). Dual enrollment programs: Legislation helps high school students enroll in college courses. *Journal of Secondary Gifted Education, 11,* 24–32.

National Consortium for Specialized Secondary Schools of Mathematics, Science and Technology. (2007). About NCSSMST. *NCSSMST Journal, 13*(1), 30.

Office of Research and Evaluation, Illinois Mathematics and Science Academy. (2005). *A pioneering educational community* (Fiscal year 2005 performance report). Aurora, IL: Illinois Mathematics and Science Academy.

Sayler, M. F. (2006). Special schools for the gifted and talented. In F. A. Dixon & S. M. Moon (Eds.), *The handbook of secondary gifted education* (pp. 547–559). Waco, TX: Prufrock Press.

Subotnik, R. F., & Jarvin, L. (2005). Beyond expertise: Conceptions of giftedness as great performance. In R. J. Sternberg & J. E. Davidson (Eds.), *Conceptions of giftedness* (2nd ed., pp. 343–357). New York: Cambridge University Press.

VanTassel-Baska, J. (1998). *Excellence in educating gifted and talented learners* (3rd ed.). Denver, CO: Love.

Von Seggern, M. (1990). Magnet music programs. *Music Educators Journal, 76*(7), 50–53. Retrieved June 1, 2007, from http://web.ebscohost.com/ehost/deliverv?vid=6&hid=22&sid=7cac7187-7593-4ded-9291-6

Authors' Note

Portions of this chapter were initially published in Olszewski-Kubilius, P., & Lee, S.-Y. (2008). Specialized programs serving the gifted. In F. A. Karnes & K. P. Stephens (Eds.), *Achieving excellence: Educating the gifted and talented* (pp. 192–208). Upper Saddle River, NJ: Pearson Education.

Chapter 9

Early College Entrance Programs

BY

PAULA
OLSZEWSKI-
KUBILIUS

RODY, MURATORI, AND STANLEY (2004) listed 17 early college entrance programs in the U.S., 10 residential and 7 commuter-only programs. Most of the residential early college entrance programs enable students to begin college 1 to 2 years earlier than would be expected. Many that are residential programs house early entrance students together in separate dorms, at least for the first year. The commuter-only early college entrance programs generally take students earlier, some as early as at the end of eighth grade.

Early college entrance programs take many different forms, but all allow students early access to college courses. Some have a particular curricular focus, such as leadership and the humanities, or science and technology. Some admit students automatically into the Honor College of the school. Some early college entrance programs, particularly those that admit students after the eighth or ninth grade, provide students with a bridging experience during the first year or summer before college studies begin so as to prepare these young students for college-level work and the college environment. Some programs are designed to enable students to finish high school during the first 2 to 3 years of the programs and do college studies during the last 1 or 2 years of enrollment in the school (e.g., combining 4 years of high school and the first 2 years of college into 4 years). A few grant high school diplomas and a few more arrange for the diploma to be granted by the students' "home" high school (see Brody et al., 2004, for a complete listing and further description). Some early entrance programs offer extracurricular programs and some do not, but many have special supports for young students, including special counselors, closer supervision (especially initially), and special social activities to foster camaraderie and support.

Early college entrance programs can offer a more advanced curriculum to students as well as some specialized opportunities that typical secondary schools cannot. These include significant authentic research opportunities, such as working in labs with scientists on their research or carrying on independent research projects via mentoring by experts, and opportunities to learn about careers via job shadowing and mentoring. Early college entrance programs thus enable gifted students to get an early start on advanced training and career preparation.

Research about early college entrance programs suggests that effects are positive and substantial for students (Gross & van Vliet, 2005). Early entrants earn higher grade point averages than regular freshman (Eisenberg & George, 1979; Janos & Robinson, 1985; Janos, Sanfilippo, & Robinson, 1986; Muratori, Colangelo, & Assouline, 2003; Noble, Robinson, & Gunderson, 1993), typically within the B+ to A- range (Stanley & McGill, 1986; Swiatek & Benbow, 1991), and equal to those of a group of National Merit Scholars at the same university (Janos & Robinson, 1985; Janos et al., 1986). Compared to typical college students, they are more likely:

1. to complete college (Pressey, 1967), and on time (Brody, Assouline, & Stanley, 1990; Stanley & McGill, 1986);
2. to earn general and departmental honors (Brody et al., 1990; Stanley & McGill, 1986);
3. to make the dean's list (Eisenberg & George, 1979);
4. to have plans to enter graduate school (Noble et al., 1993); and
5. to complete concurrent master's degrees (Brody et al., 1990).

The majority of these results are based on students who entered (1 to 2 years early) a private, selective, academically prestigious university that did not have a special early entrance program. A few are based on a large state institution that admitted students immediately after the seventh or eighth grade into a year-long transition school. Thus, the demands of these experiences, either because of the academic reputation of the institution or the age of the student, were great, yet the students were very successful. In addition, early entrance students fare well later in their educational careers and are admitted as transfer students to prestigious universities, often with scholarships, and are accepted to prestigious, selective graduate programs (Sayler & Lupkowski, 1992; Sethna, Wickstrom, Boothe, & Stanley, 2001).

Although the results of these studies are very positive, it must be remembered that students who do poorly generally leave the program and are not included in research studies. There are not much data in the published research about dropout rates, and what does exist suggest that dropout rates may be high (30 to 45%) in the initial years of a program (Callahan, Cornell, & Lloyd, 1992; Sayler, 1993), but decline rapidly to around 5 to 10% once programs have selection procedures refined (Noble et al., 1993). Regarding low achievement, again, few published statistics are available. Janos et al. (1986) reported that about 12% of students who entered college after the seventh or eighth grade were earning grade point averages 1.5 standard deviations below other similarly aged early entrants, and that under-achieving students tended to be immature or did not balance their academic and social lives. Few of these students dropped out, but they alternated between good and very poor academic terms regarding their grades and achievement. Sayler (1993) reported that 28% of students admitted to an early entrance program after the 10th grade had academic difficulties, but this was in the early years of the program, and this percentage was reduced quickly by half and then to zero. Thus, most students admitted to early college entrance programs are academically successful.

Regarding social-emotional adjustment, the picture for early college entrants is positive. Relatively few have adjustment problems (Sayler, 1993). Most find friends, initially among other early college entrants who provide an important support group in the first few years (Noble & Drummond, 1992), especially for the younger students (Janos & Robinson, 1985; Janos et al., 1986), but eventually among typically aged college students. The only study that found a high percent-age (50%) of early entrants with mental health and adjustment problems was in the early years of the program before selection procedures were refined (Cornell, Callahan, & Lloyd, 1991). Few students expressed strong regrets, and those who did tended to focus on missing social events in high school or decreased eligibility for college scholarships (Noble & Drummond, 1992; Noble et al. 1993).

Students who fared best in early college entrance programs seem to be those who:
1. have taken and succeeded in college-level classes, such as AP classes, prior to full-time college studies (Brody, Assouline, & Stanley, 1990);
2. were independent, unconventional, and less conforming (Janos & Robinson, 1985);
3. had more harmonious family relationships (Cornell et al., 1991), and
4. had well-developed study and organizational skills (Schumacker, Sayler, & Bembry, 1995).

These are not very different from predictors of success in college for typically aged college freshman.

The decision to attend college early is dependent on many factors, including but not limited to the student's desire and maturity to cope with living away from home; the lack of other alternatives within the student's local community; the degree to which a student has specific, well-identified, and developed areas of talent and interest; the student's motivation to excel and ability to work independently; family support; and the student's need for and availability of a supportive peer group.

A Synthesis of Suggested Key Points About Early College Entrance Programs

- Early entrance to college is a viable option for academically gifted students who have run out of curriculum at their secondary school and/or need the challenge of a more rigorous course of study. Students who enter early generally do well academically, exceeding the performance of the typical college student and matching those of academically talented students who enter at the typical age.
- Success in college for an early entrance student is dependent upon personal maturity, support from home, and well-developed study and organizational skills, factors that are likely to affect the adjustment of any student transitioning to college.
- Students who enter college very early (3 or 4 years) need additional support, including living at home with their families and support from counselors and programs at the university to aid their adjustment to the college environment.
- The best predictor of success in entering college early is previous success in college level classes.

Although early college entrance programs are clearly an alternative for gifted students, in reality, access to such programs is limited to those who can either pay tuition or happen to live in a state that provides such a program at no or little cost to the student. Many parents are reluctant to send younger students to programs that are out of state or far from home. This option could be more widely available to students if existing institutions of higher education were more open to younger students and willing to provide some basic and minimal supports to help them succeed.

References

Brody, L. E., Assouline, S. G., & Stanley, J. C. (1990). Five years of early entrants: Predicting successful achievement in college. *Gifted Child Quarterly, 34,* 138–142.

Brody, L. E., Muratori, M. C., & Stanley, J. C. (2004). Early entrance to college: Academic, social, and emotional considerations. In N. Colangelo, S. G. Assouline, & M. U. M. Gross (Eds.), *A nation deceived: How schools hold back America's brightest students* (Vol. 2, pp. 97–108). Iowa City: The University of Iowa, The Connie Belin & Jacqueline N. Blank International Center for Gifted Education and Talent Development.

Callahan, C. M., Cornell, D. G., & Lloyd, B. H. (1992). The academic development and personal adjustment of high ability young women in an early college entrance program. In N. Colangelo, S. G. Assouline, & D. L. Ambroson (Eds.), *Talent development: Proceedings from the 1991 Henry B. and Jocelyn Wallace National Research Symposium on Talent Development* (pp. 248–260). New York: Trillium.

Cornell, D. G., Callahan, C. M., & Lloyd, B. H. (1991). Socioemotional adjustment of adolescent girls enrolled in a residential acceleration program. *Gifted Child Quarterly, 35,* 58–66.

Eisenberg, A., & George, W. (1979). Early entrance to college: The Johns Hopkins Experience Study of Mathematically Precocious Youth. *College and University, 54,* 109–118.

Gross, M. U. M., & van Vliet, H. E. (2005). Radical acceleration and early entry to college: A review of the research. *Gifted Child Quarterly, 49,* 154–171.

Janos, P. M., & Robinson, N. M. (1985). The performance of students in a program of rapid acceleration at the university level. *Gifted Child Quarterly, 29,* 175–180.

Janos, P. M., Sanfilippo, S. M., & Robinson, N. M. (1986). "Underachievement" among markedly accelerated college students. *Journal of Youth and Adolescence, 15,* 303–311.

Muratori, M., Colangelo, N., & Assouline, S. (2003) Early-entrance students: Impressions of their first semester of college. *Gifted Child Quarterly, 47,* 219–237.

Noble, K. D., & Drummond, J. E. (1992). But what about the prom? Students' perceptions of early college entrance. *Gifted Child Quarterly, 36,* 106–111.

Noble, K. D., Robinson, N. M., & Gunderson, A. (1993). All rivers lead to the sea: A follow-up study of gifted young adults. *Roeper Review, 15,* 124–130.

Pressey, S. (1967). "Fordling" accelerates ten years after. *Journal of Counseling Psychology, 14,* 73–80.

Sayler, M. F. (1993, November). *Profiles of successful male and female early college entrants.* Paper presented at the annual conference of the National Association for Gifted Children, Atlanta, GA.

Sayler, M. F., & Lupkowski, A. E. (1992). Early entrance to college: Weighing the options. *Gifted Child Today, 15*(2), 24–29.

Schumacker, R. E., Sayler, M., & Bembry, K. L. (1995). Identifying at-risk gifted students in an early college entrance program. *Roeper Review, 18,* 126–129.

Sethna, B. N., Wickstrom, C. D., Boothe, D., & Stanley, J. C. (2001). The Advanced Academy of Georgia: Four years at a residential early-college-entrance program. *Journal of Secondary Gifted Education, 13,* 11–21.

Stanley, J., & McGill, A. (1986). More about "young entrants to college: How did they fare?" *Gifted Child Quarterly, 30,* 70–73.

Swiatek, M. A., & Benbow, C. P. (1991). Ten-year longitudinal follow-up of ability-matched accelerated and unaccelerated gifted students. *Journal of Educational Psychology, 83,* 528–538.

Author Note

Portions of this chapter were initially published in Olszewski-Kubilius, P., & Lee, S.-Y. (2008). Specialized programs serving the gifted. In F. A. Karnes & K. P. Stephens (Eds.), *Achieving excellence: Educating the gifted and talented* (pp. 192–208). Upper Saddle River, NJ: Pearson Education.

Chapter 10

Talent Search Programs for Gifted Adolescents

BY

PAULA
OLSZEWSKI-
KUBILIUS

TALENT SEARCH PROGRAMS have been in existence in the United States for more than 25 years and are designed to assist elementary- and middle-school-aged students by identifying their abilities, nurturing their talents through educational programs, and connecting schools and families to appropriate resources, services, and programs (VanTassel-Baska, 1998). At the heart of talent search programs is the practice of above-grade-level testing. Talent search testing was initiated in the early 1970s by Dr. Julian Stanley at Johns Hopkins University as part of a research project entitled the Study of Mathematically Precocious Youth (SMPY; e.g., Assouline & Lupkowski-Shoplik, 1997; Benbow, 1992a; Brody, 1998; Jarosewich & Stocking, 2003; Lee, Matthews, & Olszewski-Kubilius, 2008; Olszewski-Kubilius, 1998a, 1998c; VanTassel-Baska, 1998). Its primary goal at that time was to identify mathematically talented pre-high-school-aged students using the Scholastic Aptitude Test-Math (SAT-M). Talent search testing has expanded to include other above-grade-level tests such as the ACT and EXPLORE that assess both mathematical and verbal areas in elementary- and middle-school-aged children. It is estimated that close to 250,000 students participate annually in talent search testing.

A basic premise of talent search programs is that appropriate assessment of the abilities of gifted children requires using tests with enough ceiling to measure their advanced reasoning abilities and knowledge. Several major university-based gifted institutes, such as the Center for Talent Development at Northwestern University, the Talent Identification Program at Duke University, the Center for Talented Youth at Johns Hopkins University, and the Rocky Mountain Talent Search of the Center for Innovative and Talented Youth at the University of Denver, conduct talent search testing annually in order to provide students in grades 3–9 who score at the 95 percentile or above on nationally normed tests with more accurate information about their academic abilities.

Talent search programs typically include the diagnosis and evaluation of the area and level of students' abilities via above-level tests such as the ACT, SAT, or EXPLORE; access to further talent developing opportunities such as weekend programs, summer programs, and distance education programs; and guidance and expert advice via newsletters, magazines, and conferences (Olszewski-Kubilius, 1998a).

Talent search programs have become a major force within gifted education and are the key provider of outside-of-school, specialized programming. Lee et al. (2008) collated data from the various talent search programs to produce a comprehensive, national picture of how many children are being served by these programs annually. Based on data from 2004, almost a quarter of a million students in grades 3–9 participated in above-level testing programs offered by talent search programs. Of these, 33,900 subsequently participated in a talent search sponsored educational program in 2004. Almost half of the program participants were in summer programs, 10,300 in Saturday and weekend programs, 7,500 in distance education courses, and 460 participated in leadership programs through the talent search institutions. Males (55%) participate at slightly higher rates than females (45%) and minority students are underrepresented, more so in the educational programs than in the talent search testing. Yet, only a small proportion of the students (around 14%) identified annually through talent search testing participate in a talent-search-related educational program. Participation is limited by the tuition costs involved in these programs.

Research on the Effects of Talent Search and Talent Search Educational Programs

There is a rather substantial body of research about talent search testing and talent search participants—literally hundreds of published research studies. These studies document:

- the validity of using the ACT and SAT with advanced middle-school-aged students. Most students are not overwhelmed by these tests and on average perform similarly to the average high school student who takes the test, but below that of the average college-bound senior (Bartkovich & Mezynski, 1981; Benbow, 1992b; Olszewski-Kubilius, 1998b, 1998c);

- the predictive validity of talent search scores for later school achievement and career success; talent search participants continue to achieve at higher levels compared to other students (Barnett & Durden, 1993; Benbow, 1992a, 1992b; Benbow & Arjmand, 1990; Burton, 1988; Lubinski, Webb, Morelock, & Benbow, 2001; Webb, Lubinski, & Benbow, 2002);
- the predictive validity of talent search scores in discriminating different levels of achievement within the gifted population, in terms of degree of acceleration and indices such as income, patents earned, and tenure-track positions secured in top universities, for students scoring at the top versus bottom quartile of the top 1% (Benbow, 1992b; Wai, Lubinski, & Benbow, 2005); and
- the predictive validity of different profiles of scores on SAT-M versus SAT-V, particularly a quantitative tilt in identifying individuals who will pursue advanced scientific training and achieve success in scientific and mathematical careers (Lubinski & Benbow, 2006).

Research has documented that talent search participation gives students better knowledge about the nature of their academic abilities (Ablard, Mills, & Hoffhines, 1996; Assouline & Lupkowski-Shoplik, 1997; Brody, 1998; Jarosewich & Stocking, 2003; VanTassel-Baska, 1989) and thus can raise their educational and career aspirations (Benbow & Arjmand, 1990; Brody, 1998; Burton, 1988; VanTassel-Baska, 1989; Wilder & Casserly, 1988).

Participation in talent search testing has an impact that is magnified by also participating in talent search-sponsored educational programs subsequent to testing. Documented effects include taking Advanced Placement (AP) Calculus earlier in high school, taking more college courses while still in high school, pursuing a more rigorous course of study in mathematics, and entering more academically competitive colleges than students with similar scores who do not participate in a summer program (Barnett & Durden, 1993). Females who participate in fast-paced classes seem to particularly benefit, especially those who take mathematics in the summer (Olszewski-Kubilius & Grant, 1996). The female students subsequently accelerated themselves more in mathematics, earned more honors in math, took more AP classes of any type in high school and more math classes in college, participated more in math clubs, more often majored in math or science in college, and had higher educational aspirations. A summer program designed specifically for mathematically talented females helped them to remain competitive with mathematically talented boys in terms of accelerating themselves in math through high school (Brody & Fox, 1980; Fox, Brody, & Tobin, 1985). Additional long-term effects of summer programs for girls included a greater commitment to consistent, full-time work in the future and higher educational aspirations (Fox et al., 1985). (See Olszewski-Kubilius [1998b] for a summary of research on fast-paced summer programs.) Although a higher degree of academic acceleration and a greater level of participation in academic opportunities were found for students who participated in both talent search testing and subsequent educational programs (Barnett

& Durden, 1993), students who participated in talent search testing only were as academically successful as the former. A sizeable percentage of these talent search testing (only) students accelerated in specific subject areas especially in math and computers; performed well (usually A to B+) on college-level math or computer courses taken in high school (Kolitch & Brody, 1992); graduated from high school almost one year earlier than their age equivalent peers; and earned high grade point averages (3.4 on average) in college.

The testing in talent searches has spawned educational program models such as fast-paced summer classes. The academic performance of students in these talent search educational programs and their effects on students are strong, substantial, and positive (Ablard et al., 1996; Assouline & Lupkowski-Shoplik, 1997; Barnett & Durden, 1993; Benbow, 1992a; Benbow & Arjmand, 1990; Brody, 1998; Burton, 1988; Jarosewich & Stocking, 2003; Kolitch & Brody, 1992; Olszewski-Kubilius & Grant, 1996; VanTassel-Baska, 1989). Students in fast-paced, 3-week-long accelerated summer classes perform as well as or better than high school students who typically take the courses for a full academic year at school. Middle-school-aged students who took high school science classes in a 3-week summer program scored at or above the 70th percentile on standardized tests in biology, chemistry, and physics, compared to norms for high school juniors or seniors who had a full year of instruction (Lynch, 1992). Students with higher scores can accelerate at a faster pace. For example, mathematically talented seventh graders who scored at 600 or above on SAT-M were able to successfully complete two high school precalculus math courses in less than 50 hours of instruction (Bartkovich & Mezynski, 1981) and achieved at high levels in a special program in which 4 years of high school math were compressed into 2½ years (Benbow, Perkins, & Stanley, 1983).

Summer programs and other programs offered by talent search centers enable gifted students to augment their school programs significantly and accelerate their progress through the school curriculum. Many students choose talent-search-related programs because their schools lack classes or because they are seeking contact with intellectual peers. Research shows that learning material in a fast-paced context does not result in lower levels of mastery (Lynch, 1990), although that is a common misperception of schools. Although talent search testing has opened many opportunities for many gifted students, one of the major criticisms of the program is that it is still viewed as a primarily outside-of-school program with little impact on in-school curricula, services, and eligibility for in-school gifted programs (Olszewski-Kubilius & Lee, 2005).

Articulation of Outside-of-School Coursework With In-School Coursework

One of the issues about talent search summer programs, particularly those that offer typical high school classes, is how these are viewed and articulate with students' home school experiences. The evidence regarding this is equivocal. Many gifted students enroll in such classes for their personal and private enrichment and do not care how their schools respond to their summer coursework. But, some students are using summer courses, particularly fast-paced ones, to speed up their progress through their school curriculum, possibly to graduate early or to supplement meager offerings in their high school. Many of these students want recognition and credit for their summer coursework. The percentage of students who get credit for fast-paced classes varies across studies, with reports of 80% for subsets of students who specifically ask for credit (Lynch, 1990) and 50% for those students who achieve proficiency in the subject as measured by performance on standardized tests and thus qualified for credit (Olszewski-Kubilius, 1989). It is easier for summer students to get appropriate placement subsequently in their local schools than credit for summer coursework (Lynch, 1990; Olszewski-Kubilius, 1989). Additionally, credit rates vary by subject area and are higher for cumulatively organized subjects such as algebra or Latin, and lower for verbal classes such as writing or literature (Olszewski-Kubilius, 1989).

The awarding of credit by schools for summer courses is facilitated by accreditation of the program by an outside educational agency (Lee & Olszewski-Kubilius, 2005; Olszewski-Kubilius, Laubscher, Wohl, & Grant, 1996). Lee and Olszewski-Kubilius reported that after a summer program at a major Midwestern university had been accredited by the North Central Association of Colleges and Schools, and thus was able to award credit to middle and high school students who successfully completed high school courses, the percentage of summer students whose schools honored the credit increased significantly from 28% preaccreditation to 64% 8 years postaccreditation. How summer program experiences relate to school curricula and programming is important for students' talent development but at the present, is largely left up to parents to manage.

A Synthesis of Key Points About Talent Search Programs

- Talent search programs exist across the U.S. and have become the main providers of outside-of-school educational programs for academically gifted students.
- The research base regarding the talent search model is very strong and hundreds of studies support the efficacy of the off-level testing program, the validity of the fast-paced model of instruction, and the long-term predictive validity of SAT scores for educational and occupational choices and success.
- Despite its long history and demonstrated success, talent search programs remain largely outside-of-school programs with limited impact on in-school curricula and services for gifted students.

- Greater articulation between in-school programs and talent-search-related, outside-of-school programs is needed, including, for example, credit and recognition for summer coursework, in order to assist talented students with the development of their abilities.

Talent search programs have become entrenched within the fabric of educational opportunities available for academically gifted students. It is likely that they will remain a significant player for many students, but issues surrounding access for a broader range of students and relationships between talent search outside-of-school programs and in-school programs need to be addressed. There is great potential for schools and outside-of-school agencies, such as talent search programs, to partner to provide needed experiences for our most talented students.

References

Ablard, K. E., Mills, C. J., & Hoffhines, V. L. (1996). *The developmental study of talented youth (DSTY): The participants* (Technical Report No. 13). Baltimore: Johns Hopkins University, Institute for the Academic Advancement of Youth.

Assouline, S., & Lupkowski-Shoplik, A. (1997). Talent searches: A model for the discovery and development of academic talent. In N. Colangelo & G. A. Davis (Eds.), *Handbook of gifted education* (2nd ed., pp. 170–179). Needham Heights, MA: Allyn & Bacon.

Barnett, L. B., & Durden, W. G. (1993). Education patterns of academically talented youth. *Gifted Child Quarterly, 37,* 161–168.

Bartkovich, K. G., & Mezynski, K. (1981). Fast-paced precalculus mathematics for talented junior-high students: Two recent SMPY programs. *Gifted Child Quarterly, 25,* 73–80.

Benbow, C. P. (1992a). Mathematical talent: Its nature and consequences. In N. Colangelo, S. G. Assouline, & D. L. Ambroson (Eds.), *Talent development: Proceedings from the 1991 Henry B. and Jocelyn Wallace National Research Symposium on Talent Development* (pp. 95–123). New York: Trillium.

Benbow, C. P. (1992b). Academic achievement in mathematics and science of students between ages 13 and 23: Are there differences among students in the top one percent of mathematical ability? *Journal of Educational Psychology, 84,* 51–61.

Benbow, C. P., & Arjmand, O. (1990). Predictors of high academic achievement in mathematics and science by mathematically talented students: A longitudinal study. *Journal of Educational Psychology, 82,* 430–441.

Benbow, C. P., Perkins, S., & Stanley, J. C. (1983). Mathematics taught at a fast pace: A longitudinal evaluation of SMPY's first class. In C. P. Benbow & J. C. Stanley (Eds.), *Academic precocity: Aspects of its development* (pp. 51–78). Baltimore: Johns Hopkins University.

Brody, L. E. (1998). The talent searches: A catalyst for change in higher education. *Journal of Secondary Gifted Education, 9,* 124–133.

Brody, L., & Fox, L. H. (1980). An accelerative intervention program for mathematically gifted girls. In L. H. Fox, L. Brody, & D. Tobin (Eds.), *Women and the mathematical mystique* (pp. 164–178). Hillsdale, NJ: Erlbaum.

Burton, N. W. (1988). *Two surveys: Survey II: Test-taking history for 1980–81 young SAT-takers.* New York: College Entrance Examination Board.

Fox, L. H., Brody, L., & Tobin, D. (1985). The impact of early intervention programs upon course-taking and attitudes in high school. In S. F. Chipman, L. R. Brush, & D. M. Wilson (Eds.), *Women and mathematics: Balancing the equation* (pp. 249–274). Hillsdale, NJ: Erlbaum.

Jarosewich, T., & Stocking, V. B. (2003). Talent search: Student and parent perceptions of out-of-level testing. *Journal of Secondary Gifted Education, 14,* 137–150.

Kolitch, E. R., & Brody, L. E. (1992). Mathematics acceleration of highly talented students: An evaluation. *Gifted Child Quarterly, 36,* 78–86.

Lee, S.-Y., Matthews, M. S., & Olszewski-Kubilius, P. (2008). A national picture of talent search and talent search educational programs. *Gifted Child Quarterly, 52,* 55–69.

Lee, S.-Y., & Olszewski-Kubilius, P. (2005). Investigation of high school credit and placement for summer coursework taken outside of local schools. *Gifted Child Quarterly, 49,* 37–50.

Lubinski, D., & Benbow, C. P. (2006). Study of Mathematically Precocious Youth after 35 years: Uncovering antecedents for the development of math-science expertise. *Perspectives on Psychological Science, 1,* 316–345.

Lubinski, D., Webb, R. M., Morelock, M. J., & Benbow, C. P. (2001). Top 1 in 20,000: A 10-year follow-up of the profoundly gifted. *Journal of Applied Psychology, 85,* 718–729.

Lynch, S. J. (1990). Credit and placement issues for the academically talented following summer studies in science and mathematics. *Gifted Child Quarterly, 34,* 27–30.

Lynch, S. J. (1992). Fast-paced high school science for the academically talented: A six-year perspective. *Gifted Child Quarterly, 36,* 147–154.

Olszewski-Kubilius, P. (1989). Development of academic talent: The role of academic programs. In J. VanTassel-Baska & P. Olszewski-Kubilius (Eds.), *Patterns of influence on gifted learners: The home, the self, and the school* (pp. 214–230). New York: Teachers College.

Olszewski-Kubilius, P. (1998a). Early entrance to college: Students' stories. *Journal of Secondary Education, 10,* 226–247.

Olszewski-Kubilius, P. (1998b). Research evidence regarding the validity and effects of talent search educational programs. *Journal of Secondary Gifted Education, 9,* 134–138.

Olszewski-Kubilius, P. (1998c). Talent search: Purposes, rationale and role in gifted education. *Journal of Secondary Gifted Education, 9,* 106–114.

Olszewski-Kubilius P., & Grant, B. (1996). Academically talented women and mathematics: The role of special programs and support from others in acceleration, achievement, and aspiration. In K. D. Noble & R. F. Subotnik (Eds.), *Remarkable women: Perspectives on female talent development* (pp. 281–294). Cresskill, NJ: Hampton.

Olszewski-Kubilius, P., Laubscher, L., Wohl, V., & Grant, B. (1996). Issues and factors involved in credit and placement for accelerated summer coursework. *Journal of Secondary Gifted Education, 8,* 5–15.

Olszewski-Kubilius, P., & Lee, S.-Y. (2005). How schools use talent search scores for gifted adolescents. *Roeper Review, 27,* 233–240.

VanTassel-Baska, J. (1989). Profiles of precocity: A three-year study of talented adolescents. In J. VanTassel-Baska & P. Olszewski-Kubilius (Eds.), *Patterns of influence on gifted learners: The home, the self, and the school* (pp. 29–39). New York: Teachers College.

VanTassel-Baska, J. (1998). Key issues and problems in secondary programming. In *Excellence in educating gifted and talented learners* (3rd ed., pp. 241–259). Denver, CO: Love.

Wai, J., Lubinski, D., & Benbow, C. P. (2005). Creativity and occupational accomplishments among intellectually precocious youths: An age 13 to age 33 longitudinal study. *Journal of Educational Psychology, 97,* 484–492.

Webb, R. M., Lubinski, D., & Benbow, C. P. (2002). Mathematically facile adolescents with math-science aspirations: New perspectives on their educational and vocational development. *Journal of Educational Psychology, 94,* 785–794.

Wilder, G., & Casserly, P. L. (1988). *Survey I: Young SAT-takers and their parents.* New York: College Board.

Author Note

Portions of this chapter were initially published in Olszewski-Kubilius, P., & Lee, S.-Y. (2008). Specialized programs serving the gifted. In F. A. Karnes & K. P. Stephens (Eds.), *Achieving excellence: Educating the gifted and talented* (pp. 192–208). Upper Saddle River, NJ: Pearson Education.

Chapter 11

Study Abroad Opportunities

BY

LISA
LIMBURG-WEBER

IN PREVIOUS CENTURIES, wealthy families often provided tours of travel for young people before they settled into their adult lives (see Goodwin & Nacht, 1988). In this century, study abroad options for high school students of more ordinary economic means have steadily increased. Although most study abroad (SA) programs are not specifically marketed to academically talented students, such programs can, if used judiciously, be an excellent option in the smorgasbord of educational choices available to the highly able high school student.

Study abroad is a term that refers to a wide variety of programs providing an educational experience in another country. The most traditional program model for both high school and college students is probably the semester or year abroad. Students choosing this type of program, especially in the high school years, often combine it with a "homestay" experience, in which they live in the home of a local family who provides room and board (and sometimes other services) on either a paid or a volunteer basis. Most high school students choosing the semester or year abroad option attend a local high school in the host country for part or all of their time abroad. Their high school classes may be supplemented by language or other special classes for foreigners. Optional or required travel components may also be a part of a semester or year abroad.

The number of secondary students participating in study abroad programs is fairly large, and growing. The Council on Standards for International Educational Travel (CSIET), which maintains information on and provides accreditation for high school exchange programs, estimates that more than 31,000 secondary students from 113 different countries were served by such organizations in 2007–2008, an increase of 4,500 over 2003–2004 (Lee, 2008).

Study abroad can fill a vital role in a gifted student's academic program. Academic benefits can accrue in several areas for SA students. One study has suggested that the diversity students experience while studying abroad may increase creativity (Gurman, 1989). Students who have studied abroad also may find that their increased awareness of both their own and other cultures leads them into fascinating new areas of academic study, such as comparative literature or international politics. New career interests may emerge as students consider options requiring an in-depth knowledge of foreign affairs, a willingness to travel or live abroad, or an ability to communicate cross-culturally with professionals in one's chosen field. But, the most obvious result of a study abroad program in a non-English-speaking country is, of course, increased facility in a foreign language.

Verbally gifted students interested in adding a second or third foreign language not available in their high schools, or increasing their level of competency in a language they have already begun to study, would be well-advised to consider studying abroad to do so. Study abroad plunges language learners into an exquisitely equipped, living language-and-culture laboratory, with limitless opportunities for accelerating as quickly as one likes to new levels of learning. According to Daniel & Rayel (1982),

> The beauty of a foreign home life experience for [gifted] students is that exposure to ideas develops at a rate determined largely by the students themselves. . . . There are no routines or drills to this part of the experience and few occasions for the students to be frustrated by the pace of instruction. (p. 110)

The amount of progress an individual student makes in learning the host country's language depends, of course, on many different factors, including the following: facility in the language before the study abroad experience, length of time spent abroad, and level of engagement with native speakers. But, accelerated language learning, at whatever level, makes especially good sense for the gifted student. It can translate into time and/or credits gained at the college level, where students may be able to test out of a language requirement, accelerate directly into higher level foreign language literature courses, or even accumulate college credits through competency tests. Further, foreign language learning can help sharpen students' command of their native tongue, and each language learned seems to make learning the next language come easier (see Cox, Daniel, & Boston, 1985).

The problem of graduation requirements for students who spend part or all of a regular academic year abroad—and wish to graduate with their class—is real. On the other hand, beyond the option of enrolling in the appropriate course offered at the host high school—in the host country's language—most programs for high school students do not provide a way for students to accumulate formal credits or even stay abreast in subjects necessary for high school graduation. (One exception is School Year Abroad, offered through Phillips Academy, which provides English language instruction in what the program developers see as the "core" subjects of math and English). The dilemma underlines the critical importance of excellent pretrip planning and communication with school officials.

High school students who want to study abroad should therefore carefully consider the advantages and disadvantages of going through high school and college programs. Students who decide to go abroad in their precollegiate years should make sure they understand what the implications of their time abroad will be for both high school graduation and college matriculation. Students spending their high school senior year abroad, in particular, may need to figure out a way of accomplishing tasks like applying to and making decisions about college admission while overseas.

Practical Issues

In the initial, information-gathering stage of locating quality study abroad programs, three tools emerge as enormously useful:

- Recommendations—which can prove invaluable—from students who have been pleased with their study abroad experience;
- The most current listings of high school programs provided by the Council on Standards for International Educational Travel. Updated yearly, the *CSIET Advisory List* (available from http://www.csiet.org) provides information on U.S.-based programs that have chosen to be evaluated through CSIET's accreditation process. In a world proliferating with organizations promising high-quality study abroad programs, CSIET provides one way, although clearly not exhaustive, of locating programs meeting minimum standards for safe and responsible policies;
- The Internet, for quick-and-easy information about programs and countries.

Prospective SA students will most likely rely on the Internet to help them locate information on suitable study abroad programs; Web sites provide everything from program information to photographs of the target country. It would be impossible to provide an exhaustive list of Internet resources, but two reputable commercial sites include the following:

- http://www.studyabroad.com—Besides a searchable index of study abroad programs, this site contains extensive, non-program-specific resources, including detailed student and parent guides with information ranging from safety to packing lists.
- http://www.petersons.com—This large site, a companion to the well-known Peterson's Guides series, also provides an extensive searchable index of study abroad and summer programs.

Detailed questions that families and students should ask program representatives when considering a trip abroad are found in Table 1.

Synthesis of key points to remember concerning study abroad experiences include the following:

- Students who choose to study abroad increase their cultural awareness, which often expands their options for career choices.
- The homestay experience can be a valuable component of the study abroad experience. In many programs, students live with families while they study the language and experience the local school.
- Reputable agencies that organize study abroad opportunities often possess great expertise; they should be consulted to maximize student benefit and minimize potential problems during students' time away from home.
- Graduation requirements for the school the student leaves must be considered before travel abroad so that all considerations with credit are understood fully.
- Study abroad is a wonderful way for gifted students to incorporate several multidisciplinary areas into their academic programs.

Clearly, not every high school student has the desire, resources, and commitment necessary for a successful study abroad experience. However, study abroad should be seriously considered both for verbally gifted students committed to accelerated progress in their foreign language, and for gifted students interested in the unique and highly memorable learning opportunities available through sustained contact with another culture.

References

Cox, J., N. Daniel, & Boston, B. O. (1985). *Educating able learners: Programs and promising practices.* Austin: University of Texas Press.

Daniel, N., & Rayel, R. A. (1982). International education for gifted students. *Gifted International, 1,* 101–117.

Goodwin, C. D., & Nacht, M. (1988). *Abroad and beyond: Patterns in American overseas education.* Cambridge, UK: Cambridge University Press.

Gurman, E. B. (1989). Travel abroad: A way to increase creativity? *Educational Research Quarterly, 13*(3), 12–16.

TABLE 1

Questions for Study Abroad Programs

1. How long has the sponsoring organization been in existence?
2. Are you accredited by the CSIET or by a different accreditation agency? High-quality, nonaccredited programs certainly exist, but accreditation by a reputable agency can help ensure that the program is acknowledged by its peers as meeting basic professional standards.
3. How many students have you sent abroad in the last few years? How many of these were outgoing from the United States? Many organizations handle both incoming and outgoing exchange students, and you will want to determine that the program has devoted sufficient resources to handling American students going abroad.
4. What is your program's dropout rate? How do you handle students who are having a bad experience and want to come home?
5. What is the organizational structure of the program? Most exchange programs rely to some extent on volunteers; you will want to figure out to what extent this is true of your program of interest, and what kind of training and supervision their volunteers receive.
6. What are the criteria you use in selecting students to go abroad? You will want to ask about GPA requirements, language requirements, application procedures, and any student or family interview requirements.
7. How do you select host families (if applicable to the program) or other lodgings? How do you handle problems that come up with host families?
8. What safety policies are in place while students are abroad? How are emergencies handled? What are your provisions for medical care, including psychological care, if that should be necessary? Can the program accommodate students with disabilities (if applicable)?
9. What kind of predeparture and reentry training is provided for students? Reputable programs will devote time and resources to orienting students before they leave and preparing them to come home after the experience.
10. Who is available for students to contact for support while abroad? Who is available for students' families to contact while students are abroad? A local contact should be available for the student, and a U.S. contact for the families.
11. What countries can students choose among? How do facilities differ among the different countries? What cultural differences have proved most difficult for students to deal with in each country under consideration?
12. What kind of classes do students attend while they are abroad? Will they be studying with other foreigners, or in a local high school? What are school facilities like in the host country, and what kind of classes can students take?
13. What costs do tuition fees cover? What costs are students responsible for? Is financial aid available? Is it need-based or merit-based, and what is a typical award? How much spending money does the program recommend for a typical student?
14. Do you have the names of some program alumni (and their families) that we could speak with? Preferably, you should try to speak with alumni who visited the country in which you are interested.

Lee, J. (2008). *International youth exchange statistics: Semester and academic year programs 2007–2008 cycle.* Alexandria, VA: Council on Standards for International Educational Travel. Retrieved May 29, 2008, from http://www.csiet.org/mc/page.do?sitePageId=2486.

Author Note

This chapter was adapted from the following article: Limburg-Weber, L. (1999/2000). Send them packing: Study abroad as an option for gifted students. *Journal of Secondary Gifted Education, 11,* 43–51. The adaptation is reprinted with permission from Prufrock Press Inc. (http://www.prufrock.com).

Chapter 12

Distance Education

BY

PAULA
OLSZEWSKI-
KUBILIUS

DISTANCE EDUCATION is now widespread, especially at the college level. It is being utilized for transmitting instruction across geographic boundaries and extending educational opportunities nationally and internationally (Timpson & Jones, 1989). Distance education programs for K–12 students have also increased dramatically in recent years, largely due to ever-improving technologies that can connect students with teachers easily and efficiently, and because of demand on the part of parents and educators for educational alternatives. For example,

- a recent book aimed at helping high-school-aged students find an online high school lists 113 such programs (Kiernan, 2005);
- forty-two states have significant online learning programs to supplement school programs, significant full-time programs (complete cyber schools), or both (Kiernan, 2005); and
- the majority of online programs for K–12 students reported growth of 25% or more in enrollments in 2006–2007 compared to the previous year; 20% of these programs reported growth of 50% or higher (Watson & Ryan, 2007).

More recently, distance education programs for pre-college-aged students have been designed to serve students who were not succeeding in a traditional school setting or were unable to attend a regular school (Olszewski-Kubilius & Limburg-Weber, 2002; Timpson & Jones, 1989) for a variety of reasons including illness or because they had special talents that required full-time training during the day (e.g., elite tennis players).

Distance education transcends the constraints of time and space through media such as computer- or Internet-based programs, which enable educators and learners to "interact," but not necessarily in face-to-face situations ("Accessing Distance Learning," 1995; Hofmeister, 1994; Washington, 1997). Distance education programs may never replace existing classrooms and schools but can be used to compensate for educational deficits and lack of advanced coursework in schools (Adams & Cross, 1999/2000; Ravaglia & Sommer, 2000; Washington, 1997; Wilson, Litle, Coleman, & Gallagher, 1997/1998) or as part of a home-schooling program (Ravaglia & Sommer, 2000; Washington, 1997).

Distance education historically was designed primarily for students who were not succeeding in a traditional school setting or were unable to attend a regular school (Olszewski-Kubilius & Limburg-Weber, 2002; Timpson & Jones, 1989). As a result, studies on the effectiveness of distance education have been limited to these groups of students (Adams & Cross, 1999/2000; Belcastro, 2001; Lewis, 1989; McBride & Lewis, 1993; Ravaglia & Sommer, 2000; Threlkeld, 1991) and have not focused on gifted students enrolled in such programs. Although distance education programs are proliferating, there are only a few that are specifically designed for gifted students, enabling them to obtain advanced courses earlier than usual, proceed through a course at an accelerated rate, or craft a more appropriate individualized program.

Need for Distance Education Programs for Gifted Students

Despite the scarcity of research on distance education for gifted students, gifted educators appear interested in distance education as a means to increase their ability to serve gifted learners, especially those with limited access to advanced courses (Adams & Cross, 1999/2000; Olszewski-Kubilius & Limburg-Weber, 2002). Distance education programs may be a good option for a range of gifted students, including students who attend rural schools where advanced courses and gifted programs are limited, students who cannot obtain "early" access to advanced courses, students who want to take additional advanced courses but cannot fit them into their school schedules, gifted students who are not thriving in a typical school setting (Goodrich, 1994; Lewis, 1989; Lewis & Talbert, 1990; McBride, 1991b; McBride & Lewis, 1993; Ravaglia & Sommer, 2000; Savage & Werner, 1994; Wilson et al., 1997/1998), or homebound or home-schooling learners (Ravaglia & Sommer, 2000). One of the significant advantages of distance education for schools is the ability to provide appropriate courses for gifted students without having to remove them from their peers or regular school environment, thus avoiding transportation costs and problems associated with placing younger students in classes with older students (Ravaglia & Sommer, 2000).

In a sample of middle and high school (grades 6–12) gifted students, most of whom (83%) were enrolled in public schools, students' interests in specific subjects, a desire to enrich or add to their home-school curriculum, a desire to accelerate or move faster through the curriculum, and the unavailability of the courses in their home schools were the major reasons for enrolling in the distance education program (Olszewski-Kubilius & Lee, 2004). Less salient (less than 10% of students) were reasons such as a desire to accumulate another Advanced Placement (AP) credit for college or a desire to take a course offered in their schools but unavailable to their age group. Parents who enrolled their 4th through 6th graders in enrichment classes in a distance education program did so primarily because they desired academic challenge for their children and because of their children's interest in the subject matter. Other less significant reasons for this age group were the lack of courses in their school and a desire by parents that their children spend more time on academic pursuits (Dershewitz, Lee, & Johnson, 2006).

It is difficult to gauge how many gifted students are participating in distance education programs. A national study of four talent search centers that offer distance education programs found that 34,644 students in grades 3 through 12 had participated in distance education courses since their inception in the 1990s, and 7,468 participated in 2003-2004 (Lee, Matthews, & Olszewski-Kubilius, 2008). For the year 2003-2004, males (53.9%) surpassed females (45.9%) in their participation in these courses. More than half (54.2%) of the students were 7th through 9th graders, 43.1% were 3rd through 6th graders, and 2.8% were 10th through 12th graders.

Many other gifted students may be participating in distance education programs through state-supported virtual high schools. A recent book aimed at helping high school students find an online high school lists 113 programs (Kiernan, 2005). Although the overwhelming majority of these are not geared specifically or exclusively toward gifted learners, individual programs may have courses appealing to or appropriate for them. Additionally, growing numbers of gifted students are enrolling in online college courses, for example, through Stanford University's Education Program for Gifted Youth, which offers both an online high school and college credit courses, and/or earning college credits through AP courses online, through programs such as APEX or state-supported virtual high schools.

Distance Education Program Features and Models

Contrary to most people's beliefs that distance education is passive, distance education programs are actually based on the premise that students are active

participants and collaborators (McLoughlin, 1999) who construct their own knowledge (Hull, Bull, Montgomery, May, & Overton, 2000). Hull et al. contended
that distance education, such as online courses, entails authentic problem solving,
which assumes learners are able to transform given information into knowledge. It
is comparable to a student-centered learning approach, in which learners are central
to the learning process and take responsibility for their learning. Teachers assist
learners as an "educational resource" and encourage students to engage in learning
activities as active participants (Wilson et al., 1997/1998). Thus, students enrolling
in distance education must be independent problem solvers and take initiative and
responsibility for their academic activities ("Accessing Distance Learning," 1995;
University of Plymouth, 2006; Wilson et al., 1997/1998). Indeed, research has
shown that students are more likely to "challenge" their teachers in a setting where
geographic distance and lack of face-to-face contact lessens their concern about
actively questioning their teachers (McBride, 1991a).

Distance education often is thought of as a lonely or a solitary type of experience, but this is not necessarily the case with current technologies. By posting discussions or participating in real-time class discussions online, students can actively
engage with others. Although researchers (Glennan & Melmed, 1996) have alleged
that limited access to and use of computers and other educational technologies are
still a problem for many students, they also suggested that technologies make distance education programs active and engaging learning experiences for students.

With the development of various forms of communication technologies—
especially Internet and broadband technologies—distance education has not only
spread in the past few years ("Accessing Distance Learning," 1995), but there are
now multiple venues and delivery modes available. Most courses currently are
provided online or with some kind of computer teleconferencing. The technologies
enable students to have a variety of learning experiences beyond classes, including
virtual field trips to cultural institutions and historical sites that can allow students
to have broader cultural exposure to the arts. Technologies also can enable students
the opportunity to communicate and collaborate with a more diverse group of
students, thereby cultivating an understanding of multicultural perspectives via
interactions across classrooms, countries, and continents (Cifuentes, Murphy, &
Davis, 1998).

Some university-based gifted centers have distance education programs
designed specifically for gifted students of precollege age. The Center for Talented
Youth (CTY) program at Johns Hopkins University offers computer-based mul-
timedia courses in mathematics and computer science for elementary through
beginning college level, writing classes for students beginning in fifth grade, and
some Advanced Placement courses. Students interact with their instructors using
e-mail, telephone, or an interactive, Internet-based whiteboard. Students can earn
high school credit for high-school-level classes.

The Duke University Talent Identification Program (Duke TIP) offers distance
education courses through its e-Studies program to gifted students in grades 8–12.
Courses are Web-based, and students interact with their instructors and peers

through online discussions, virtual lectures, and real-time collaborations. Currently eight courses are offered, including Anatomy and Physiology, History of the Ancient World, JAVA for Video Games, Mathematical Problem-Solving, Academic Writing, Social Psychology, and Short Fiction Workshops I and II. Duke TIP does not grant credit for successful completion of e-Studies courses, but students may seek this on their own from their local schools.

The Center for Talent Development (CTD) at Northwestern University has offered a distance education program, Gifted LearningLinks, for gifted students in grades 3–12 for more than 20 years. Classes include 22 enrichment classes (e.g., The Wonders of Ancient Egypt, Classic American Novels, Writing Workshops, Latin, Topics in Math) for younger students, 30 or more high school honors-level classes (e.g., Creative Writing, Literary Analysis, Economics, U.S. History, Biology, Chemistry), and 19 different AP classes. Students receive "textboxes" (boxes filled with needed course materials) that include introductory course materials, textbooks, course syllabi, and more. Courses are Web-based, and students participate with others in online discussions and communicate with teachers via e-mail. Some college-level classes also are available and students earn credit for high-school-level classes.

Stanford University recently inaugurated its online high school. This is a diploma-granting, 3-year online independent high school within the Education Program for Gifted Youth (EPGY). Courses are rigorous and distinguishing features include enhanced mathematical content in the natural science and social science courses; an emphasis on writing, discussion, and argumentation within courses; a college-style class schedule; and self-paced, directed study courses. The current set of course offerings include core courses such as Democracy, Freedom and the Rule of Law; History of Science and Culture; and Grammar, Rhetoric, and Argument. University-level courses include Differential Equations, Complex Analysis, and Quantum Mechanics; and online high school courses include AP courses and honors-level courses. Optional intensive residential summer courses at the Stanford campus also are available for students, as are advising and extracurricular activities.

Research About the Effects of Distance Education Programs

Empirical research about the effectiveness of distance education programs is sparse, specifically regarding gifted students. Not all gifted students are good candidates for a distance education course. Several characteristics that may contribute to success in a distance education course include the ability to work independently, a strong desire to take the course, motivation to persist in the course to completion, and having the appropriate prerequisite content knowledge and skills (Wilson et al., 1997/1998). National completion rates for distance education courses are about 30 to 40% (Huerta, d'Entremont, & Gonzalez , 2006), but some programs that are open to all learners have much higher rates and attribute this to curricula that are systemically designed and interactive in nature, assessment and monitoring of students' progress, and specific training for teachers in online instruction. Little data are available on completion rates for distance education programs designed specifically for gifted learners, although one program reports completion rates around 66 to 80% percent (lower for AP classes, higher for enrichment classes), and grades of A or B for more than 95% of students (L. Dershewitz, personal communication, January 25, 2006; Olszewski-Kubilius & Lee, 2004). Olszewski-Kubilius and Lee found that students who took AP classes via a distance education program specifically designed for gifted students reported that the classes prepared them well for their AP examinations (64% of students followed through with the AP exam, 63% of whom earned a 4 or 5).

Despite limited data on how successful gifted students actually are in distance education courses, researchers have documented evidence about the positive effects of distance education programs on gifted and talented students academically and socially, primarily through self-reports of students on questionnaires and surveys after the program. Effects found include:

- greater independence on the part of students regarding their learning and the development of close relationships with peers for rural gifted students who took advanced high school mathematics courses in a telelearning program (Lewis, 1989);

- enhanced independent study and thinking skills, new means of communication, academic challenge and growth, and a more realistic assessment of how one's abilities compared to others among high-school-aged students from multiple schools participating in a distance education program through a state-supported residential school (Wilson et al., 1997/1998);

- increases in students' collaboration skills and higher order thinking skills, such as logical explanation, critical inquiry, interpretation, and reflection as a result of participation in a program that augmented teaching with audiographic conference technology for secondary students (McLoughlin, 1999);

- increases in students' problem-solving abilities, logical thinking skills, collaborative learning skills, motivation, task commitment, leadership ability, and responsibility for learning in a program that connected elementary and gifted secondary students from multiple schools (Ewing, Dowling, & Coutts, 1997); and

- higher interest in the subject studied, increased confidence in one's academic abilities, and improved study and organizational skills for fourth through sixth graders who took enrichment classes via a distance education program (Dershewitz, Lee, & Johnson, 2006).

Regarding gifted students' preferences for certain features of their distance education classes, Olszewski-Kubilius and Lee (2004) found that among gifted students who took either honors or AP courses through a distance education program, the lack of interactions with teachers was a source of dissatisfaction for some students and that most students wanted to use computer technologies that enabled them to have easy communication with teachers, other students, and course information, but still desired to have traditional textbooks and written course materials as part of the learning tools. Thus, students need to know and understand their learning styles and preferences in order to find those distance education classes appropriate for them.

There continues to be concerns about distance education on the part of both educators and students. Concerns include the inability to use students' body language as an indication of student engagement and understanding (Gallagher, 2001), technological problems (Lewis & Talbert, 1990), and insufficient contact with, and therefore support from, other students and the teacher (University of Plymouth, 2006). Also, distance education programs suffer from some of the same articulation issues as summer and other outside-of-school programs. Olszewski-Kubilius and Lee (2004) found that 20% of students who took a distance education course and wanted credit did not get it from their high schools, but only 6% of those who asked for placement in the next course in sequence were denied. However, almost half of the students could not skip ahead to the next course because none was available.

A Synthesis of Key Points About Distance Education Programs

- Distance education is a growing phenomenon in the U.S. and worldwide. One advantage is that learning opportunities can transcend the limitations of time and space.
- Distance education is a growing alternative for gifted students because it allows students to take courses that are commensurate with their abilities and readiness without leaving their home or school and without having to be placed with older students.
- Distance education is being used by gifted students to take classes earlier than is typical, to take additional classes they cannot fit into their schedule, or to take classes that are not available in their school or district.
- Although research is sparse, what is available suggests that benefits for gifted students from distance learning classes include acquiring greater independence in their learning, and enhancing skills such as collaboration with others and problem solving. Some distance education classes may offer students a more individualized and personalized educational experience, yet students and teachers alike do see the lack of face-to-face interaction as a negative aspect of distance learning classes.

- Distance education programs for gifted students must deal with similar issues as other types of service models, including articulation between them and in-school programs, credit, and access for all students.

With technologies to support instruction and communication becoming more numerous as well as more advanced and more available, distance education is likely to grow as an option for students of all ages. The key to its use and success with gifted students will be distance education providers' openness to including advanced courses and allowing students to proceed through courses at their own, accelerated rate.

References

Accessing distance learning. (1995, November/December). *Imagine, 3,* 1–4.

Adams, C. M., & Cross, T. L. (1999/2000). Distance learning opportunities for academically gifted students. *Journal of Secondary Gifted Education, 11,* 88–96.

Belcastro, F. P. (2001). Electric technology and its use with rural gifted students. *Roeper Review, 25,* 14–16.

Cifuentes, L., Murphy, K., & Davis, T. (1998, February). *Cultural connections: Promoting self-esteem, achievement, and multicultural understanding through distance learning.* Paper presented at the Association for Educational Communications and Technology, St. Louis, MO. (ERIC Document Reproduction Service No. ED423831)

Dershewitz, L., Lee, S.-Y., & Johnson, P. (2006, February). *Parents' perceptions of the effects of distance education on gifted children.* Paper presented at the Illinois Association for Gifted Children, Chicago.

Ewing, J., Dowling, J., & Coutts, N. (1997). *STARS: Report on superhighway teams across rural school projects.* Dunhee, Scotland: Northern College. (ERIC Document Reproduction Service No. ED421319)

Gallagher, J. J. (2001). Personnel preparation and secondary education programs for gifted students. *Journal of Secondary Gifted Education, 12,* 133–138.

Glennan, T. K., & Melmed, A. (1996). *Fostering the use of educational technology: Elements of a national strategy.* Santa Monica, CA: RAND Corporation. Retrieved April 9, 2008, from http://rand.org/pubs/monograph_reports/MR682/contents.html

Goodrich, B. E. (1994). Creating a "virtual" magnet school. *T.H.E. Journal, 21*(10), 73–75.

Hofmeister, A. (1994). Technological tools for rural special education. *Exceptional Children, 50,* 326–331.

Huerta, L. A., d'Entremont, C., Gonzalez, M.-F. (2006). Cyber charter schools: Can accountability keep pace with innovation? *Phi Delta Kappan, 88,* 23–30.

Hull, D. F., Bull, K. S., Montgomery, D., May, J. R., & Overton, R. (2000, March). *Designing an online, introductory gifted education.* Paper presented at the Capitalizing on Leadership in Rural Special Education conference, Alexandria, VA. (ERIC Document Reproduction Service No. ED439873)

Kiernan, V. (2005). *Finding an online high school: Your guide to more than 4,500 high school courses offered over the Internet.* Alexandria, VA: Mattily.

Lee, S.-Y., Matthews, M. S., & Olszewski-Kubilius, P. (2008). A national picture of talent search and talent search educational programs. *Gifted Child Quarterly, 52,* 55–69.

Lewis, G. (1989). Telelearning: Making maximum use of the medium. *Roeper Review, 11,* 195–198.

Lewis, G., & Talbert, M. (1990). Telelearning: Reaching out to the gifted in rural schools. *Educating Able Learners, 15*(1), 2–3, 10.

McBride, R. (1991a). Courses offered despite cutbacks. *American School Board Journal, 178,* A26.

McBride, R. (1991b). Strategies for implementing teletraining systems in education K–12. In C. Steinfield & T. Ehlers (Eds.), *ITCA teleconferencing yearbook.* Washington, DC: International Teleconferencing Association.

McBride, R. O., & Lewis, G. (1993). Sharing the resources: Electronic outreach programs. *Journal for the Education of the Gifted, 16,* 372–386.

McLoughlin, C. (1999). Providing enrichment and acceleration in the electronic classroom: A case study of audiographic conferencing. *Journal of Special Education Technology, 14*(2), 54–69

Olszewski-Kubilius, P., & Lee, S.-Y. (2004). Gifted adolescents' talent development through distance learning. *Journal for the Education of the Gifted, 28,* 7–35.

Olszewski-Kubilius, P., & Limburg-Weber, L. (2002). *Designs for excellence: A guide to educational program options for academically talented middle and secondary school students.* Evanston, IL: Northwestern University, The Center for Talent Development.

Ravaglia, R., & Sommer, R. (2000). Expanding the curriculum with distance learning. *Principal, 79*(3), 10–13.

Savage, L., & Werner, J. (1994). *Potpourri of resources to tap gifted education in rural areas.* Austin, TX: American Council on Rural Education. (ERIC Document Reproduction Service No. ED369601)

Threlkeld, R. (1991). Increasing educational options through distance learning. *Gifted Education Communicator, 21*(1), 12–14.

Timpson, W. M., & Jones, C. S. (1989). Increased education choices for the gifted: Distance learning via technology. *Gifted Child Today, 12*(5), 10–11.

University of Plymouth. (2006). *Distance education: Why distance learning?* Retrieved April 9, 2008, from http://www2.plymouth.ac.uk/distancelearning

Washington, M. F. (1997). Real hope for the gifted. *Gifted Child Today, 20*(6), 20–22.

Watson, J., & Ryan, J. (2007). *Keeping pace with K–12 online learning: A review of state-level policy and practice.* Retrieved July 1, 2008, from http://nacol.org/resources

Wilson, V., Litle, J., Coleman, M. R., & Gallagher, J. (1997/1998). Distance learning: One school's experience on the information highway. *Journal of Secondary Gifted Education, 9,* 89–100.

Author Note

Portions of this chapter were initially published in Olszewski-Kubilius, P., & Lee, S.-Y. (2008). Specialized programs serving the gifted. In F. A. Karnes & K. P. Stephens (Eds.), *Achieving excellence: Educating the gifted and talented* (pp. 192–208). Upper Saddle River, NJ: Pearson Education; and Adams, C. M., & Olszewski-Kubilius, P. (2007). Distance learning and gifted students. In J. VanTassel-Baska (Ed.), *Serving gifted learners beyond the traditional classroom: A guide to alternative programs and services* (pp. 169–188). Waco, TX: Prufrock Press.

A **Visionary Statement** for the **Education** of **Gifted Students** in **Secondary Schools**

BY

FELICIA A. DIXON,

SHELAGH A. GALLAGHER

AND

PAULA OLSZEWSKI-KUBILIUS

PREVIOUS CHAPTERS presented a picture of the gifted adolescent and the services he or she may receive. Part I provided an overview of current knowledge about intellectual and emotional development. Essentially important to note is that gifted adolescents' capacities for qualitative differences in thinking suggest a need for marked differences in their academic careers. Psychologically stable overall, gifted adolescents still face unique social and emotional challenges that can stymie them without proper support. These challenges are exacerbated when there is no outlet for, nor appreciation of, their curiosity. The intertwined issues of college and career also present pressures and problems for gifted students that others are much less likely to face. Part II described current knowledge about gifted adolescents' achievement levels and existing service models. Here the news is disturbing; especially disturbing is the recognition that national data about achievement and persistence among talented high school students are virtually nonexistent. Current services for gifted adolescents give evidence of powerful outcomes that result when proper attention is given to a gifted adolescent's academic and emotional needs. The jewel in this crown is the network of magnet programs and state-supported residential schools of the NCSSSMST, but even they are too few in number and too specific in focus to meet more than a fraction of the overall need. Typical high schools still serve a majority of gifted adolescents, even in states with residential schools, and the typical high school gifted education offerings are dominated by summer programs, competitions, and effective, but short-lived, grant-based projects.

Gifted students cannot be prepared adequately either for postsecondary education or for future careers solely with afterschool and summer programs. Therefore, this section moves the discussion from "what is" to "what could be" for high-ability adolescents. Before presenting this vision, however, it is important to acknowledge the three factors that make high school a particularly difficult time to program for gifted students. First, even among gifted students there are varying levels of ability; many are advanced, some are highly gifted. Differences in level of ability affects program needs: Although advanced students may be eager for AP U.S. History, a student who already has sophisticated knowledge of political policy may need something more. Second, gifted students' interests change as they grow, sometimes becoming very precise and focused—sometimes spanning the breadth of several disciplines. Increasing specificity creates dilemmas in that it is easier to program for five students who are, broadly speaking, gifted in mathematics than it is to program for four different mentorships in differential equations, mathematical modeling, inferential statistics, and string theory. The challenge only grows with a fifth student in the class who is passionate about understanding the connection among mathematics, music, and poetic rhythms. Third, the structure of high school creates barriers to programming. Rigid divisions between subjects make interdisciplinary study difficult, the need for adequate class sizes mitigates against small honors classes, and the pressure of college preparation extinguishes excitement over creative course options. School size also makes a difference: Providing services in all subjects for both advanced and highly gifted students would be a mammoth task in any high school and is well beyond the scope of smaller, poorer, or more rural schools. Recognizing this, Table 1 both summarizes the recommendations discussed below and presents reasonable adaptations from the ideal for smaller or less affluent schools.

Identification: Recognizing and Acknowledging Abilities

Formal identification of giftedness is rare at the high school level. The only time students take tests to determine ability is for admission into special programs such as the talent search (see Chapter 10 in this monograph) or specialized academic programs. In a typical high school, "identification" takes the form of recognizing and acknowledging students' abilities. Although informal, many of the standard recommendations for identification still apply. First, it is essential that a variety of information is used that accurately assesses level of talent, including prior grades, assessment of significant products, observation of behavioral traits, and indicators of student interest in the discipline. Second, it is important that students' prior knowledge allows them to advance either through the award of course credit, including course hours, or allowing the student to advance to complete graduation credits in more advanced classes. An example is the case of a student who qualifies for a talent search program by virtue of strong performance on the SAT in middle school. The student attends a summer talent search program and completes a fast-paced high-school-level geometry course. In this single case, there are several opportunities for identification: Being invited to participate in the talent search identifies the student as a very high achiever in need of honors-level coursework in mathematics. Qualifying for a talent search summer program identifies him or her as an exceptional achiever, perhaps requiring some independent projects in specific areas in math. Most importantly, successful completion of a talent search course should "identify" the young mathematician as having the requisite skills to receive high school credit—assuming that the courses are reasonably comparable and this young scholar has met the criteria for passing the class. Several chapters in this monograph (e.g., 1, 3, 7, and 10) mentioned the difficulty students have trying to gain this kind of recognition. It is time to address these systemic issues that impede maximal progress for our most capable students.

Another important feature of recognizing talent in high school is open-mindedness. Chapter 1 presents compelling evidence that adolescents are in a period of radical change. Adults involved with adolescents may well see the sudden emergence of talent in students who had previously shown no sign of giftedness. Open-mindedness also is necessary regarding placement. Prior knowledge acquires heightened importance as advanced programs become more academic and disci-pline specific. Adults must create a delicate balance between holding high content standards and allowing students with potential but insufficient backgrounds to advance. For example, a student who has never before taken an advanced section of a course, nor participated in a gifted program, can still be ready for advanced coursework if he or she performs exceptionally well on assignments relevant to the abstract type of materials that are present in the advanced course. Hence, even without the required prerequisite course, advanced understanding at any time may signal the need for flexibility in identification of adolescents for advanced programs. In short, identification for gifted services will take the highly individual nature of talent into account. At the high school level it is particularly important to have strong alignment between the mode of identification and the services provided. Because teacher recommendations are, formally or informally, an important gate-keeper to program and service decisions, it is important that teachers are aware of the subtler, culturally relevant, behavioral indicators of talent and ability. Crucial to the promotion of equity in high school gifted education services is active col-laboration with feeder schools to create strong vertical curricular alignment and proactive services to help students transition from middle to high school gifted services. Following the guidelines recommended by research in equity in Advanced

Table 1

Recommendations for Gifted Secondary Education Programs and Services

	Ideal	Standard	Minimum
	For affluent schools with large populations of above average and many highly gifted students, magnet programs, or specialized secondary schools.	Could be considered "ideal" for a typical high school.	Lowest acceptable standards for any high school, could be considered "ideal" for impoverished, rural, or small high schools.
	• Multifaceted program that responds to different individual subjects and also interdisciplinary study. • Opportunities for early specialization. • Contact with domain-specific mentors. • Some portion of the day set aside for self-contained study. • Direct instruction in epistemology. • Access to distance learning and college courses. • Opportunity to place out of courses based on rigorous independent/summer study. • Required immersion in second language. • Flexible access based on ability scores and/or demonstrated achievement. • Required use of discipline-specific advanced technology. • Options for both extremely gifted and above-average (honors-level) students.	• Opportunity for discipline-specific study in at least one math/science field and one field in the humanities. • Easy access to independent study. • AP and or IB options. • Distance education available. • Opportunity to place out of courses based on rigorous independent/summer study. • Consistent technology use. • Required second language. • A few options for extremely gifted and comprehensive honors offerings. • Differentiation in the regular classroom. • Flexible access based on ability scores and/or demonstrated achievement. • Required advanced study in a second language.	• AP and/or IB options. • Independent study. • Access to distance education. • Opportunity to place out of courses based on rigorous independent/summer study. • Required advanced study in a second language. • Differentiation in the regular classroom. • Flexible access based on ability scores and/or demonstrated achievement. • Students capable of moving faster/higher than average.
Social and Emotional	• Time with ability peers. • Mentorships available. • Direct instruction on the psychological aspects of advanced ability.		

	Ideal	Standard	Minimum
Career Counseling and Training			College.
Personnel Preparation	• Advanced subject matter content. • Interdisciplinary understanding. • Conceptual orientation. • Epistemological understanding. • Characteristics of gifted adolescents. • Curriculum and instruction models for gifted students. • Connections with discipline-specific professionals.	• Advanced subject-matter content. • Interdisciplinary understanding. • Conceptual orientation. • Epistemological understanding. • Characteristics of gifted adolescents. • Curriculum and instruction models for gifted students. • Connections with discipline-specific professionals.	

Placement classes, it seems advisable to combine strong 6–12 program alignment with open access to *consideration* for advanced courses and established criteria to actually *enroll* in advanced courses.

Program Essentials

Formal gifted "programs" at the high school level are rare; those that exist have eclectic, individual structures to fit specific subjects and students. However, those that work share one or more of the following characteristics: flexible structure, professional experience, and well-qualified personnel.

Flexible Structure

The typical 4-year, lock-step high school model is not appropriate for many gifted adolescents, many of whom require options such as grade skipping, independent study, or early college entrance. There also must be flexibility regarding meeting graduation requirements, particularly for students who specialize during high school. Students who indicate unusual talent in a specialized area (e.g., math, science, literature, foreign language, art, or music, or any other highly focused area) should be able to take more courses in their area of specialization rather than a broader array of courses across a variety of disciplines. Similarly, there must be greater latitude with respect to elective courses. If a talent is identified in a specific area, counselors, teachers, and administrators must work to meet the needs of the individual student with this manifest talent. Flexibility is key here.

Students who have both advanced knowledge in and clear commitment to a subject should be allowed the opportunity to specialize. This focus was suggested by Jarvin and Subotnik (2006), who advocated the development of talents that lead to competence and then to expertise, finally manifesting in scholarly productivity or artistry. They use the Juilliard School of Music as an exemplar that identifies students based on expressed talent and commitment to excellence, without specific regard to age. The school offers a range of academic subjects to ensure that students have a solid academic background. However, the goal of the program is to create musicians, so intensive, advanced music study is the core of the program. Jarvin and Subotnik argued that models like this are needed in science and other disciplines. This model comes to life in the New York-based program called Authentic Science Research, developed by Dr. Robert Pavlica, and reported by Robinson (2004). Students who opt for this program enter in their sophomore year and spend the subsequent 3 years working on a single research topic, beginning with a comprehensive literature review and ending with the completion of original research in the area. Throughout, students work with an expert mentor and participate in activities that engage them in a research community with other students in the program.

Specialization can take a variety of forms serving different regions, schools, and populations of students. Specialized residential schools are an essential component of a comprehensive state gifted education offering, and each state in the nation should have at least one, and ideally several, with different disciplinary emphasis. However, not all students are ready to live away from home, so residential schools cannot completely meet the needs of even the highest ability students. Whole- or half-day regional magnet programs, such as the network of Governor's Schools in Virginia, provide opportunity for students to work with like-minded peers and faculty. Some high schools create mini-magnets in a "school-within-a-school" model. In Charlotte, NC, a network of high schools offer school-within-a-school magnets in a wide range of subjects including foreign language immersion; communication arts; math, science, and technology; visual and performing arts; and International Baccalaureate options. In these programs, students are broadly educated, but the magnet focus serves as a unifying force across the curriculum.

Specialization is a crucial option, but should not be the only option. Interdisciplinary study that demonstrates connections across fields provides fertile ground for creative minds to cultivate innovative ideas and is immensely attractive to gifted students who are global thinkers and/or whose interests are not yet well defined. Indeed, adolescence is an ideal time to awaken new interests; all gifted students, whether specializing or pursuing general advanced studies, should be exposed to new and original ideas, interdisciplinary connections, and unique career options. In some cases, students broaden the scope of their talent when they forge connections among disciplines. They can see the synthesis of possibilities among disciplines when many others could not begin to imagine such connections.

Whenever possible, the program services for gifted high school students should be tiered, offering options to both advanced and extremely gifted students. Advanced offerings would include honors classes, within-subject grade skipping, and in some cases, Advanced Placement and International Baccalaureate, especially when operated under a philosophy of open enrollment. Offerings for extremely gifted students would include more radical acceleration, curriculum telescoping, specialized curriculum, and early, intensive independent studies.

One example of a well-tiered program is presented by Ngoi and Vondracek (2004). At Evanston Township High School, separate science options are available for advanced students and science-prone students. Advanced students have access to well-designed, complex, accelerated curriculum. Science-prone students have a choice of three options including enrollment in a university course, independent study with a school faculty member, or independent, original research. Student response to the two tiers suggests a widespread appreciation for the recognition of the differences between advanced and extremely gifted students.

Professional Experience

In a parallel to vocational education, gifted students need experience in professions related to their academic interests using internships, mentorships, shadowing, or similar models. Direct access to professional practice gives students experience with authentic work and socializes them into the culture of employment. Immersion in the actual practice of a field also proves invaluable for learning the tacit knowledge in a field; the ways of professional thinking and acting are best learned through immersion in the workplace. Gifted students drawn to science must learn the diverse skills entailed in modern science, including collaboration and communication skills, but they also must learn the necessity of fundraising as well. The reality is that they will need these skills to advance their creative thoughts. Students interested in the visual arts must understand the career path of an artist and that options that are available for making a living with their art. Ideally, their experiences will reveal that some aspects of day-to-day practice in any given field cannot be learned from a book, but must be acquired through experience. Similarly, they need to consider early on where their discipline is practiced. Being interested in engineering is very different from actually being an engineer for a large corporation, government agency, a think tank, or for work as an independent consultant.

In an optimal program, career counseling is built into internships and flows naturally from more authentic class work. Internships and mentorships are natural venues in which students develop and conduct original investigations.

Well-Qualified Personnel

Decisive gatekeepers controlling access to advanced courses, all high school faculty should understand traditional and nontraditional indicators of giftedness. Likewise, all high school faculty should be familiar with the social and emotional dimensions of giftedness, and especially understand underachievement as a marker of emotional distress or academic disenchantment. Teachers of advanced courses, including AP and IB, should be required to take courses in characteristics of gifted adolescents or to have ongoing professional development investigating the implications these characteristics have for curriculum and instruction. Regardless of whether they teach in heterogeneous or self-contained classrooms, high school teachers should understand the fundamentals of curriculum differentiation. As discussed in previous chapters, even AP and IB classes can have widely diverse ability levels, and particular care is essential to ensuring that academic rigor is maintained for the highest ability students.

It is not important that teachers in high school gifted programs know more about their subject than their students; however, they should be deeply familiar with disciplinary content and structure. Understanding disciplinary structure entails content knowledge, conceptual underpinnings, interdisciplinary connections, and epistemological beliefs. They should be comfortable working with students who know more than they do about specific topics and, ideally, will be comfortable with uncertainty. Supporting an inquiry-based approach to instruction, especially at advanced levels, compels teachers to have training in questioning strategies generally, as well as sequencing questions to support higher order thinking. Teachers working directly with gifted students should be comfortable contacting and working with professionals active in their discipline.

Personnel preparation will ideally go beyond classroom instructors. Gifted adolescents benefit from the presence of specifically trained counselors. Chapter 2 outlines the social and emotional challenges associated with giftedness that can inhibit academic and personal growth for gifted teens; a trained counselor could provide direct intervention and have links to local professional services as needed. Specific supports are needed for gifted girls, underrepresented gifted, gifted with nontraditional career choices, and underachievers. Ongoing career counseling should be provided beginning at the start of secondary school, especially for students who want to specialize early. College and career choices for gifted students also require a different kind of advising. Some gifted students, having been accepted to six colleges, are overwhelmed by the need to select only one to attend; other gifted students have interests so specific and narrow that finding a suitable program is like searching for a needle in a haystack.

Building administrators ideally understand enough about gifted students to realize the importance of cultivating a school climate that values intellectual pursuits equally with the current value placed on athletic pursuits. To that end, the school culture must emphasize excellence in all areas. Administrators should promote programs that help sustain equitable access to advanced courses for any qualified students and be prepared to adjust schedules in order to create a "critical mass" of gifted students in advanced sections to support traditionally underrepresented groups. Administrators should know or designate a person responsible for being familiar with ongoing research and development in the field.

Integrated Essentials

Gifted secondary students in the beginning of the 21st century have never known life without computer technology. They are tech-savvy and invent and create on the computer as well as in other media. A curriculum that incorporates technology is an integral part of a program for gifted high school students. Such curriculum must focus on programming, gaming, technology applications, and computing in biology and the other sciences, as well as the appropriate applications used in the other content domains. Instruction must use technology to enable students to conduct research, access Internet resources and tools (e.g., virtual laboratories and simulations) for learning, and create peer networks that connect students globally with others with similar interests to facilitate collaborative projects (i.e., across schools). Technology also can be used to provide access to experts and to pursue accelerated or specialized study through distance education.

Foreign language training is another critical component to any gifted program. The workplace is increasingly global, and America is increasingly multilingual. It is essential that the nation's most able students, ostensibly future leaders, are prepared to communicate with at least some colleagues in their native language.

Ethics is the final essential to integrate across the curriculum. Specific and deliberate attention to ethics is crucial to ensure that students are prepared to reason through the complex issues associated with advanced technology and international human relations.

Curriculum and Instruction Within the Program

Flexibility, professional experiences, and well-qualified personnel provide the guideposts for gifted secondary programming; the center of activity is curriculum and instruction. Developing and delivering high-quality curriculum is the heart of any program.

Curriculum

All students, gifted or otherwise, learn best when they feel their education has use and meaning. However, gifted students define "useful" and "meaningful" in ways dramatically different from their peers. Although typically developing students will tend to find pragmatic, concrete, and sequential courses useful, gifted students find more meaning from curriculum that uses ideas, questions, and complexity as the context for learning facts.

Secondary curriculum for gifted students should place a premium on authenticity. Research by Csikszentmihalyi, Rathunde, and Whalen (1993) showed that gifted performing arts students enrolled in art courses generally found their classes motivating and engaging. However, students gifted in math and science did not find their classes motivating or stimulating; their persistence—and resulting success—were due to the students' ability to understand the long-term benefits of high school achievement. Gifted secondary education must not rely upon the existing motivation of students; to do so runs the risk that students will achieve but cease to pursue learning when it is no longer necessary. Rather, gifted secondary education should be designed to build motivation through engagement. For most students, motivation is built by involving them in learning that either is authentic or models authenticity; often this means it will be problem focused.

Integrated along with advanced content and authentic structure should be direct instruction in the structure of the discipline. Discussions about the nature of investigation across different fields, the advanced standards of practice (elegance, fecundity), and the assumptions that undergird current theories should be interspersed throughout the students' studies.

A pinnacle of school-based authentic learning is an individual investigation that requires sustained, systematic study and an original product. Senior projects are an excellent example of this kind of individual investigation, as are competitions such as the high-powered Intel Science Talent Search. Numerous similar competitions are available in other disciplines and are easily found on the Hoagies'

Gifted Education Web site (http://www.hoagiesgifted.org/contests.htm). Rigorous, authentic senior projects or competitions have the added advantage of being demonstrable evidence of intellectual effort: A major commonality among the 2007 top 20 seniors identified by *USA Today* was the submission of a major project. These academic all stars are described on the Web site (http://www.usatoday.com/news/education/2007-05-16-high-school-allstars_N.htm).

With careful attention to rigorous content and inquiry-based delivery, Advanced Placement and International Baccalaureate still can be options for gifted secondary students. AP in particular is still a very cost-effective means of providing accelerated curriculum to students in rural areas or smaller schools. However, whenever possible, AP and IB should not be the only avenue to advanced study, especially in schools where open access to those courses and programs is encouraged.

A Dire Need for Additional Advanced Curriculum

The AP and IB programs have provided excellent evidence that programs are easier to mount when curriculum is readily available. The lack of readily available advanced high school curriculum is a severe deficit in the field. Innovative courses often are tied directly to the passion of specific instructors and fade away when the teacher is no longer involved. Although there is no substitute for the magic created when a passionate teacher shares his or her love of the discipline with engaged and eager students, having a body of advanced, original curriculum materials may be the easiest path to increasing services to gifted students nationwide.

Instruction

Instruction for gifted students should emphasize moving quickly through facts in order to allow time for higher order thinking. This applies equally for courses that emphasize acceleration and inquiry. Acceleration that only moves students through a new set of facts does not adequately train their minds. Similarly, the goals of authentic, inquiry-based curriculum are seriously undercut when instruction is dominated by teacher lectures. Instruction should be directed increasingly by students' questions whenever possible, and an emphasis on helping students become independent, self-reflective learners should permeate all instruction.

Conclusion

In sum, the field of high school programming for gifted students is rich territory for advocacy, exploration, innovation, research, and development. We advocate for changes that value individual differences and celebrate talent development that leads to creative productivity and expertise. Secondary students clearly are able to accomplish much greater feats than schools allow them to do. We must not hold them back but must understand their abilities, enable their talents, and celebrate their successes in all talent domains. This is both our challenge and our mandate if we are to create meaningful learning experiences for high-ability secondary students in the 21st century.

We suggest that:

- all states should have at least one residential school,
- each large urban area should have a magnet school to serve its most able students, and
- all high schools should have programs that provide flexibility in access for high-ability adolescents; revision of the programs and flexibility are paramount.

References

Csikszentmihalyi, M., Rathunde, K., & Whalen, S. (1993). *Talented teenagers: The roots of success & failure.* New York: Cambridge University Press.

Jarvin, L., & Subotnik, R. (2006). Understanding elite talent in academic domains: A developmental trajectory from basic abilities to scholarly productivity/artistry. In F. A. Dixon & S. M. Moon (Eds.), *The handbook of secondary gifted education* (pp. 203–220). Waco, TX: Prufrock Press.

Ngoi, M., & Vondracek, M. (2004). Working with gifted science students in a public high school environment: One school's approach. *Journal of Secondary Gifted Education, 15,* 141–147.

Robinson, G. (2004). Replicating a successful Authentic Science Research Program: An interview with Dr. Robert Pavlica. *Journal of Secondary Gifted Education, 15,* 148–155.

About the Editor

Felicia A. Dixon is professor of psychology in the Department of Educational Psychology at Ball State University. She formerly directed the master's degree program in educational psychology and the license/endorsement in gifted education. She received her doctorate from Purdue University and specializes in gifted education. Author of more than 30 articles and chapters, Felicia Dixon coedited the important *The Handbook of Secondary Gifted Education* in 2006 and received the Early Scholar Award from NAGC in 2004. She has served as a member of the Board of Directors of NAGC and is currently Chairman of the Task Force on Gifted Secondary Education of NAGC, and chairs the awards committee for NAGC. Her research interests include critical thinking, cognitive abilities, self-concept of gifted adolescents, perfectionism, and curriculum. Her special interest is in the advancement of gifted education for secondary students. Correspondence should be addressed to Felicia A. Dixon at her e-mail address: fdixon@ bsu.edu.

About the Authors

Shelagh A. Gallagher received her Ph.D. in special education, with an emphasis in gifted education, at the University of North Carolina (UNC). She works as in independent consultant in gifted education, conducting workshops nationwide on a number of topics. Prior to her current job she served for 10 years as associate professor in UNC Charlotte's Department of Special Education and Child Development. While there, Dr. Gallagher directed two Javits grants: Project Insights and Project P-BLISS (Problem-Based Learning in the Social Sciences). She also worked for a year at The College of William and Mary, where she was project manager of the Javits grant that produced the respected William and Mary science units. For 3 years Shelagh worked as Director of Research and Assessment at the Illinois Mathematics and Science Academy (IMSA). Shelagh has served two terms on the NAGC Board of Directors, has twice won NAGC Curriculum Division awards for exemplary curriculum, and once won the NAGC Article of the Year award. She and her father, James J. Gallagher, coauthored *Teaching the Gifted Child*.

M. Katherine Gavin is an associate professor at the Neag Center for Gifted Education and Talent Development at the University of Connecticut where she serves as the math specialist. She is currently the principal investigator and director of a 6-year Javits Grant, Project M³: Mentoring Mathematical

Minds that involves the development of math curriculum units for talented students in grades 3, 4, and 5. These units have won the National Association for Gifted Education (NAGC) Curriculum Division Award in 2004, 2005, 2006, and 2007. Dr. Gavin received the Early Leader Award from NAGC in 2006. She is also principal investigator and director of a 5-year National Science Foundation Grant, Project M²: Advanced Math Curriculum for Primary Students. Dr. Gavin received her Ph.D. in educational psychology specializing in gifted and talented education from the University of Connecticut. She has 30 years of experience in education as a mathematics teacher and curriculum coordinator, elementary assistant principal, assistant professor of mathematics education, and currently associate professor in educational psychology. She has written numerous articles and book chapters on gifted mathematics education and is presently coauthoring a middle school mathematics textbook series, is a member of the writing team for the National Council of Teachers of Mathematics *Navigations* series, and has coauthored a series of creative problem solving books.

Marcia Gentry is the director of the Gifted Education Resource Institute at Purdue University, a position she holds due to the excellent education she received from the faculty at the University of Connecticut where she received her Ph.D. in 1996. Her research has focused on the use of cluster grouping and differentiation; the application of gifted education pedagogy to improve teaching and learning; student perceptions of school; and nontraditional services and underserved populations. Dr. Gentry developed and studied the Total School Cluster Grouping Model and is engaged in continued research on its effects concerning student achievement and identification and on teacher practices. She is active in AERA and NAGC, frequently contributes to the gifted education literature, and regularly serves as a speaker and consultant. Prior to her work in higher education, she spent 12 years as a teacher and administrator in K–12 settings.

Lisa Limburg-Weber worked for more than 14 years at the Center for Talent Development (CTD) at Northwestern University, during which she served many roles, most recently as an assistant director. During her tenure at CTD, she designed and implemented many different types of educational programs for varying groups of gifted learners including underserved students. Dr. Limburg-Weber also is the coeditor, with Paula Olszewski-Kubilius and Steven Pfeiffer, of *Early Gifts: Recognizing and Nurturing Children's Talents*. She drew on her own international educational experience as well as existing research and literature to write the chapter on study abroad in this book.

Paula Olszewski-Kubilius is currently the director of the Center for Talent Development at Northwestern University and a professor in the School of Education and Social Policy. She earned her bachelor's degree in elementary education from St. Xavier University in Chicago and her master's and doctorate degrees from Northwestern University in educational psychology. Dr. Olszewski-Kubilius has worked at the Center for 25 years, during which she has designed and conducted educational programs for learners of all ages including summer programs, weekend programs, distance learning programs, and programs for underrepresented gifted students, as well as workshops for parents and teachers. She is active in national- and state-level advocacy organizations for gifted children in the Midwest. She currently serves on the board of directors of the National Association for Gifted Children and the Illinois Association for Gifted Children and serves on the Board of Trustees of the Illinois Mathematics and Science Academy. She has conducted research and published more than 80 articles or book chapters on issues of talent development, particularly the effects of accelerated educational programs and the needs of special populations of gifted children. She has served as the editor of *Gifted Child Quarterly* and as a coeditor of *the Journal of Secondary Gifted Education*. She also has served on the editorial advisory boards of the *Journal for the Education of the Gifted* and *Gifted Child International,* and was a consulting editor for *The Roeper Review.* She currently is a member of the editorial board of *Gifted Child Today* and *Gifted Child Quarterly.*

Scott J. Peters is a doctoral candidate in gifted education at Purdue University. He currently serves as a coordinator of student programs for the Gifted Education Resource Institute, administering student enrichment programs. His research interests include educational research methodologies with particular focus on advanced measurement techniques such as structural equation modeling, multi-level modeling, and growth curve modeling. His research interests also include nontraditional giftedness and secondary student programming outcomes. He has contributed articles to *Gifted Child Quarterly, Journal of Advanced Academics, Career and Technical Education Research, Educational Leadership, Pedagogies,* and *Teaching for High Potential,* and is a frequent presenter at state and national conferences on gifted education and research methodology.

Susannah Wood is currently an assistant professor at the University of Iowa, where she teaches both doctoral students and students who are pursing their master's in school counseling with an emphasis in gifted education. Dr. Wood received her bachelor's degree in psychology and English from the University of Richmond and her master's degree in school counseling from The College of William and Mary. She completed her doctorate at The College of William and Mary in counselor education with a cognate in gifted education and won the Margaret, The Lady Thatcher Medallion for academic excellence. Dr. Wood was a middle school counselor who worked with sixth- and seventh-grade students in Newport News, VA, during the academic year, and spent summers as a residential counselor for programs such as Johns Hopkins' Center for Talented Youth, and the Virginia Governor's School for the Visual and Performing Arts and Humanities.

CPSIA information can be obtained at www.ICGtesting.com
Printed in the USA
LVOW09s2034200816

501188LV00022B/432/P